# EASY GENIUS MATH
# RATIOS
# AND PERCENTS

### IT'S EASY!

Rebecca Wingard-Nelson

**Enslow Publishers, Inc.**
40 Industrial Road
Box 398
Berkeley Heights, NJ 07922
USA

http://www.enslow.com

Original edition published as *Ratios and Percents* in 2008.

**Library of Congress Cataloging-in-Publication Data**

Wingard-Nelson, Rebecca.
    Ratios and percents : it's easy / Rebecca Wingard-Nelson.
        pages cm.—(Easy genius math)
    Previously published as: Ratios and percents. c2008.
    Summary: "Learn about ratios and percents including equivelent ratios, proportions, scale drawings, rates, and percent change"—Provided by publisher.
    Includes bibliographical references and index.
    ISBN 978-0-7660-4289-6
    1.  Ratio and proportion—Juvenile literature.  2.  Percentage—Juvenile literature.  I. Title.
    QA117.W567 2008
    513.2'4—dc23

                                                                    2012040790

Future editions:
Paperback ISBN: 978-1-4644-0527-3                EPUB ISBN: 978-1-4645-1269-8
Single-User PDF ISBN: 978-1-4646-1269-5        Multi-User PDF ISBN:  978-0-7660-5901-6

Printed in the United States of America

102013 Lake Book Manufacturing, Inc., Melrose Park, IL

10 9 8 7 6 5 4 3 2 1

**To Our Readers:** We have done our best to make sure all Internet addresses in this book were active and appropriate when we went to press. However, the author and the publisher have no control over and assume no liability for the material available on those Internet sites or on other Web sites they may link to. Any comments or suggestions can be sent by e-mail to comments@enslow.com or to the address on the back cover.

♻ Enslow Publishers, Inc., is committed to printing our books on recycled paper. The paper in every book contains 10% to 30% post-consumer waste (PCW). The cover board on the outside of each book contains 100% PCW. Our goal is to do our part to help young people and the environment too!

**Illustration Credits:** © Clipart.com, p. 23, 72; Hemera/Thinkstock, p. 18; iStockphoto/Thinkstock, pp. 11, 20, 21, 41, 48; Shutterstock.com, pp. 9, 14, 17, 26, 29, 31, 33, 37, 39, 43, 51, 53, 55, 57.

**Cover Photo:** Shutterstock.com

# CONTENTS

# Introduction

Not every person is an accountant, engineer, rocket scientist, or math teacher. However, every person does use math.

Most people never think, "I just used math to decide if I have enough milk for this week!" But that is exactly what they did. Math is everywhere; we just don't see it because it doesn't always look like the math we do at school.

Math gives you the power to:
• determine the best route on a trip
• keep score in a game
• compare prices
• figure how much paint to buy
• plan a vacation schedule

Ratios and percents describe how amounts relate to each other. You can compare the number of boys to the number of girls in a class with a ratio. A percent grade on a test compares the right answers to all of the answers. Percents can also tell you how much you can save by purchasing items on sale.

This book will help you understand ratios and percents. It can be read from beginning to end, or used to review a specific topic.

# ① Ratios

Ratios are a way to compare two numbers, quantities, or measurements.

## Reading and Writing Ratios

Ratios can be written in three ways.

| | |
|---|---|
| 1. Using the word "to": | **3 to 2** |
| 2. Using a colon: | **3 : 2** |
| 3. Using the fraction bar: | $\dfrac{3}{2}$ |

No matter how you write a ratio, it is always read the same way, **"three to two."**

The numbers in a ratio are called **terms.** In the ratio 3 : 2, 3 is the **first term**, and 2 is the **second term.**

## Parts and Wholes

*Jerry has 8 blue marbles and 4 green marbles. Marie has 7 red marbles and 4 green ones.*

*Write a ratio using the word "to" that compares Jerry's blue and green marbles.*

**Step 1:** Jerry has 8 blue marbles. This is the first term.          **8 to**

**Step 2:** Jerry has 4 green marbles. This is the second term.   **8 to 4**
**The ratio of Jerry's blue marbles to his green ones is 8 to 4.**
This ratio compares two parts (blue marbles and green marbles) of one whole thing (all of Jerry's marbles).

***Write a ratio using a colon (:)
that compares Jerry's blue
marbles to all of his marbles.***

**Step 1:** Jerry has 8 blue marbles.
This is the first term.

     **8 :**

**Step 2:** Jerry has a total of
12 marbles, 8 blue + 4 green.
This is the second term.

     **8 : 12**

**The ratio of Jerry's blue marbles to all of his marbles is 8 : 12.**
This ratio compares one part (Jerry's blue marbles) to the whole
thing (all of his marbles).

***Write a ratio using the fraction bar that compares
Jerry's marbles to Marie's marbles.***

**Step 1:** Jerry has 12 marbles (8 blue and 4 green).      **12**
This is the first term (the top number).

**Step 2:** Marie has 11 marbles (7 red and 4 green).      $\dfrac{12}{11}$
This is the second term (the bottom number).

**The ratio of Jerry's marbles to Marie's marbles is $\dfrac{12}{11}$.**

This ratio compares one whole thing (Jerry's marbles) to another
whole thing (Marie's marbles).

Ratios can
look like fractions,
but they are not always the same.
The denominator in a fraction always
tells how many equal parts are in one whole.

$\dfrac{8}{12}$ blue marbles      $\dfrac{8}{4}$ blue marbles
     total marbles         green marbles

Here $\dfrac{8}{12}$ is a ratio     Here $\dfrac{8}{4}$ is a ratio

and a fraction.       but not a fraction.

# ② Equivalent Ratios

Ratios that have the same value are called equivalent ratios. *Equivalent* means "equal to."

## Equivalent Ratios

Let's look at an example to help understand equivalent ratios. Here is a pattern of dots.

⚫ ⚫ ⚫ ⚫ ⚫ ⚫ ⚫ ⚫ ⚫

There are 6 blue dots and 3 pink dots.
The ratio of blue to pink is **6 to 3.**

You can see that for every 2 blue dots there is 1 pink dot.
The ratio of each set of dots is **2 to 1.**

| 1 | 2 | 1 | 1 | 2 | 1 | 1 | 2 | 1 |
|---|---|---|---|---|---|---|---|---|
| ⚫ | ⚫ | ⚫ | ⚫ | ⚫ | ⚫ | ⚫ | ⚫ | ⚫ |

If you add one more set of dots, 2 blue and 1 pink, there are 8 blue dots and 4 pink dots. The ratio of blue to pink is **8 to 4.**

⚫ ⚫ ⚫ ⚫ ⚫ ⚫ ⚫ ⚫ ⚫ ⚫ ⚫ ⚫

Each of these ratios, **6 to 3**, **2 to 1**, and **8 to 4**, describes the same pattern. They are equal, or **equivalent ratios.**

# Finding Equivalent Ratios

*Jacinda can skate around the roller rink 15 times for every 10 times Moe can skate around. Write 2 ratios that are equivalent to 15 : 10.*

**Step 1:** You can rename ratios by multiplying both terms by the same number. Let's multiply both terms by 2.

$$15 : 10$$
$$15 \times 2 : 10 \times 2$$
$$30 : 20$$

**15 : 10 is equivalent to 30 : 20.**

**Step 2:** You can rename ratios by dividing both terms by the same number. Let's divide both terms by 5.

$$15 : 10$$
$$15 \div 5 : 10 \div 5$$
$$3 : 2$$

**15 : 10 is equivalent to 3 : 2.**

If you have 20 girls and 10 boys in a class, the ratio is 20 to 10. This can also be written as 2 to 1.

The ratio 2 to 1 tells you that for every two girls in the class, there is one boy. However, it does not tell you exactly how many girls and boys are in the class.

So, do not rewrite a ratio if you need to know the actual numbers.

# ③ Reducing Ratios

Knowing the factors of numbers
will help you reduce ratios.

## Factors

**factor**—A number that divides evenly into a given number.

The number 3 divides evenly into 12 ($12 \div 3 = 4$).

3 is a factor of 12.

**common factor**—A number that divides evenly into more than one given number.

The factors of 12 are **1**, **2**, **3**, 4, **6**, and 12.

The factors of 6 are **1**, **2**, **3**, and **6**.

The common factors of 12 and 6 are **1**, **2**, **3**, and **6**.

**greatest common factor**—The largest number that divides evenly into more than one given number.

The greatest common factor of 12 and 6 is **6**.

## Reducing Ratios

**_Reduce 24 : 6 to lower terms._**

**Step 1:** Reducing a ratio means writing it using smaller numbers. To reduce a ratio, find a common factor of the terms.

The terms 24 and 6 are both divisible by 3, so a common factor of 24 and 6 is 3.

**Step 2:** Divide both terms by the common factor, 3.

$$24 : 6$$
$$24 \div 3 : 6 \div 3$$
$$8 : 2$$

**24 : 6 can be reduced to 8 : 2.**

## Lowest Terms

*Serena made 36 quesadillas and 12 salads. Write the ratio of quesadillas to salads in lowest terms.*

A ratio is in **lowest terms** when it cannot be reduced any more. In lowest terms, the only common factor of the terms is 1.

**Step 1:** Write the ratio of quesadillas to salads.
There are 36 quesadillas—this is the first term.
There are 12 salads—this is the second term.

**36 : 12**

**Step 2:** Find the greatest common factor of 36 and 12.

List the factors of 36:    **1, 2, 3, 4, 6**, 9, **12**, 18, 36
List the factors of 12:    **1, 2, 3, 4, 6, 12**

The greatest common factor of 36 and 12 is 12.

**Step 3:** Divide both terms by the greatest common factor, 12.

$$36 : 12$$
$$36 \div 12 : 12 \div 12$$
$$3 : 1$$

**In lowest terms, the ratio of quesadillas to salads is 3 : 1.**

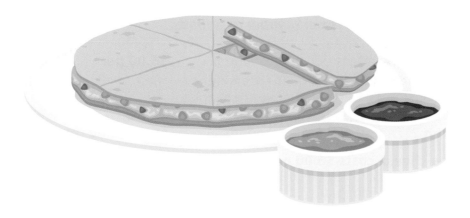

# ④ Rates

Rates are ratios that compare two different kinds of quantities, such as distance and time.

## Reading and Writing Rates

The types of quantities, called units, are included when you write a rate. Rates are usually written in two ways.

1. Using the word "per":       **35 students per 2 teachers**

2. Using the fraction bar:     $\dfrac{\textbf{35 students}}{\textbf{2 teachers}}$

Rates are read using the word "per" and the units.

    **"Thirty-five students per two teachers"**

## Finding Rates

*A 2-pound package of cheese costs $6.00. Write a rate showing the price of cheese per number of pounds.*

**Step 1:** The rate is price per pounds, so the first term is the price. Write a dollar sign ($) to show the units are dollars.     **$6.00 per**

**Step 2:** The second term is pounds.     **$6.00 per 2 pounds**

**The cheese costs $6.00 per 2 pounds.**

# Reducing Rates

*A 2-pound package of cheese costs $6.00.*
*Write the rate in lowest terms.*

**Step 1:** Write the rate.                    **$6.00 per 2 pounds**

**Step 2:** Find the greatest common factor of 6 and 2.

List the factors of 6:          **1, 2**, 3, 6
List the factors of 2:          **1, 2**

The greatest common factor of 6 and 2 is 2.

**Step 3:** Divide both terms          **$6.00  per  2 pounds**
by the greatest common              **6.00 ÷ 2  2 ÷ 2**
factor, 2.                          **$3.00 per 1 pound**

**In lowest terms, the cheese costs $3.00 per pound.**

Rates are used every day.
Some even have their own names.

**Speed** compares how far you go to how
long it takes you (55 miles per hour).

**Mileage** compares how many miles you drive to
how much fuel you use (20 miles per gallon).

**Density** compares the amount of something to
the amount of space it takes up.
(10 seeds per square foot).

# ⑤ Ratios and Fractions

Ratios with fractions are sometimes easier to use if they are changed to ratios with whole numbers.

## Multiples

Multiples help you change fraction ratios to whole number ratios.

**multiple**—The product of a given number and any whole number is a multiple of that number.

**common multiples**—Numbers that are multiples of two or more given numbers.

**least common multiple**—The smallest common multiple, other than zero, of two or more given numbers.

## Fractions in Ratios

*When Omar practices his clarinet for $\frac{1}{4}$ hour, his mother lets him play video games for $\frac{1}{2}$ hour. Write a whole number ratio showing Omar's practice time to his game time.*

**Step 1:** Write the ratio of hours of practice time to hours of game time.

$$\frac{1}{4} \text{ to } \frac{1}{2}$$

**Step 2:** Find the least common multiple of the denominators.

List the multiples of 4:  **4, 8**, 12, 16, . . .
List the multiples of 2:  2, **4**, 6, **8**, . . .
**The least common multiple is 4.**

**Step 3:** Multiply each term by the least common multiple of the denominators.

$$\frac{1}{4} \times 4 \text{ to } \frac{1}{2} \times 4$$

To multiply fractions and whole numbers, change the whole numbers to fractions by writing them with a denominator of one.

$$\frac{1}{4} \times \frac{4}{1} \text{ to } \frac{1}{2} \times \frac{4}{1}$$

Reduce before you multiply by cancelling out common factors.
Cancel out 4s in the first term.
Cancel out 2s in the second term.

$$\frac{1}{\cancel{4}} \times \frac{\cancel{4}^{\,1}}{1} \text{ to } \frac{1}{\cancel{2}} \times \frac{\cancel{4}^{\,2}}{1}$$

Multiply the numerators.
Multiply the denominators.

$$\frac{1 \times 1}{1 \times 1} \text{ to } \frac{1 \times 2}{1 \times 1}$$

$$\frac{1}{1} \text{ to } \frac{2}{1}$$

**Step 4:** Reduce the ratio to lowest terms.          **1 to 2**

**The ratio of Omar's practice time to his game time is 1 to 2.**

## Mixed Numbers in Ratios

*Write the ratio $3\frac{1}{2}$ to 2 as a whole number ratio.*

**Step 1:** Write the original ratio.          $3\frac{1}{2}$ to 2

**Step 2:** Write mixed number terms as improper fractions.          $\frac{7}{2}$ to 2

**Step 3:** The second term is a whole number. When only one of the terms is a fraction, multiply each of the terms by the denominator of the fraction.
Multiply each term by 2.

$$\frac{7}{2} \times 2 \text{ to } 2 \times 2$$

$$\frac{7}{\cancel{2}} \times \frac{\cancel{2}^{\,1}}{1} \text{ to } 2 \times 2$$

$$\frac{7}{1} \text{ to } 4$$

**Step 4:** Reduce the ratio to lowest terms.          **7 to 4**

**$3\frac{1}{2}$ to 2 is the same as 7 to 4.**

# ⑥ Ratios and Decimals

Sometimes ratios contain decimals.
The decimals can be changed to whole
number ratios by moving the decimal points.

## Powers of Ten and Decimals

When a decimal is multiplied by a power of ten (like 10 or 100),
the decimal point moves to the right one place for each zero.

$$4.127 \times 10 = 41.27$$

$$4.127 \times 100 = 412.7$$

$$4.127 \times 1,000 = 4127$$

## Decimal Ratios

*Write the ratio 4 : 5.2 as a whole number ratio.*

**Step 1:** There is one decimal place in 5.2.
To move the decimal point one place right,
you can multiply by 10.

$$5.2 \times 10 = 52$$

**Step 2:** To find equivalent ratios, multiply
both terms by the same number.
Multiply both terms by 10.

$$4 : 5.2$$
$$4 \times 10 : 5.2 \times 10$$
$$40 : 52$$

**Step 3:** Reduce the ratio to lowest terms.
Divide 40 and 52 by their
greatest common factor, 4.

$$40 : 52$$
$$40 \div 4 : 52 \div 4$$
$$10 : 13$$

**4 : 5.2 is the same as 10 : 13.**

# Move the Decimal Point

*A picture is 4.5 centimeters tall and 6.75 centimeters wide. Write the ratio of height to width as a whole number ratio.*

**Step 1:** Write the original ratio.　　　　　　　　**4.5 to 6.75**

**Step 2:** Move the decimal point right the same number of places in each term. Since 6.75 has two decimal places, move each decimal point two places to the right.

**4.5 to 6.75**

**450 to 675**

**Step 3:** Reduce the ratio to lowest terms. When the greatest common factor is large, or hard to find, you can reduce more than one time. Divide 450 and 675 by 5 first.
Reduce again by dividing 90 and 135 by 5.

$\dfrac{450}{5}$ to $\dfrac{675}{5}$

**90 to 135**

$\dfrac{90}{5}$ to $\dfrac{135}{5}$

**18 to 27**

Reduce again by dividing 18 and 27 by 9.

$\dfrac{18}{9}$ to $\dfrac{27}{9}$

**2 to 3**

**For this picture, the whole number ratio of height to width is 2 to 3.**

# Unit Ratios and Rates

Unit ratios and unit rates always
have one unit in the second term.

## Unit Ratios and Rates

When the second term in a ratio is one unit (like one person or
one hour), the ratio is called a **unit ratio.**
25 students to 1 teacher is a unit ratio.

When the second term in a rate is one unit, the rate is called a
**unit rate.** $6 per 1 hour is a unit rate.

Unit rates usually do not include the 1 in the second term.
Instead of saying 50 miles per 1 hour, you say 50 miles per hour.

## Unit Ratios

*Sam mixed 5 parts of red paint and 2 parts of blue paint.
How many times as much red paint did he use as blue paint?*

To solve this problem, find the unit ratio. A unit ratio tells you how
many times larger or smaller the first term is than the second term.
.........................................................................................................................

**Step 1:** Write the original ratio of
red paint to blue paint.

**5 : 2**
.......................................................................................................

**Step 2:** To find a unit ratio, divide both
terms by the second term.

**5 ÷ 2 : 2 ÷ 2**

**2.5 : 1**

**The ratio of red paint to blue paint is
2.5 to 1. This means Sam used 2.5 times
as much red paint as he did blue paint.**

# Unit Rates

*A painter earns $600.00 per 40-hour week.*
*How much does the painter earn per hour?*

To solve this problem, find the unit rate, or rate per one hour.

**Step 1:** Write the original rate.                  $600.00 per 40 hours

**Step 2:** Divide both terms by the     $\frac{$600.00}{40}$ per $\frac{40}{40}$ hours
second term, 40.

$15.00 per hour

**The painter earns $15.00 per hour.**

*Darlene used 4 gallons of fuel to drive 70 miles. What was her fuel mileage?*

Problems that ask you to find the mileage, speed, or any other common rate are asking for the unit rate.

To solve this problem, find the unit rate. Fuel mileage is the unit rate for the number of miles driven per gallon of fuel.

**Step 1:** Write the original rate.                  **70 miles per 4 gallons**

**Step 2:** Divide both terms by the     $\frac{70}{4}$ miles per $\frac{4}{4}$ gallons
second term, 4.

$17\frac{1}{2}$ miles per gallon

**Darlene's fuel mileage was $17\frac{1}{2}$ miles per gallon.**

Unit ratios can be written using decimals or fractions in the first term.

$17\frac{1}{2}$ miles per hour
or
**17.5 miles per hour**

# ⑧ The **Better** Buy

Unit prices let you compare prices
when items are sold in different sizes.

## Unit Prices

The **price** of an item is usually the total price for a can, bottle, box, or container of something. For example, the price of a 6-ounce can of juice might be $0.78.

**Unit price** is the price of one measurement unit, like a pound, an ounce, a quart, or any other weight or volume unit. The unit price for the can of juice is $0.13 per ounce ($0.78 ÷ 6 ounces = $0.13 per ounce).

## The Better Buy

*A 9-ounce bottle of water costs $0.99. A 20-ounce bottle of water costs $1.60. Which is the better buy?*

To solve this problem, compare the unit prices.

**Step 1:** Write a rate for each bottle that shows the cost per number of units. The units in this problem are ounces of water.

$0.99 per 9 ounces       $1.60 per 20 ounces

**Step 2:** Find the unit rate for each package by dividing each by its second term.

$$\frac{\$0.99}{9} \text{ per } \frac{9}{9} \text{ ounces} \qquad \frac{\$1.60}{20} \text{ per } \frac{20}{20} \text{ ounces}$$

$0.11 per ounce          $0.08 per ounce

**Step 3:** Compare.       $0.08 is less than $0.11

**The 20-ounce bottle of water is the better buy because each ounce of water costs $0.08.**

*One package of 8 hotdog buns costs $1.20. A package of 12 buns costs $1.68. Which package is the better buy?*

**Step 1:** Write a rate for each package that shows the cost per number of units. The units in this problem are hotdog buns.

**$1.20 per 8 buns**       **$1.68 per 12 buns**

**Step 2:** Find the unit rate for each package by dividing each by its second term.

$\dfrac{\$1.20}{8}$ per $\dfrac{8}{8}$ buns       $\dfrac{\$1.68}{12}$ per $\dfrac{12}{12}$ buns

**$0.15 per bun**       **$0.14 per bun**

**Step 3:** Compare.

**$0.15 is more than $0.14.**

**The package with 12 buns is the better buy.**

## Other Rates

*Clara typed 128 words in 4 minutes. Zachary typed 165 words in 5 minutes. Who typed faster?*

You can compare any kind of rates by finding the unit rates first.

> Unit price is only part of smart shopping. If you only have 8 hotdogs, you will not use 12 buns. The smaller package is the better buy because it costs less, and you won't waste any buns. If you don't like the taste of one kind of bun, it may be worth spending more for the kind you like.

**Step 1:** Write the original typing rate for each person.

| **Clara** | **Zachary** |
|---|---|
| **128 words per 4 minutes** | **165 words per 5 minutes** |

**Step 2:** Find the unit rate each person typed.

$\dfrac{128}{4}$ words per $\dfrac{4}{4}$ minutes       $\dfrac{165}{5}$ words per $\dfrac{5}{5}$ minutes

**32 words per minute**       **33 words per minute**

**Step 3:** Compare.       **32 words per minute is less than 33 words per minute.**

**Zachary typed faster than Clara.**

# ⑨ Distance, Rate, and Time

Speed is a rate that tells how fast you do something. Speed compares how much you do or how far you go to the amount of time it takes.

## Speed

*Harold drove 234 miles in 4.5 hours. What was his average speed?*

**Step 1:** Write the original rate.    **234 miles per 4.5 hours**

**Step 2:** Divide both terms by the second term, 4.5.

$$\frac{234}{4.5} \text{ miles per } \frac{4.5}{4.5} \text{ hours}$$

**52 miles per hour**

**Harold's average speed was 52 miles per hour.**

## The Distance Formula

A **formula** is an equation that uses words or symbols to show a relationship that is always true.

The relationship between distance, rate, and time is so important that it has its own formula.

The distance formula is **distance = rate × time.**

You can always find how far something goes (distance) by multiplying how fast it moves (a unit rate) by how much time it takes (time).

# The Distance Formula

*You are walking at a rate of 3 mph (miles per hour). If you walk for 2 hours, how many miles will you have walked?*

**Step 1:** The distance formula tells you that if you multiply a unit rate (3 mph) by a time (2 hours), you can find the distance traveled. Multiply 3 miles per hour by 2 hours.

$$3 \times 2 = 6$$

**You will have walked 6 miles.**

The units used in a problem must match.

If the speed is in miles per **hour**, you can't use **minutes** for the time. Change the time to hours first.

If the speed uses kilometers, the distance is in **kilometers**, not **miles**.

*Gina rode an ATV for $\frac{1}{2}$ hour at a steady rate of 60 km per hour.*

*How many kilometers did she ride?*

**Step 1:** Multiply the unit rate (60 km per hour) by the time ($\frac{1}{2}$ hour).

$$60 \times \frac{1}{2} = 30$$

**Gina rode 30 kilometers.**

# Proportions

Proportions are used to
show that two ratios are equal.

## Proportions

A **proportion** is an equation that shows equivalent ratios.
Proportions are usually written using fraction bars.

$$\frac{2}{3} = \frac{4}{6}$$

Proportions can also be written using colons.

$$2 : 3 = 4 : 6$$

No matter how you write a proportion, it can always be read the same way.

**"Two is to three as four is to six."**

Proportions have **four** terms.
$$\frac{\textbf{first } \text{term}}{\textbf{second } \text{term}} = \frac{\textbf{third } \text{term}}{\textbf{fourth } \text{term}}$$

## Proportional

*Are the ratios $\frac{2}{6}$ and $\frac{6}{18}$ proportional?*

**Step 1:** Write the two ratios as a proportion.
$$\frac{2}{6} = \frac{6}{18}$$

**Step 2:** Reduce each ratio to lowest terms. The proportion is **true** because the ratios are equivalent. If the ratios were not equivalent, you would say the proportion is **NOT true**.

$$\frac{2 \div 2}{6 \div 2} = \frac{6 \div 6}{18 \div 6}$$
$$\frac{1}{3} = \frac{1}{3}$$

**Yes, the ratios $\frac{2}{6}$ and $\frac{6}{18}$ are proportional.**

# Cross Multiplication

**Cross multiplication** means to multiply diagonally. Multiply the first term by the fourth term and multiply the second term by the third term. The answers, called **cross products**, are the same in a true proportion. If the answers are not the same, the proportion is not true.

$$\frac{1}{4} \diagdown \frac{2}{8} \qquad \begin{array}{l} 4 \times 2 = 8 \\ 1 \times 8 = 8 \end{array} \Big\rangle 8 = 8$$

Cross multiplication is written as:

**first term × fourth term = second term × third term**

$$1 \times 8 = 4 \times 2$$

## Cross Products

*A picture is 3 inches tall and 2 inches wide. Jerry used his computer to change the size of the picture to 4 inches tall and 6 inches wide. Are the pictures proportional?*

**Step 1:** Write the ratio of height to width for each picture.

| original | new |
|---|---|
| $\dfrac{3\text{ in}}{2\text{ in}}$ | $\dfrac{4\text{ in}}{6\text{ in}}$ |

**Step 2:** Cross multiply. If the cross products are equal, the ratios are proportional. The cross products are NOT equal, so the proportion is NOT true.

$$\frac{3}{2} \overset{?}{=} \frac{4}{6}$$

$$3 \times 6 \overset{?}{=} 2 \times 4$$

$$18 \neq 8$$

**The pictures are not proportional.**

25

# ⑪ Solving Proportions

You can use what you know about proportions to find an unknown term.

## Simple Proportions

*The ratio of boys to girls in Megan's class is 2 to 3.*
*If there are 12 boys in the class, how many girls are there?*

**Step 1:** You can find the number of girls in the class by setting up a proportion. The ratio given is boys to girls, so the ratio on the other side of the proportion should also be boys to girls. Fill in the ratios with the numbers given in the problem.

$$\frac{\text{boys}}{\text{girls}} = \frac{\text{boys}}{\text{girls}}$$

$$\frac{2}{3} = \frac{12}{?}$$

**Step 2:** You can solve a proportion by finding equivalent ratios using mental math. To change the first term (2) to 12, you multiply by 6. Do the same to the second term (3). $3 \times 6 = 18$.

$$\frac{2}{3} = \frac{12}{18}$$

**There are 18 girls in Megan's class.**

Remember:
To find equivalent
ratios, multiply
or divide both
terms by the
same number.

# Cross Products

*Inez uses 2 cups of flour to make 12 biscuits. How many cups of flour does she need to make 18 biscuits?*

**Step 1:** Set up a proportion.

$$\text{flour} \longrightarrow \frac{2}{12} = \frac{?}{18} \longleftarrow \text{biscuits}$$

**Step 2:** In proportions, the cross products are equal. Show the cross multiplication. Multiply 2 × 18.

$$2 \times 18 = 12 \times ?$$
$$36 = 12 \times ?$$

**Step 3:** You need to find the number that when multiplied by 12 equals 36. Divide 36 by 12.
The solved proportion is $\frac{2}{12} = \frac{3}{18}$

$$36 = 12 \times ?$$
$$36 \div 12 = 3$$

**Inez needs 3 cups of flour to make 18 biscuits.**

# Proportions Shortcut

*Inez uses 2 cups of flour to make 12 biscuits. How many biscuits can she make using 1 cup of flour?*

**Step 1:** Set up a proportion.

$$\text{flour} \longrightarrow \frac{2}{12} = \frac{1}{?} \longleftarrow \text{biscuits}$$

**Step 2:** Cross multiply only the two terms that are given.
These give you a cross product of 12.

$$\frac{2}{12} \nearrow \frac{1}{?}$$
$$12 \times 1 = 12$$

**Step 3:** Divide this cross product (12) by the known term that is left (2).
The result is the unknown term.
The solved proportion is $\frac{2}{12} = \frac{1}{6}$

$$\frac{2}{12} \nearrow \frac{1}{?} \quad 12$$
$$12 \div 2 = 6$$

**Inez can make 6 biscuits with 1 cup of flour.**

# ⑫ Ratios in Geometry

Anything related to the shape or size of something is also related to geometry.

## Similar Shapes

*In geometry, similar shapes have measurements that are in proportion. They have the same ratio. These two rectangles are similar. How tall is the blue rectangle?*

**Step 1:** Set up a proportion relating the height and width of each rectangle. Write in the measurements you know from the rectangles.

$$\frac{\text{height}}{\text{width}} = \frac{\text{height}}{\text{width}}$$

$$\frac{5 \text{ cm}}{4 \text{ cm}} = \frac{?}{6 \text{ cm}}$$

**Step 2:** Cross multiply the terms that are both known, 5 and 6.

$$\frac{5 \text{ cm}}{4 \text{ cm}} \quad \frac{?}{6 \text{ cm}}$$

$$5 \times 6 = 30$$

**Step 3:** Divide by the term that is left, 4. The solved proportion is $\frac{5}{4} = \frac{7.5}{6}$

$$30 \div 4 = 7.5$$

**The blue rectangle is 7.5 cm tall.**

The word **geometry** comes from the Greek root words geo, meaning earth, and metron, meaning measure.

# Shadow Problems

*Alex is standing beside a statue. Alex is 54 inches tall. His shadow is 9 inches long. The shadow of the statue is 21 inches long. How tall is the statue?*

**Step 1:** Heights of objects and the lengths of their shadows are proportional when they are measured at the same time of day. Set up a proportion using the measurements in the problem.

| Alex | | Statue |
|:---:|:---:|:---:|
| $\dfrac{\text{height}}{\text{shadow length}}$ | = | $\dfrac{\text{height}}{\text{shadow length}}$ |
| $\dfrac{54 \text{ in}}{9 \text{ in}}$ | = | $\dfrac{?}{21 \text{ in}}$ |

**Step 2:** You can reduce the ratio that you know to make cross multiplication easier.

$$\frac{54 \text{ in} \div 9}{9 \text{ in} \div 9} \quad \text{becomes} \quad \frac{6 \text{ in}}{1 \text{ in}}$$

**Step 3:** Write the proportion using the reduced ratio.

$$\frac{6 \text{ in}}{1 \text{ in}} = \frac{?}{21 \text{ in}}$$

**Step 4:** Cross multiply the terms that are both known, 6 and 21.

$$6 \times 21 = 126$$

**Step 5:** Divide by the term that is left, 1.

$$126 \div 1 = 126$$

The solved proportion is

$$\frac{54 \text{ inches}}{9 \text{ inches}} = \frac{126 \text{ inches}}{21 \text{ inches}}$$

**The statue is 126 inches tall.**

Check the answer to the shadow problem by reducing each ratio to lowest terms.

$$\frac{54 \div 9}{9 \div 9} = \frac{126 \div 21}{21 \div 21}$$

$$\frac{6}{1} = \frac{6}{1}$$

The proportion is true.

# ⑬ Scale Drawings and Models

Scale drawings and models are used to show big or small objects in a manageable size.

## Scale

A **scale** is a ratio that compares the measurements of a drawing or model to the measurements of the object it represents.
The model or drawing measurement is always the first term.
The real object measurement is the second term

Scales are written like other ratios. The scale **1 inch to 2 feet** means if an object is 2 feet tall, the drawing will be 1 inch tall. Sometimes a scale is written using the = sign, **1 inch = 2 feet.**

There are two kinds of scale drawings and models.
A **reduction** makes a model that is smaller than the object.
An **enlargement** makes a model that is larger than the object.

## Reduction

*Jennifer is making a map of her town. The map scale is 1 inch to 2 miles. Jennifer's house is exactly 4 miles from the school. On her map, how far should her house be from the school?*

**Step 1:** Maps are reductions. The scale tells you that on the map, 1 inch is the same as 2 miles in real distance.

Set up a proportion. Use the scale as the first ratio.
Fill in the part of the second ratio that you know.

scale inches $\longrightarrow$
real miles $\longrightarrow$ $\dfrac{1}{2} = \dfrac{?}{4}$

30

**Step 2:** This is a simple proportion. Solve it by finding equivalent ratios. To change the second term (2) to 4, you multiply by 2. Do the same to the first term (1). $1 \times 2 = 2$.

$$\frac{1 \, (\times 2)}{2 \, (\times 2)} = \frac{2}{4}$$

**On the map, Jennifer's house should be 2 inches from the school.**

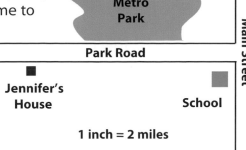

Park Road

Jennifer's House

School

Metro Park

Main Street

1 inch = 2 miles

## Enlargement

*A model of a ladybug is made at a scale of 1 meter = 0.5 cm. The model is 0.8 meters long. How many centimeters long is the real ladybug?*

**Step 1:** Remember, the scaled measurement is the first term, and the real life measurement is the second term. The scale tells you that for every 1 meter of the model, the ladybug measures 0.5 cm. Since the model is larger than the real ladybug, this is an enlargement.

Set up a proportion. Use the scale as the first ratio. Fill in the part of the second ratio that you know.

scale meters $\longrightarrow$
real centimeters $\longrightarrow$ $\dfrac{1}{0.5} = \dfrac{0.8}{?}$

**Step 2:** Cross multiply the terms that are both known, 0.5 and 0.8.

$0.5 \times 0.8 = 0.4$

**Step 3:** Divide by the term that is left, 1.

$0.4 \div 1 = 0.4$

scale meters $\longrightarrow$
real centimeters $\longrightarrow$ $\dfrac{1}{0.5} = \dfrac{0.8}{0.4}$

**The real ladybug is 0.4 centimeters long.**

# ⑭ The Golden Ratio

One ratio is seen repeating itself in art, biology, nature, architecture and mathematics. It is called the golden ratio.

## The Golden Ratio

The golden ratio is a special ratio that is about **1 : 1.62**.

The modern idea of the golden ratio was discovered, but not invented, by a man named **Leonardo Fibonacci**. The ancient Egyptians, Mayans, and Greeks used the golden ratio in their art and architecture.

## The Golden Rectangle

*A golden rectangle looks nice. Its length and width are in a ratio that is close to the golden ratio. A computer screen is 15 inches tall. Find the width if the screen is a golden rectangle.*

**Step 1:** Set up a proportion using the golden ratio as the first term. The height (length) of a computer screen is smaller than the width. Write the length as the corresponding term to the smaller term, 1. The length to width ratio is 1 to 1.62. Fill in the part of the second ratio that you know.

$$\text{length} \longrightarrow \quad \text{width} \longrightarrow \quad \frac{1}{1.62} = \frac{15 \text{ in}}{?}$$

**Step 2:** Cross multiply the terms that are both known, 1.62 and 15.

$$1.62 \times 15 = 24.3$$

**Step 3:** Divide by the term that is left, 1.

$$24.3 \div 1 = 24.3$$

$$\text{length} \longrightarrow \quad \text{width} \longrightarrow \quad \frac{1}{1.62} = \frac{15 \text{ in}}{24.3 \text{ in}}$$

**The screen is 24.3 inches wide.**

# The Golden Ratio in Your Body

*An average adult hand is about 18 cm long from the tip of the middle finger to the wrist. The length of an average adult forearm (wrist to elbow) is about 29 cm. Is the ratio of hand length to forearm length the golden ratio?*

**Step 1:** Write the golden ratio and the ratio of hand length to forearm length as a proportion.

$$\frac{1}{1.62} = \frac{18 \text{ cm}}{29 \text{ cm}}$$

**Step 2:** Cross multiply. The cross products are not equal, so the ratios are not proportional. However, the ratios are VERY close. When you measure a person's hand length and forearm length, the ratio is usually close to the golden ratio.

$$\frac{1}{1.62} = \frac{18}{29}$$
$$1 \times 29 = 1.62 \times 18$$
$$29 = 29.16$$

The golden ratio can also be found in other parts of your body.

Try comparing the length of the segments in your fingers.

Try the length from your foot to your belly button and from your foot to the top of your head.

Remember, everyone is different, so the ratios will not be exactly the same. But they will be close. And they will be close to the golden ratio.

# Alternate Proportions

A proportion can be written
another way and still be true.

## Corresponding Terms

There are two ratios and four terms in a proportion.
Terms that are in the same place in each ratio are called
**corresponding terms.**

$$\frac{\textbf{first}}{\textbf{second}} = \frac{\textbf{third}}{\textbf{fourth}}$$

The **first** and **third** term are corresponding terms.
The **second** and **fourth** term are corresponding terms.

## Find Corresponding Terms

*What are the corresponding terms in the proportion 1 : 3 = 5 : 15?*

**Step 1:** Corresponding terms are in the
same place in each ratio.
1 is the first term in the first ratio.
5 is the first term in the second ratio.

$1 : 3 = 5 : 15$
or
$\frac{1}{3} = \frac{5}{15}$

**1 and 5 are corresponding terms.**

3 is the second term in the first ratio.
15 is the second term in the second ratio.

$1 : 3 = 5 : 15$
or
$\frac{1}{3} = \frac{5}{15}$

**3 and 15 are corresponding terms.**

# Alternate Proportion

Corresponding terms in a true proportion are also in proportion. The proportion made by corresponding terms is called the **alternate proportion.**

$$\frac{1}{2} = \frac{3}{6}$$ can be written as $$\frac{1}{3} = \frac{2}{6}$$

## Alternate Proportions

*The proportion 3 : 25 = 12 : 100 is true. Write the alternate proportion, and check to make sure it is true.*

**Step 1:** Write the original proportion using fraction bars. This makes it easier to find the corresponding terms.

$$\frac{3}{25} = \frac{12}{100}$$

**Step 2:** The first set of corresponding terms is 3 and 12. Write 3 and 12 as the first ratio in the alternate proportion.

$$\frac{3}{25} = \frac{12}{100} \qquad \frac{3}{12} = \underline{\qquad}$$

**Step 3:** The second set of corresponding terms is 25 and 100. Write 25 and 100 as the second ratio.

$$\frac{3}{25} = \frac{12}{100} \qquad \frac{3}{25} = \frac{25}{100}$$

The alternate proportion is $\frac{3}{12} = \frac{25}{100}$.

**Step 4:** Check the alternate proportion. Reduce each ratio to lowest terms.

$$\frac{3 \div 3}{12 \div 3} = \frac{25 \div 25}{100 \div 25}$$

$$\frac{1}{4} = \frac{1}{4}$$

**The reduced ratios are the same, so the alternate proportion is true.**

You can also check to see if a proportion is true by seeing if the cross products are equal.

35

# ⑯ Percents and Ratios

Percents are ratios that have 100 as the second term. The word *percent* means *per hundred*.

## Percents

Percents are written using the percent sign, %.

25% is read as twenty-five percent.
25% means 25 per 100, or 25 : 100.

| | |
|---|---|
| Percents can be less than 100. | 42% or 42 : 100 |
| Percents can be equal to 100. | 100% or 100 : 100 |
| Percents can be greater than 100. | 150% or 150 : 100 |

## Modeling Percents

**Use a model to show 35%.**

**Step 1:** One way to model percents is to use a grid with 100 squares. 35% means 35 per hundred, so color 35 of the 100 squares.

**35% of the grid is colored.**

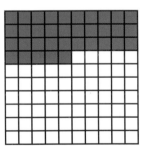

**Use a model to show 100%.**

**Step 1:** 100% means 100 per hundred, so color 100 of the 100 squares.

**100% of the grid is colored.**

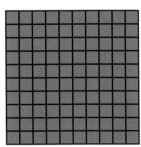

# Writing a Ratio as a Percent

*On Ray's mp3 player, the ratio of jazz music to all of his music is 78 to 100. What percent of the music is jazz?*

**Step 1:** Write the ratio of jazz music to all music.    **78 : 100**

**Step 2:** When the second term is 100, you can replace the term with the percent symbol, %.    **78%**

To write a fraction or ratio as a percent when the second term is not 100, see pages 39 and 46.

**78% of the music on Ray's mp3 player is jazz.**

# Writing a Percent as a Ratio

*Write 48% as a ratio.*

**Step 1:** The first term of the ratio is the number part of the percent, 48.    **48 :**

**Step 2:** The second term is always 100.    **48 : 100**

**Step 3:** Reduce the ratio to lowest terms. Divide both terms by their greatest common factor, 4.

**48 ÷ 4 : 100 ÷ 4**

**12 : 25**

**48% as a ratio is 12 : 25.**

*Write 150% as a ratio.*

**Step 1:** The first term of the ratio is the number part of the percent, 150.    **150 :**

**Step 2:** The second term is always 100.    **150 : 100**

**Step 3:** Reduce the ratio to lowest terms. Divide both terms by their greatest common factor, 50.

**150 ÷ 50 : 100 ÷ 50**

**3 : 2**

**150% as a ratio is 3 : 2.**

# ⑰ Percents, Fractions, and Decimals

Percents can be written as fractions and decimals.

## Rewriting Percents

| As fractions: | 89% | 151% |
|---|---|---|
| A percent is written as a fraction with a denominator of 100. The percentage, or number part of the percent, is the numerator. | $\frac{89}{100}$ | $\frac{151}{100}$ |

| As decimals: | 89% | 151% |
|---|---|---|
| A percent is written as a decimal by dropping the percent sign and moving the decimal point two places left. | 0.89 | 1.51 |

## Rewriting a Percent

***Write 35% as a fraction and a decimal.***

**Step 1:** Write 35% as a fraction. Write the number part, 35, in the numerator.
Write 100 in the denominator.

$$\frac{35}{100}$$

Reduce the fraction to lowest terms by dividing the numerator and denominator by their greatest common factor, 5.

$$\frac{35 \div 5}{100 \div 5} = \frac{7}{20}$$

**Step 2:** Write 35% as a decimal.
Drop the percent sign.
In a whole number, like 35, the decimal point is on the right of the ones digit.
Move the decimal point two places left.

35%
35.
0.35

$$35\% = \frac{35}{100} = 0.35$$

# Decimals as Percents

*Write 0.23, 0.6, and 1.27 as percents.*

**Step 1:** Multiply each decimal by 100%. When you multiply by 100, the decimal point moves 2 places to the right.

$$0.23 \quad 0.6 \quad 1.27$$
$$23 \quad\quad 60 \quad\quad 127$$

**Step 2:** Write the percent signs.     **23%   60%   127%**

**0.23 = 23%, 0.6 = 60%, and 1.27 = 127%.**

# Fractions as Percents

*In Bob's office, $\frac{1}{20}$ of the employees have beards. What percent of the employees have beards?*

**Step 1:** Multiply the fraction by 100.

$$\frac{1}{20} \times 100 = \frac{1}{20} \times \frac{100}{1} = \frac{100}{20}$$

**Step 2:** Reduce the fraction to lowest terms.

$$\frac{100}{20} = 5$$

**Step 3:** Write the percent sign.          **5%**

**5% of the employees have beards.**

> You can also write a fraction as a percent by writing it as a decimal first.
>
> 1. Write the fraction as a decimal by dividing the numerator by the denominator.
>
> 2. Write the decimal as a percent.

# Percents and Proportions

Proportions can be used to solve percent problems. Just use the percent as one of the ratios.

## Proportions in Percent Problems

Percent problems relate a percent, a part, and a whole. You can solve percent problems by writing the percent as a ratio and setting up a proportion.

$$\frac{\text{percentage}}{100} = \frac{\text{part}}{\text{whole}}$$

## Using Proportions

*Dr. Price saw 20 patients on Monday. Of those patients, 60% had cavities. How many of the patients on Monday had cavities?*

**Step 1:** Set up a proportion.
Write 60% as a ratio.

$$\frac{60}{100} = \underline{\quad\quad}$$

**Step 2:** The second ratio compares the patients with cavities to all of the patients. You know there were a total of 20 patients on Monday. You are trying to find how many of them had cavities.

$$\frac{60}{100} = \frac{\text{part}}{\text{whole}}$$

$$\frac{60}{100} = \frac{?}{20}$$

**Step 3:** Solve the proportion.
Cross multiply the terms you know.
Divide by the term that is left.
The solved proportion is $\frac{60}{100} = \frac{12}{20}$

$$60 \times 20 = 1{,}200$$
$$1{,}200 \div 100 = 12$$

**12 of the patients on Monday had cavities.**

# Percents and Money

*A $3.00 tube of toothpaste is marked 40% off this week. How much will you save if you buy toothpaste this week?*

**Step 1:** Set up a proportion. Write 40% as a ratio.

$$\frac{40}{100} = \underline{\hspace{2cm}}$$

**Step 2:** This problem compares part of the price to the whole price of the toothpaste. You know the regular price is $3.00 (whole). You want to find the amount you can save (part) if you buy the toothpaste this week.

$$\frac{40}{100} = \frac{part}{whole} \qquad\qquad \frac{40}{100} = \frac{?}{\$3.00}$$

**Step 3:** Solve the proportion. A money value is treated like any other decimal. Remember, the terms of a ratio can be decimals or fractions. Cross multiply the terms you know. Divide by the term that is left. The solved proportion is

$$40 \times \$3.00 = \$120.00$$
$$\$120.00 \div 100 = \$1.20$$

$$\frac{40}{100} = \frac{\$1.20}{\$3.00}$$

You can save $1.20 if you buy the toothpaste this week.

Error Buster:
Always include the decimal point and dollar sign in the answer when you solve a money problem.

# ⑲ The Percent Equation

You can use a multiplication
statement to find the percent of a number.

## The Percent Equation

Remember, percent problems relate three numbers: a whole,
a percent, and a part. This statement relates the numbers
to each other.

**Percent of whole is part.**

**50% of 20 is 10.**

You can change this statement to an equation.
"Of" means multiplication and "is" means equals.

**percent × whole = part**

**50% × 20 = 10**

## Finding the Percent of a Number

*What is 25% of 60?*

**Step 1:** Write the percent equation.　　**percent × whole = part**
Put in the numbers that you know.　　　**25% × 60 = \_\_**

**Step 2:** Write the percent as a decimal.

**0.25 × 60 = \_\_**

**Step 3:** Multiply.　　**0.25 × 60 = 15**

**25% of 60 is 15.**

> You can write
> the percent as a
> decimal or a fraction.
> 25% is 1/4.
> 1/4 × 60 = 15.

# Word Problem Percents

*Marci wants to put 15% of her paycheck in a savings account. If her paycheck is $200.00, how much should she put in savings?*
To solve this problem, find 15% of $200.00.

**Step 1:** Write the percent equation. Put in the numbers you know.

$$\text{percent} \times \text{whole} = \text{part}$$
$$15\% \times 200.00 = \underline{\quad}$$

**Step 2:** Write the percent as a decimal.

$$0.15 \times 200.00 = \underline{\quad}$$

**Step 3:** Multiply.

$$0.15 \times 200.00 = 30.00$$
$$15\% \text{ of } 200.00 \text{ is } 30.00$$

**Marci should put $30.00 in a savings account.**

## Fractions in Percents

*What is $\frac{1}{3}$ % of 1,200?*

**Step 1:** Write the percent equation. Put in the numbers you know.

$$\text{percent} \times \text{whole} = \text{part}$$
$$\frac{1}{3}\% \times 1,200 = \underline{\quad}$$

**Step 2:** Write the percent as a fraction. Percents are written as fractions by dividing the percent by 100.

$$\frac{1}{3}\% = \frac{1}{3} \div 100$$

To divide fractions, multiply the first number by the reciprocal of the second.

$$\frac{1}{3} \div 100 = \frac{1}{3} \times \frac{1}{100}$$
$$= \frac{1}{300}$$

**Step 3:** Put the fraction into the percent equation, then multiply. When multiplying fractions, you can cancel out like factors before you multiply.

$$\frac{1}{300} \times 1,200 = \underline{\quad}$$
$$\frac{1}{\cancel{300}} \times \frac{\cancel{1200}^{12}}{1} = \underline{\quad}$$
$$\frac{1}{\cancel{3}} \times \frac{\cancel{12}^{4}}{1} = \frac{4}{1} = 4$$

$\frac{1}{3}$% of 1,200 is 4.

# Percents Larger Than 100%

In most problems, the part is less than the whole. Some problems have a part that is equal to or greater than the whole.

## 100%

*D'Jon set a goal to sell 72 used cars last year. He sold 100% of his goal. How many used cars did D'Jon sell?*

To solve this problem, find 100% of 72.

**Step 1:** Write the percent equation. Put in the numbers you know.

$$\text{percent} \times \text{whole} = \text{part}$$
$$100\% \times 72 = \underline{\quad}$$

**Step 2:** Write the percent as a decimal.

$$1.00 \times 72 = \underline{\quad}$$

**Step 3:** Multiply.

$$1.00 \times 72 = 72$$

100% of 72 is 72.

When the percent is 100%, the part is always equal to the whole.

**D'Jon sold 72 used cars last year.**

**Think about it:**
100% as a fraction is $\frac{100}{100}$, or 1.
100% as a decimal is 1.00, or 1.

What *do* you get when you multiply one by a number?

The same number!

# Percents Larger Than 100%

*Phillip needs new jeans. The price of a pair of jeans today is 130% of what is was last month. If the jeans cost $27.00 last month, how much do they cost today? What is the difference in price?*

**Step 1:** Write the percent equation. Put in the numbers you know.

**percent × whole = part**
130% × $27.00 = ___

**Step 2:** Write the percent as a decimal.

1.30 × $27.00 = ___

**Step 3:** Multiply.

1.30 × $27.00 = $35.10

**Today, the jeans cost $35.10**

**Step 4:** Find the difference in price. Subtract the cost last month from the cost today.

$35.10
− $27.00
$ 8.10

**The jeans cost $8.10 more today.**

## Use a Proportion

*What is 150% of 200?*

**Step 1:** Set up a proportion. Write 150% as a ratio.

$$\frac{150}{100} = \frac{part}{whole}$$

**Step 2:** You can use the percent statement to decide which number is the part, and which is the whole.

Percent statement:  percent of whole is part
Problem statement:  150% of 200 is ___
200 is the whole. Write it in the proportion.

$$\frac{150}{100} = \frac{part}{200}$$

When the percent is over 100%, the part is greater than the whole.

300 > 200

**Step 3:** Solve the proportion. Cross multiply the terms you know.

150 × 200 = 30,000
Divide by the term that remains.

30,000 ÷ 100 = 300
The solved proportion is

$$\frac{150}{100} = \frac{300}{200}$$

**150% of 200 is 300.**

45

You can find what percent one number is of another by using what you already know about percents.

## First Write a Ratio

*There are 40 students in the marching band. Of those students, 7 play trombones. What percent of the marching band students play trombones?*

**Step 1:** Write the ratio of students who play trombones to the total number of students in the marching band.

$$\frac{\textbf{trombones}}{\textbf{total band}} \qquad \frac{7}{40}$$

**Step 2:** Write the ratio as a decimal by dividing the first term by the second term.

$$\frac{7}{40} = 7 \div 40$$

$$\frac{7}{40} = 0.175$$

```
      0.175
40)7.000
  − 40
    300
  − 280
    200
  − 200
      0
```

**Step 3:** Write 0.175 as a percent. Move the decimal point 2 places right. Write the percent symbol.

$$0.175 = 17.5\%$$

**17.5% of the marching band students play trombones.**

# Use a Proportion

*What percent of 48 is 30?*

**Step 1:** Set up a proportion. Remember, a percent is a ratio with a second term of 100.

$$\frac{percentage}{100} = \frac{part}{whole}$$

**Step 2:** Fill in what you know.

$$\frac{percentage}{100} = \frac{30}{48}$$

**Percent Buster:**
Use the percent statement to decide which number is the part, and which is the whole.

Percent of whole is part.
What percent of 48 is 30?

**Step 3:** Solve the proportion to find the percentage.

Cross multiply the terms you know.

$100 \times 30 = 3{,}000$

Divide by the term that is left, 48.

$3{,}000 \div 48 = 62.5$

The solved proportion is

$$\frac{62.5}{100} = \frac{30}{48}$$

**30 is 62.5% of 48.**

# Fractional Percents

*What percent of 3 is 1?*

**Step 1:** Set up a proportion.

$$\frac{percentage}{100} = \frac{part}{whole}$$

**Step 2:** Fill in what you know.

$$\frac{percentage}{100} = \frac{1}{3}$$

**Step 3:** Solve the proportion.
Cross multiply the terms you know, 100 and 1.
Divide by the term that is left, 3.

$100 \times 1 = 100$

$100 \div 3 = 33\frac{1}{3}$

$$\frac{33\frac{1}{3}}{100} = \frac{1}{3}$$

**1 is $33\frac{1}{3}$% of 3.**

$$\begin{array}{r} 33\frac{1}{3} \\ 3\overline{)100} \\ -9 \\ \hline 10 \\ -9 \\ \hline 1 \end{array}$$

**Write the remainder as $\frac{1}{3}$.**

# ㉒ Finding the Total

Sometimes you know the percent and the part, and you need to find the whole.

## Use a Proportion

*One serving of tomato soup contains 1 gram of fiber. This is 4% of the amount of fiber recommended for one day. How many grams of fiber are recommended for one day?*

**Step 1:** Set up a proportion.

$$\frac{percentage}{100} = \frac{part}{whole}$$

**Step 2:** Fill in what you know.

$$\frac{4}{100} = \frac{1}{whole}$$

**Step 3:** Solve the proportion.
Cross multiply the terms you know, 100 and 1.
Divide by the term that is left, 4.

$$100 \times 1 = 100$$
$$100 \div 4 = 25$$
$$\frac{4}{100} = \frac{1}{25}$$

**25 grams of fiber are recommended for one day.**

Proportion Buster:

Proportions can be used to solve any percent problem.

You can find the part, whole, or percent with a proportion.

# The Percent Statement

*Complete this statement.*
*50% of ____ is 60.*

**Step 1:** Write the problem. The problem is written using the percent statement. Change the statement to an equation.

50% of ____ is 60.
50% × ____ = 60

**Step 2:** Write the percent as a decimal.

0.50 × ____ = 60

**Step 3:** You can write a multiplication with a missing factor as a division problem. Divide the product by the factor you know.

60 ÷ 0.50 = ____

**Step 4:** Divide. When you divide by a decimal, make the decimal a whole number by moving the same number of places in each number.

60.0 ÷ 0.50 = ____

600 ÷ 5 = ____

600 ÷ 5 = 120

so, 0.50 × 120 = 60

**50% of 120 is 60.**

*A serving of crackers contains 720 mg of sodium. This is 30% of the sodium recommended for one day. How many milligrams of sodium are recommended for one day?*

**Step 1:** Write the percent equation. Put in the numbers you know.

**percent × whole = part**
30% × ____ = 720

**Step 2:** Write the percent as a decimal.

0.30 × ____ = 720

**Step 3:** Write the problem as division.

720 ÷ 0.30 = ____

**Step 4:** Divide.

720.0 ÷ 0.30 = ____

7,200 ÷ 3 = ____

7,200 ÷ 3 = 2,400

so, 0.30 × 2,400 = 720

**2,400 milligrams of sodium are recommended for one day.**

# (23) Percent of Change

This year, you have one more pet than you did last year. Is that a big change? It *is* if you only had one pet last year. It *is not* if you already had 20 pets. A percent of change compares an amount of change to the original amount.

## Percent of Increase

*A high school had 240 students last year. This year, there are 261 students at the same school. What is the percent of increase in the number of students?*

> **Percent of increase** is the percent of change when an amount goes up.

**Step 1:** Subtract to find the change between the new number of students and the original number of students.

$$\text{new} - \text{original} = \text{change}$$
$$261 - 240 = 21$$

**Step 2:** Write a ratio of the change to the original.

$$\frac{\text{change}}{\text{original}} \quad \frac{21}{240}$$

**Step 3:** Reduce the ratio to lowest terms.

$$\frac{21}{240} = \frac{7}{80}$$

**Step 4:** Write the ratio as a percent.
Multiply the ratio by 100.
Reduce.
Add the percent sign.

$$\frac{7}{80} \times 100 = \frac{7}{\underset{4}{80}} \times \frac{\overset{5}{100}}{1} = \frac{35}{4}$$

$$= 8\frac{3}{4}$$

**The percent of increase in the number of students is $8\frac{3}{4}$%.**

$$\frac{21}{240} = 8\frac{3}{4}\%$$

# Percent of Decrease

*For the final football game of the year, the price of a cup of hot chocolate went down from $1.25 to $1.00. What was the percent of decrease?*

**Step 1:** Subtract to find the change between the new price and the original price.

**original − new = change**
**$1.25 − $1.00 = $0.25**

**Step 2:** Write a ratio of the change to the original.

$$\frac{\text{change}}{\text{original}} \qquad \frac{0.25}{1.25}$$

**Step 3:** Write the ratio as a decimal by dividing the first term by the second term.

**0.25 ÷ 1.25 = 0.2**

$$1.25\overline{)0.250}$$

$$\begin{array}{r} 0.2 \\ 125\overline{)25.0} \\ -\,250 \\ \hline 0 \end{array}$$

12   12

**Step 4:** Write 0.2 as a percent. Move the decimal point 2 places right. Write the percent symbol.

**0.2 = 20%**

**The percent of decrease was 20%.**

# ㉔ Sales Tax and Discounts

When you buy an item sometimes it costs you more than the marked price. Sales tax is money collected by the government when you buy certain things.

## Sales Tax

*Marita spent the day at the mall. She bought a sweater with a price of $30.00. The sales tax was 7.5%. How much was the sales tax on the sweater?*

To solve this problem, find 7.5% of $30.00.

**Step 1:** Write the percent equation. Put in the numbers you know.

$$\text{percent} \times \text{whole} = \text{part}$$
$$7.5\% \times \$30.00 = \underline{\quad}$$

**Step 2:** Write the percent as a decimal.

$$0.075 \times \$30.00 = \underline{\quad}$$

**Step 3:** Multiply.

$$0.075 \times \$30.00 = \$2.25$$

**7.5% of $30.00 is $2.25.**

## Total Cost

*What was the total cost of Marita's sweater from the problem above?*

**Step 1:** To find the total cost of an item, add the price and the sales tax.

| | |
|---|---|
| price: | $30.00 |
| sales tax: | + $ 2.25 |
| total cost: | $32.25 |

**The total cost of the sweater was $32.25.**

> Sales tax percents are set by state and local governments.
>
> Items with the same price may have a different total cost in different states or cities.

## What Is a Discount?

A **discount** is an amount that is taken off the original price of an item. Some discounts are a dollar amount, like $2 off the price of a meal. Other discounts are a percent, like 10% off the price of an oil change.

## Discounts

*Every Monday, tropical fish at the pet store are discounted 25%. If the original price of a fish is $2.60, how much is the discount?*

To solve this problem, find 25% of $2.60.

**Step 1:** Write the percent equation. Put in the numbers you know.

percent × whole = part
25% × $2.60 = ____

**Step 2:** Write the percent as a decimal.

0.25 × $2.60 = ____

**Step 3:** Multiply.

0.25 × $2.60 = $0.65

**The discount on a fish that costs $2.60 is $0.65.**

## Sale Price

*What is the sale price of the fish from the problem above?*

**Step 1:** To find the sale price of an item, subtract the discount from the original price.

original price:     $2.60
discount:         − $0.65
sale price:         $1.95

**The sale price of the fish is $1.95.**

53

# ㉕ Commission and Income

Some jobs are paid on commission. When a salesperson receives a certain percent of sales, the amount is called his or her commission.

## Sales Commission

*Jameson is a real estate agent. He earned a commission of $5,200 for the sale of a $130,000 house. What percent of the sale was his commission?*

**Step 1:** Write the ratio comparing commission (part) to sale price (whole).

$$\frac{\text{part}}{\text{whole}} \quad \frac{\$5,200}{\$130,000}$$

**Step 2:** Write the ratio as a decimal.

$$\frac{\$5,200}{\$130,000} = \$5,200 \div \$130,000$$
$$= 0.04$$

Large even amounts of money, like $5,200 and $130,000 can be written without a decimal point. All of the zeros at the end can get confusing!

**Step 3:** Write the decimal, 0.04, as a percent.  **0.04 = 4%**

**Jameson's commission was 4% of the sale.**

## Use a Proportion

*At an appliance store, the salespeople earn a 12% commission when they sell an extended warranty. If the warranty costs $200.00, how much is the commission?*

**Step 1:** Set up a proportion.

$$\frac{\text{percentage}}{100} = \frac{\text{part}}{\text{whole}}$$

**Step 2:** Fill in what you know.

$$\frac{2}{100} = \frac{\text{part}}{\$200.00}$$

**Step 3:** Solve the proportion. Cross multiply the terms you know. Divide by the term that is left.

$$12 \times 200.00 = 2400.00$$
$$2400.00 \div 100 = 24.00$$

**The commission is $24.00.**

# Income

**gross income**—The total amount of income before taxes and other deductions are taken out.

**net income**—The amount that is left over after taxes and other deductions are taken out.

## Income

*Jameson earned $5,200 in commission. If 21% was taken out of his pay in deductions, how much was his net income?*

To solve this problem, first find the amount of deductions. Then subtract the deductions from $5,200.

**Step 1:** Find the amount of deductions by finding 21% of $5,200.
Write the percent equation.       **percent × whole = part**
Put in the numbers you know.      **21% × $5,200 = \_\_\_\_**

**Step 2:** Write the percent as a decimal.    **0.21 × $5,200 = \_\_\_\_**

**Step 3:** Multiply.                      **0.21 × $5,200 = $1,092**
                                             **deductions = $1,092**

**Step 4:** Subtract the deductions, $1,092,        **$5,200**
from Jameson's gross pay, $5,200.         **− $1,092**
                                            **$4,108**

**Jameson's net income was $4,108.**

# ㉖ Tips

Some jobs are paid by the hour. Some are paid on commission. Part of the pay for other jobs is from the tips given by customers.

## What is a Tip?

People who provide a service are often given a **tip**.

Some service people are porters, waiters, and hairdressers.

Tips are usually given as a percent of the cost of the service.

For example, if a haircut costs $10.00, you might give the hairdresser a tip of 20%, or $2.00.

## Tips

*Cheyenne ate dinner at a restaurant. Her meal cost $17.89. She wants to give the waitress a tip that is close to 15%. About how much should she tip the waitress?*

**Step 1:** A tip is not usually a set amount, or a set percent. By rounding amounts to the nearest dollar, you can quickly decide how much to tip.

Round $17.89 to the nearest whole dollar.

$$\$17.89 \xrightarrow{\text{Rounds to}} \$18.00$$

**Step 2:** Find 15% of $18.00.

$$15\% \times \$18.00 = \underline{\hspace{1cm}}$$

$$0.15\% \times \$18.00 = \$2.70$$

**Cheyenne should tip about $2.70**

> You could also round the tip amount to the nearest dollar. $2.70 rounds to $3.00.

## Multiplying by 10%

Look at 10% of some amounts. Do you see a pattern?

**10% of $70.00 is $7.00**      **10% of $7.00 is $0.70**

**10% of $42.00 is $4.20**      **10% of $4.20 is $0.42**

To find 10% of an amount, you can move the decimal point one place to the left.

## Mental Math

*A haircut costs $25.00. Use mental math to find the amount of a 20% tip on the haircut.*

**Step 1:** Think:     **I can find 10% of $25.00 by moving the decimal point one place left.**

**10% of $25.00 is $2.50**

**Step 2:** Think:     **20% is the same as 10% + 10%**

**20% = $2.50 + $2.50 = $5.00**

**A 20% tip on $25.00 is $5.00.**

# ㉗ Simple Interest

For some bank accounts, like savings accounts, a bank will pay you a set percent to borrow your money.

## Interest Terms

**principal**—The amount of money in an account.

**interest rate**—The percent that is paid by the borrower.

**simple interest**—Interest that is found one time on the principal. To find simple interest multiply the principal, interest rate, and time in years.

**Interest = Principal × Rate × Time, or**

$$I = P \times R \times T$$

## Simple Interest

*Find the simple interest on $300.00 for 2 years at 6%.*

**Step 1:** Write the equation for simple interest. Fill in the amounts you know.

**Interest = Principal × Rate × Time**
**Interest = $300.00 × 6% × 2 years**

**Step 2:** Change the percent to a decimal. Write it in the equation.

**6% = 0.06**
**Interest = $300.00 × 0.06 × 2**

**Step 3:** Multiply.

**Interest = ($300.00 × 0.06) × 2**
**= ($18.00) × 2**
**= $36.00**
**The simple interest is $36.00.**

# Time

Since interest is found using years, change all time values to years. For example, to change months to years, divide the number of months by the number of months in a year, 12.

These are some terms used for time when finding interest.

**annually**—One time a year.

**semiannually**—Every six months. $6 \div 12 = {}^1/_2$ or 0.5.

**quarterly**—Every three months. $3 \div 12 = {}^1/_4$ or 0.25.

**monthly**—Every month. $1 \div 12 = {}^1/_{12}$ or about 0.08.

## Semiannual Interest

*Find the semiannual interest on $1,000.00 at 8%.*

**Step 1:** Write the equation for simple interest. Semiannual means every six months. Fill in the amounts you know.

**Interest = Principal × Rate × Time**
**Interest = $1,000.00 × 8% × 6 months**

**Step 2:** Change months to years. Write it in the equation.

**6 months = 0.5 years**
**Interest = $1,000.00 × 8% × 0.5**

**Step 3:** Change the percent to a decimal. Write it in the equation.

**8% = 0.08**
**Interest = $1,000.00 × 0.08 × 0.5**

**Step 4:** Multiply.

**Interest = ($1,000.00 × 0.08) × 0.5**
**= ($80.00) × 0.5**
**= $40.00**

**The semiannual simple interest is $40.00.**

# ㉘ Compound Interest

Compound interest is interest that is paid on principal *and* interest that has already been earned.

## Compound Interest

*Find the compound interest on $300.00 for 2 years at 6% compounded annually.*

**Step 1:** To find compound interest, find the simple interest for each period of time the amount is compounded. This account is compounded annually, or yearly, so find the simple interest for the first year.

| | |
|---|---|
| Write the equation for simple interest. Fill in the amounts you know. | **Interest = Principal × Rate × Time**<br>**Interest = $300.00 × 6% × 1 year** |

**Step 2:** Change the percent to a decimal. Write it in the equation.

$$6\% = 0.06$$
$$\textbf{Interest} = \$300.00 \times 0.06 \times 1$$

**Step 3:** Multiply. This is the interest earned the first year.

$$\textbf{Interest} = (\$300.00 \times 0.06) \times 1$$
$$= (\$18.00) \times 1$$
$$= \$18.00$$

**Step 4:** Add the principal and the interest from the first year. This is the new principal.

| | |
|---|---|
| **principal** | $300.00 |
| **interest** | + $ 18.00 |
| **new principal** | $318.00 |

**Step 5:** Find the interest earned the second year using the new principal.

| | |
|---|---|
| Write the equation for simple interest. Fill in the amounts you know. | **Interest = Principal × Rate × Time**<br>**Interest = $318.00 × 6% × 1 year** |

**Step 6:** Change the percent to a decimal. Write it in the equation.

$$6\% = 0.06$$
$$\textbf{Interest} = \$318.00 \times 0.06 \times 1$$

**Step 7:** Multiply. This is the interest earned the second year.

$$\text{Interest} = (\$318.00 \times 0.06) \times 1$$
$$= (\$19.08) \times 1$$
$$= \$19.08$$

**Step 8:** The question asked for the compound interest over 2 years.

| first year | $ 18.00 |
|---|---|
| second year | + $ 19.08 |
| | $ 37.08 |

**The compound interest is $37.08.**

## Compounding

*If you save money in an account that compounds quarterly for 3 years, how many times will it compound?*

**Step 1:** Multiply the number of times the money compounds each year by the number of years the money is saved.

Compound interest earns more money than simple interest when the interest rate and time are the same. On page 58, using simple interest, the same savings account earned $36.

Some accounts compound daily. That's 365 times every year! Calculator, anyone?

When an account compounds quarterly, it compounds 4 times every year.
**4 times a year × 3 years = 12 times**

**The money will compound 12 times.**

# Further Reading

**Books**

Howett, Jerry. *New Basic Skills with Ratios and Percents*. Cambridge, 1998.

McKellar, Danica. *Math Doesn't Suck: How to Survive Middle School Math Without Losing your Mind or Breaking a Nail*. New York: Penguin Group, 2008.

———. *Math At Hand: A Mathematics Handbook*. Wilmington, MA: Great Source Education Group, 2004.

———. *Steck-Vaughn Middle School Collection: Math: Student Edition Grades 5 - 8 Fractions, Ratios, & Percents*. New York: Steck-Vaughn, 2006.

Zev, Marc, Kevin B. Segal, and Nathan Levy. *101 Things Everyone Should Know About Math*. Washington, D.C.: Science, Naturally!, 2010.

**Internet Addresses**

Math.com. "Pre-Algebra." © 2000–2012.
<http://www.math.com/homeworkhelp/PreAlgebra.html>

The Math Forum. "Ask Dr. Math." © 1994–2012.
<http://mathforum.org/library/drmath/sets/elem_golden.html>
<http://mathforum.org/library/drmath/sets/mid_fractions.html>

Spector, Lawrence. *The Math Page*. "Skill in Arithmetic." © 2001–2012.
<http://www.themathpage.com/ARITH/arithmetic.htm>

# Index

# THE 100 MOST INFLUENTIAL
# MUSICIANS
## OF ALL TIME

# THE 100 MOST INFLUENTIAL
# MUSICIANS
## OF ALL TIME

EDITED BY GINI GORLINSKI, ASSOCIATE EDITOR, MUSIC AND DANCE

Britannica®
Educational Publishing

IN ASSOCIATION WITH

ROSEN
EDUCATIONAL SERVICES

Published in 2010 by Britannica Educational Publishing
(a trademark of Encyclopædia Britannica, Inc.)
in association with Rosen Educational Services, LLC
29 East 21st Street, New York, NY 10010.

Distributed exclusively by Rosen Educational Services.
For a listing of additional Britannica Educational Publishing titles, call toll free (800) 237-9932.

First Edition

Britannica Educational Publishing
**Michael I. Levy: Executive Editor**
Marilyn L. Barton: Senior Coordinator, Production Control
Steven Bosco: Director, Editorial Technologies
Lisa S. Braucher: Senior Producer and Data Editor
Yvette Charboneau: Senior Copy Editor
Kathy Nakamura: Manager, Media Acquisition
Gini Gorlinski, Associate Editor, Music and Dance
Diana Solomon, Copy Editor

Rosen Educational Services
Hope Lourie Killcoyne: Senior Editor and Project Manager
Nelson Sá: Art Director
Nicole Russo: Designer
Introduction by Chris Hayhurst

**Library of Congress Cataloging-in-Publication Data**

The 100 most influential musicians of all time / edited by Gini Gorlinski.
   p. cm.—(The Britannica guide to the world's most influential people)
"In association with Britannica Educational Publishing, Rosen Educational Services."
Includes index.
ISBN 978-1-61530-006-8 (library binding)
1. Musicians—Biography. I. Gorlinski, Gini. II. Title: One hundred most influential musicians of all time.
ML385A15 2010
780.92'2—dc22
[B]

2009029076

*Manufactured in the United States of America*

Cover credit: Carlos Spottorno/Photonica/Getty Images; p. 8 © www.istockphoto.com/Neil Sullivan; p. 16 © www.istockphoto.com.

# CONTENTS

44

91

148

# INTRODUCTION

What is influence? Is it the power that one individual holds to change the world? Is it prestige—the glimmering reputation earned by those who have achieved excellence or superiority? Or is it that sense of immortality bestowed on certain people who, through their lives, their actions, and their accomplishments, have climbed pedestals so high and prominent that they are virtually guaranteed a place in the books of history?

Influence can mean so many things and is therefore hard to define. But this much is clear: in a book such as this, where the subject is influential musicians, an exact definition hardly matters. Such artists may exert themselves in all kinds of ways—through their compositions, lyrics, performances, or even through "extracurricular" activities such as raising funds for charitable causes and organizations.

Just by taking the stage—whether in a local church or on the 50-yard line during halftime at the Super Bowl—musicians have instant influence. They command the ability to make people stop what they are doing—to have them clap, dance, and sing along. If musicians are truly great—be it composer Igor Stravinsky, classic rocker Eric Clapton, hip-hop rapper Jay-Z, "King of Rock and Roll" Elvis Presley, or "King of Juju" King Sunny Ade—their creations have the ability to transcend time and space, culture and nationality.

Simply put, great music is more than just music. It makes us think; it makes us feel. And over twenty, thirty, even hundreds of years, it continues to make us listen. In the world of music, that is influence.

Within these pages readers will also discover how the work of one musician inspired and motivated that of others, sometimes in groundbreaking ways. In 1791, having heard the moving oratorios of George Frideric Handel,

Austrian composer Joseph Haydn set to work on his own compositions in this genre, eventually creating a composition believed to be the first musical work written for two languages, in this case, German and English. Haydn also became good friends with musical genius Wolfgang Amadeus Mozart, the two composers finding camaraderie in each other's company and inspiration in each other's work. Mississippi native Robert Johnson, who legend holds acquired his musical genius by way of having made a deal with the devil, is known to have had a major impact on musicians from Muddy Waters to the Rolling Stones.

Some musicians were inspired by influences beyond music. The art of English painter J. M. W. Turner and French painter Claude Monet struck a chord with seminal French composer Claude Debussy, prompting him to create his orchestral seascape *La Mer*. Visits to Paris prompted a young George Gershwin to create his famous orchestral composition *An American in Paris*. And it was John Steinbeck's *The Grapes of Wrath* that provided the impetus for "Tom Joad," Woody Guthrie's classic entry in the American songbook.

There are, of course, those musicians who, as childhood prodigies, seem not to have needed outside influence to exert their own. Frédéric Chopin began playing piano at age seven, gave his first concert a year later, and at age eleven performed for the Russian tsar Alexander I. Mozart, whose life was all too short although with an extraordinary influence, was composing from the age of five.

Little is known about Johann Sebastian Bach's early musical education, but in his prime he was recognized by his peers as being a talented harpsichordist, organist, violinist, and singer. He is now recognized as being one of the greatest composers of all time. By bringing together the musical traditions that preceded him and then melding those traditions to create music that was all his own, Bach built his legacy around unique innovation. After his death, students of classical music excavated, analyzed, incorporated, and emulated his work. Today Bach's "voice" is heard everywhere, from big-city symphony halls to high school auditoriums. It is even heard in the music of Beethoven, who is said to have studied Bach's works closely. Musicians the world over have been influenced by, and owe a debt of gratitude to, Bach.

Luciano Pavarotti is considered one of the greatest operatic tenors ever. Teaming his athletic vocal range with a lively, energizing personality, Pavarotti earned such popularity over the seven decades of his life that many credit him with single-handedly opening the traditionally upper-class world of opera to the everyday masses. In his prime, Pavarotti performed before live audiences approaching half a million people. He also won five Grammys, sang at the opening ceremony of the 2006 Winter Olympics, and became a fixture, along with Plácido Domingo and José Carreras, in the aptly named traveling opera group "The Three Tenors." That Pavarotti, who died in 2007, will have a lasting influence on opera is unquestioned. His millions of fans, many of whom would never have listened to opera were it not for him, are a testament to his legacy. So, too, are the new opera singers in line to be his successors. Audiences worldwide will hear a hint of Pavarotti's voice every time the next generation of tenors performs.

Aretha. Her first name alone is instantly recognizable, conjuring the image and sound of this singular musician. The undeniably sensational Aretha Franklin, better known to many as the "Queen of Soul," was the first woman to be inducted into the Rock and Roll Hall of Fame (1987). An electrifying performer since she premiered as a teenager in the mid-1950s, Aretha Franklin has used her unprecedented vocal talent to stir deep emotions in audiences at venues as varied and far-reaching as Detroit churches, Fillmore West in San Francisco, and the 2009 presidential inauguration of Barack Obama in Washington, D.C. Millions have bought her albums; millions more have not only heard but felt the energy of her voice. With songs such as "Respect," which she borrowed from Otis Redding in 1967 and then made her own, she instantly defined the women's rights movement, the Civil Rights movement, and the right of one performer to shout out her soul. A passionate, perennial performer, it is no wonder that she has more Top 40 singles than any other female singer.

The great Irish rock band U2 all but defines what it means to be influential. Bono, the band's lead singer, is also cofounder of the grassroots advocacy organization ONE and a regular contributor to newspapers. Through ONE, Bono has brought together millions of people committed to fighting extreme poverty and disease, especially in Africa. But it is the band's rock music, which Bono and a tight-knit group of friends (including David "the Edge" Evans; Larry Mullen, Jr.; and Adam Clayton) started in 1977, that has the most influence. Beginning with their first breakthrough album, *War*, in 1983, and continuing through *How to Dismantle an Atomic Bomb* in 2004 and *No Line on the Horizon* in 2009, U2 has over the years created music that is so instantly recognizable as theirs, yet also so innovative and so technologically cutting-edge, that you are practically compelled to listen. Influential? Certainly. How so? That is hard to say. In that they have reduced hunger? In that they have inspired teenagers to pick up an instrument? Or in the music that has followed their lead, from one new band to the next, and which clearly demonstrates a reverence for this celebrity group of post-punk rock stars.

For an example of this type of astronomical influence, consider Bob Dylan. Part American folksinger, part poet, part rock star, and part living icon, Dylan wields lyrics as a soldier wields his sword (or Shakespeare his pen). Throughout his career, Dylan has used the stage to deliver a full range of commentary on the issues of the day. Witty, biting, damning, and always interesting, every word he sings is laced with meaning, and every sentence he speaks comes layered like an onion waiting to be peeled. He sings of love, politics, war, exploration, and exploitation. And if an issue of import is being ignored when it should be front and center, or has been forgotten, Dylan sings about it. With his lyrics, he pulls the world together, even as he rips apart the status quo. Without a doubt, Dylan will continue to be a legend as long as people listen to music.

As for the music experience and its delivery, today is quite different than just a few short years ago. Records and tapes are all but gone, and CDs are on their way out. In the 21st century, we have ear buds and iPods, we download MP3s, and we listen to music online at Web sites such as Pandora, Jango, and YouTube. Music can enter our lives in previously unimagined ways: a new generation is being introduced to musicians and their work via various gaming platforms and programs, from a handheld gaming device such as Game Boy to the simulated guitar-playing experience of *Rock Band*. Music today is digital. It is fast, at our fingertips, and often it is free. The current profile will undoubtedly change in the future—it always does.

But then again, you can also be sure that much will be the same. We will always listen to music, through whatever device we choose. Music will always be a part of our lives, ringing through our ears even when it is silent and nothing but a memory. People will always sing as they shower, turn it up as they drive, and "tune out" as they try to ignore everything else in their lives. That is music, and that is the influence it has on us.

Those musicians featured in this book span hundreds of years, countless musical genres, and immeasurable distances in style, technique, and purpose. Nevertheless, they have all been, and continue to be, influential. Some are influential because they brought a unique approach to their art that others later followed. Others were leaders of an influential movement in their field—a movement that led future musicians to improvise, change, and ultimately re-create music itself. And still others, through their work, brought about social reform and societal change that has forever shaped the landscape in which we now live.

For these influential people, music was and is life. Tchaikovsky, Stravinsky, Rachmaninoff. Springsteen, Sinatra, Madonna. They devoted their careers to the art, spending countless hours writing, creating, and fine-tuning. They have performed for great crowds, spoken on their beliefs, stood up for just causes, and above all, brought pleasure to the people who have listened. In doing so, each has left a mark, a stamp of influence, on the world.

# GUIDO D'AREZZO

(b. *c.* 990, Arezzo? [Italy]—d. 1050, Avellana?)

Guido d'Arezzo was a medieval music theorist whose principles served as a foundation for modern Western musical notation.

Educated at the Benedictine abbey at Pomposa, Guido evidently made use of the music treatise of Odo of Saint-Maur-des-Fossés and apparently developed his principles of staff notation there. He left Pomposa in about 1025 because his fellow monks resisted his musical innovations, and he was appointed by Theobald, bishop of Arezzo, as a teacher in the cathedral school and commissioned to write the *Micrologus de disciplina artis musicae.* The bishop also arranged for Guido to give (*c.* 1028) to Pope John XIX an antiphonary he had begun in Pomposa.

Guido seems to have gone to the Camaldolese monastery at Avellana in 1029, and his fame developed from there. Many of the 11th-century manuscripts notated in the new manner came from Camaldolese houses.

The fundamentals of the new method consisted in the construction by thirds of a system of four lines, or staff, and the use of letters as clefs. The red F-line and the yellow C-line were already in use, but Guido added a black line between the F and the C and another black line above the C. The neumes could now be placed on the lines and spaces between and a definite pitch relationship established. No longer was it necessary to learn melodies by rote, and Guido declared that his system reduced the 10 years normally required to become an ecclesiastical singer to a year.

Guido was also developing his technique of solmization, described in his *Epistola de ignoto cantu.* There is no evidence that the Guidonian hand, a mnemonic device associated with his name and widely used in the Middle Ages, had any connection with Guido d'Arezzo.

Guido is also credited with the composition of a hymn to St. John the Baptist, *Ut queant laxis*, in which the first syllable of each line falls on a different tone of the hexachord (the first six tones of the major scale); these syllables, *ut*, *re*, *mi*, *fa*, *sol*, and *la*, are used in Latin countries as the names of the notes from *c* to *a* (*ut* was eventually replaced by *do*). His device was of immense practical value in teaching sight-reading of music and in learning melodies. Singers associated the syllables with certain intervals; *mi* to *fa*, in particular, always represented a half step.

Before Guido an alphabetical notation using the letters from *a* to *p* was used in France as early as 996. Guido's system used a series of capital letters, small letters, and double small letters from *a* to *g*. Guido's system also came to be associated with the teaching of the gamut—the whole hexachord range (the range of notes available to the singer).

In addition to his innovations Guido also described a variety of organum (adding to a plainchant melody a second voice singing different pitches) that moved largely, but not completely, in parallel fourths. Guido's work is known through his treatise the *Micrologus*.

## JOSQUIN DES PREZ

(b. *c.* 1450, Condé-sur-l'Escaut?, Burgundian Hainaut [France]—d. Aug. 27, 1521, Condé-sur-l'Escaut)

Josquin des Prez was one of the greatest composers of Renaissance Europe.

Josquin's early life has been the subject of much scholarly debate, and the first solid evidence of his work comes from a roll of musicians associated with the cathedral in Cambrai in the early 1470s. During the late 1470s and early '80s, he sang for the courts of René I of Anjou and Duke Galeazzo Maria Sforza of Milan, and from 1486 to about 1494 he performed for the papal chapel. Sometime between then and 1499, when he became choirmaster to Duke Ercole I of Ferrara, he apparently had connections with the Chapel Royal of Louis XII of France and with the Cathedral of Cambrai. In Ferrara he wrote, in honour of his employer, the mass *Hercules Dux Ferrariae*, and his motet *Miserere* was composed at the duke's request. He seems to have left Ferrara on the death of the duke in 1505 and later became provost of the collegiate church of Notre Dame in Condé.

Josquin's compositions fall into the three principal categories of motets, masses, and chansons. Of the 20 masses that survive complete, 17 were printed in his lifetime in three sets (1502, 1505, 1514) by Ottaviano dei Petrucci. His motets and chansons were included in other Petrucci publications, from the *Odhecaton* (an anthology of popular chansons) of 1501 onward, and in collections of other printers. Martin Luther expressed great admiration for Josquin's music, calling him "master of the notes, which must do as he wishes; other composers must do as the notes wish." In his musical techniques he stands at the summit of the Renaissance, blending traditional forms with innovations that later became standard practices. The expressiveness of his music marks a break with the medieval tradition of more abstract music.

Especially in his motets, Josquin gave free reign to his talent, expressing sorrow in poignant harmonies, employing suspension for emphasis, and taking the voices gradually into their lowest registers when the text speaks of death. Josquin used the old cantus firmus style, but he also developed the motet style that characterized the 16th century after him. His motets, as well as his masses, show an approach to the modern sense of tonality. In his later works

Josquin gradually abandoned cantus firmus technique for parody and paraphrase. He also frequently used the techniques of canon and of melodic imitation.

In his chansons Josquin was the principal exponent of a style new in the mid-15th century, in which the learned techniques of canon and counterpoint were applied to secular song. He abandoned the fixed forms of the rondeau and the ballade, employing freer forms of his own device. Though a few chansons are set homophonically—in chords—rather than polyphonically, a number of others are examples of counterpoint in five or six voices, maintaining sharp rhythm and clarity of texture.

## ANTONIO VIVALDI

(b. March 4, 1678, Venice, Republic of Venice [Italy]—d. July 28, 1741, Vienna, Austria)

Antonio Lucio Vivaldi was an Italian composer and violinist who left a decisive mark on the form of the concerto and on the style of late Baroque instrumental music.

### LIFE

Vivaldi's main teacher was probably his father, Giovanni Battista, who in 1685 was admitted as a violinist to the orchestra of the San Marco Basilica in Venice. Antonio, the eldest child, trained for the priesthood and was ordained in 1703. He made his first known public appearance playing violin alongside his father in the basilica in 1696. He became an excellent violinist, and in 1703 he was appointed violin master at the Ospedale della Pietà, a home for abandoned or orphaned children. The Pietà specialized in the musical training of its female wards, and those with musical aptitude were assigned to its excellent choir and orchestra.

Vivaldi had dealings with the Pietà for most of his career: as violin master (1703–09; 1711–15), director of instrumental music (1716–17; 1735–38), and paid external supplier of compositions (1723–29; 1739–40).

Vivaldi's earliest musical compositions date from his first years at the Pietà. Printed collections of his trio sonatas and violin sonatas respectively appeared in 1705 and 1709, and in 1711 his first and most influential set of concerti for violin and string orchestra (Opus 3, *L'estro armonico*) was published by the Amsterdam music-publishing firm of Estienne Roger. In the years up to 1719, Roger published three more collections of his concerti (opuses 4, 6, and 7) and one collection of sonatas (Opus 5).

Vivaldi made his debut as a composer of sacred vocal music in 1713, when the Pietà's choirmaster left his post and the institution had to turn to Vivaldi and other composers for new compositions. He achieved great success with his sacred vocal music, for which he later received commissions from other institutions. Another new field of endeavour for him opened in 1713 when his first opera, *Ottone in villa*, was produced in Vicenza. Returning to Venice, Vivaldi immediately plunged into operatic activity in the twin roles of composer and impresario. From 1718 to 1720 he worked in Mantua as director of secular music for that city's governor, Prince Philip of Hesse-Darmstadt. This was the only full-time post Vivaldi ever held; he seems to have preferred life as a freelance composer for the flexibility and entrepreneurial opportunities it offered. Vivaldi's major compositions in Mantua were operas, though he also composed cantatas and instrumental works.

The 1720s were the zenith of Vivaldi's career. Based once more in Venice, but frequently traveling elsewhere, he supplied instrumental music to patrons and customers throughout Europe. Between 1725 and 1729 he published five new collections of concerti (opuses 8–12). After

1729 Vivaldi stopped publishing his works, finding it more profitable to sell them in manuscript to individual purchasers.

In the 1730s Vivaldi's career gradually declined. The French traveler Charles de Brosses reported in 1739 with regret that his music was no longer fashionable. Vivaldi's impresarial forays became increasingly marked by failure. In 1740 he traveled to Vienna, but he fell ill and did not live to attend the production there of his opera *L'oracolo in Messenia* in 1742. The simplicity of his funeral on July 28, 1741, suggests that he died in considerable poverty.

## Instrumental Music

Almost 500 concerti by Vivaldi survive. More than 300 are concerti for a solo instrument with string orchestra and continuo. Of these, approximately 230 are written for solo violin, 40 for bassoon, 25 for cello, 15 for oboe, and 10 for flute. There are also concerti for viola d'amore, recorder, mandolin, and other instruments. Vivaldi's remaining concerti are either double concerti (including about 25 written for two violins), concerti grossi using three or more soloists, concerti ripieni (string concerti without a soloist), or chamber concerti for a group of instruments without orchestra.

Vivaldi perfected the form of what would become the Classical three-movement concerto. Indeed, he helped establish the fast-slow-fast plan of the concerto's three movements. Perhaps more importantly, Vivaldi was the first to employ regularly in his concerti the ritornello form, in which recurrent restatements of a refrain alternate with more episodic passages featuring a solo instrument. Vivaldi's bold juxtapositions of the refrains (ritornelli) and the solo passages opened new possibilities for virtuosic display by solo instrumentalists. The fast movements in his concerti are notable for their rhythmic drive and the boldness of their themes, while the slow movements often present the character of arias written for the solo instrument.

Several of Vivaldi's concerti have picturesque or allusive titles. Four of them, the cycle of violin concerti entitled *The Four Seasons* (Opus 8, no. 1–4), are programmatic in a thoroughgoing fashion, with each concerto depicting a different season of the year, starting with spring. Vivaldi's effective representation of the sounds of nature inaugurated a tradition to which works such as Ludwig van Beethoven's *Pastoral Symphony* belong. Vivaldi also left more than 90 sonatas, mainly for stringed instruments.

## Vocal Music

More than 50 authentic sacred vocal compositions by Vivaldi are extant. They range from short hymns for solo voices to oratorios and elaborate psalm settings in several movements for double choir and orchestra. He composed some 50 operas (16 of which survived in their entirety) as well as nearly 40 cantatas. Many of Vivaldi's vocal works exhibit a spiritual depth and a command of counterpoint equal to the best of their time. Moreover, the mutual independence of voices and instruments often anticipates the later symphonic masses of Joseph Haydn and Wolfgang Amadeus Mozart.

## GEORGE FRIDERIC HANDEL

(b. Feb. 23, 1685, Halle, Brandenburg [Germany]—d. April 14, 1759, London, Eng.)

A German-born English composer of the late Baroque era, George Frideric Handel—or, Georg Friedrich Händel, as he was known for the first 30 years of his life—was noted particularly for his operas, oratorios, and instrumental compositions. He wrote the most famous of all oratorios, *Messiah* (1741), and is also known for such occasional pieces as *Water Music* (1717) and *Music for the Royal Fireworks* (1749).

## LIFE

The son of a barber-surgeon, Handel showed a marked gift for music and became a pupil in Halle of the composer Friedrich W. Zachow, from whom he learned the principles of keyboard performance and composition. In 1702 Handel enrolled as a law student at the University of Halle. He also became organist of the Reformed (Calvinist) Cathedral in Halle but served for only one year before going north to Hamburg. In Hamburg he joined the violin section of the opera orchestra and also took over some of the duties of harpsichordist; early in 1705 he presided over the premiere in Hamburg of his first opera, *Almira*.

Handel spent the years 1706–10 traveling in Italy, where he met many of the greatest Italian musicians of the day. He composed many works in Italy, including two operas, numerous Italian solo cantatas (vocal compositions), *Il trionfo del tempo e del disinganno* (1707) and another oratorio, the serenata *Aci, Galatea e Polifemo* (1708), and some Latin (i.e., Roman Catholic) church music. His opera *Agrippina* enjoyed a sensational success at its premiere in Venice in 1710.

Also in 1710 Handel was appointed Kapellmeister to the elector of Hanover, the future King George I of England, and later that year he journeyed to England. Handel's opera *Rinaldo* was performed in London in 1711 and was greeted with great enthusiasm. Over the next two years his operas *Il pastor fido* (1712) and *Teseo* (1713) were also staged in London. In 1713 he won his way into royal favour by his *Ode for the Queen's Birthday* and the *Utrecht Te Deum* and *Jubilate* in celebration of the Peace of Utrecht, and he was granted an annual allowance of £200 by Queen Anne.

On the death of Queen Anne in 1714, the elector George Louis became King George I of England, and Handel subsequently made England his permanent home. In 1718 he became director of music to the duke of Chandos, for whom he composed the 11 *Chandos Anthems* and the English masque *Acis and Galatea*, among other works. Another masque, *Haman and Mordecai*, was to be the effective starting point for the English oratorio. In 1726 Handel officially became a British subject, which enabled him to be appointed a composer of the Chapel Royal. In this capacity he wrote much music, including the *Coronation Anthems for George II* in 1727 and the *Funeral Anthem for Queen Caroline* 10 years later.

From 1720 until 1728 the operas at the King's Theatre in London were staged by the Royal Academy of Music, and Handel composed the music for most of them. Among those of the 1720s were *Floridante* (1721), *Ottone* (1723), *Giulio Cesare* (1724), *Rodelinda* (1725), and *Scipione* (1726). From 1728, after the sensation caused by John Gay's *Beggar's Opera* (which satirized serious opera), the Italian style went into decline in England, largely because of the impatience of the English with a form of entertainment in an unintelligible language sung by artists of whose morals they disapproved. But Handel went on composing operas until 1741, by which time he had written more than 40 such works. As the popularity of opera declined in England, oratorio became increasingly popular. The revivals in 1732 of Handel's masques *Acis and Galatea* and *Haman and Mordecai* (renamed *Esther*) led to the establishment of the English oratorio—a large musical composition for solo voices, chorus, and orchestra, without acting or scenery, and usually dramatizing a story from the Bible in English-language lyrics. Handel first capitalized on this genre in 1733 with *Deborah* and *Athalia*.

In 1737 Handel suffered what appears to have been a mild stroke. After a course of treatment in Aachen (Germany), he was restored to health and went on to compose the *Funeral Anthem for Queen Caroline* (1737) and two of his most celebrated oratorios, *Saul* and *Israel in Egypt*, both of which were performed in 1739. He also wrote the *Twelve Grand Concertos*, Opus 6, and helped establish the Fund for the Support of Decayed Musicians (now the Royal Society of Musicians).

Handel was by this time at the height of his powers, and the year 1741 saw the composition of his greatest oratorio, *Messiah*, and its inspired successor, *Samson*. *Messiah* was given its first performance in Dublin on April 13, 1742, and created a deep impression. Handel's works of the next three years included the oratorios *Joseph and His Brethren* (first performed 1744) and *Belshazzar* (1745), the secular oratorios *Semele* (1744) and *Hercules* (1745), and the *Dettingen Te Deum* (1743), celebrating the English victory over the French at the Battle of Dettingen. Handel had by this time made oratorio and large-scale choral works the most popular musical forms in England. Even during his lifetime Handel's music was recognized as a reflection of the English national character, and his capacity for realizing the common mood was nowhere better shown than in the *Music for the Royal Fireworks* (1749), with which he celebrated the peace of the Treaty of Aix-la-Chapelle. Handel now began to experience trouble with his sight. He managed with great difficulty to finish the last of his oratorios, *Jephtha*, which was performed at Covent Garden Theatre, London, in 1752. He kept his interest in musical activities alive until the end. After his death on April 14, 1759, he was buried in Poets' Corner in Westminster Abbey.

## MUSIC

The first basis of Handel's style was the north German music of his childhood, but it was soon completely overlaid by the Italian style that he acquired in early adulthood during his travels in Italy. The influences of Arcangelo Corelli and Alessandro Scarlatti can be detected in his work to the end of his long life, and the French style of Jean-Baptiste Lully and, later, that of the English composer Henry Purcell are also evident. There is a robustness in Handel's later music that gives it a very English quality. Above all, his music is eminently vocal. His choral writing is remarkable for the manner in which it interweaves massive but simple harmonic passages with contrapuntal sections of great ingenuity, the whole most effectively illustrating the text. His writing for the solo voice is outstanding in its suitability for the medium. Handel had a striking ability to depict human character musically in a single scene or aria, a gift used with great dramatic power in his operas and oratorios.

Though the bulk of his music was vocal, Handel was nevertheless one of the great instrumental composers of the late Baroque era. His long series of overtures (mostly in the French style), his orchestral concertos (Opus 3 and Opus 6), his large-scale concert music for strings and winds (such as the *Water Music* and the *Fireworks Music*), and the massive double concertos and organ concertos all show him to have been a complete master of the orchestral means at his command.

Handel had a lifelong attachment to the theatre—even his oratorios were usually performed on the stage rather than in church. Like other composers of his time, he accepted the conventions of Italian opera, with its employment of male sopranos and contraltos and the formalized sequences of stylized recitatives and arias upon which opera seria was constructed. Using these conventions, he produced Italian operas, such as *Giulio Cesare* (1724), *Sosarme* (1732), and *Alcina* (1735), which still make impressive stage spectacles.

But Handel's oratorios now seem even more dramatic than his operas, and they can generally be performed on the stage with remarkably little alteration. Most of them, from early attempts such as *Esther* to later works such as *Saul*, *Samson*, *Belshazzar*, and *Jephtha*, treat a particular dramatic theme taken from the Hebrew Bible that illustrates the heroism and suffering of a particular individual. The story line is illustrated by solo recitatives and arias and underlined by the chorus. With *Israel in Egypt* and *Messiah*, however, the emphasis is quite different, *Israel* because of its uninterrupted chain of massive choruses, which do not lend themselves to stage presentation, and *Messiah* because it is a meditation on the life of Christ the Saviour rather than a dramatic narration of his Passion. Handel also used the dramatic oratorio genre for a number of secular works, chief among which are *Semele*, *Hercules*, and *Acis and Galatea*, all based on stories from Greek mythology.

Handel's most notable contribution to church music is his series of large-scale anthems. Foremost of these are the 11 *Chandos Anthems*. Closely following these works are the four *Coronation Anthems for George II*, the most celebrated of which is *Zadok the Priest*.

Most of the orchestral music Handel wrote consists of overtures, totaling about 80 in number. Handel was equally adept at the concerto form, especially the concerto grosso. His most important works of this type are the *Six Concerti Grossi* (known as *The Oboe Concertos*), Opus 3, and the *Twelve Grand Concertos*, which represent the peak of the Baroque concerto grosso for stringed instruments. The *Water Music* and *Fireworks Music* suites, for wind and string band, stand in a special class in the history of late Baroque music by virtue of their combination of grandeur and melodic bravura.

Handel also published harpsichord music, of which two sets of suites, the *Suites de pièces pour le clavecin* of 1720 and the *Suites de pièces* of 1733, containing 17 sets in all, are his finest contribution to that instrument's repertoire. Handel's finest chamber music consists of trio sonatas, notably those published as *Six Sonatas for Two Violins, Oboes, or German Flutes and Continuo*, Opus 2 (1733). He also wrote various sonatas for one or more solo instruments with basso continuo accompaniment for harpsichord. In addition, he composed more than 20 organ concertos.

## JOHANN SEBASTIAN BACH

(b. March 21, 1685, Eisenach, Thuringia, Ernestine Saxon Duchies [Germany]—d. July 28, 1750, Leipzig)

A prolific composer of the Baroque era, Johann Sebastian Bach was the most celebrated member of a large family of northern German musicians. Although he was admired by his contemporaries primarily as an out-standing harpsichordist, organist, and expert on organ building, Bach is now generally regarded as one of the greatest composers of all time and is celebrated as the creator of the *Brandenburg Concertos*, *The Well-Tempered Clavier*, the *Mass in B Minor*, and numerous other masterpieces of church and instrumental music.

### EARLY YEARS

J.S. Bach was the youngest child of Johann Ambrosius Bach and Elisabeth Lämmerhirt. Ambrosius was a string player, employed by the town council and the ducal court of Eisenach. Although Johann Sebastian started school in 1692 or 1693, nothing definite is known of his musical

*The prolific Baroque composer Johann Sebastian Bach, seen here, was also a skilled organist and harpsichordist.* Getty Images/Time & Life Pictures

education at that time. By 1695 both his parents were dead, and he was looked after by his eldest brother, Johann Christoph (1671–1721). Christoph was the organist at Ohrdruf, and he apparently gave Johann Sebastian his first formal keyboard lessons. In 1700 the young Bach secured a place in a select choir of poor boys at the school at Michaelskirche, Lüneburg.

Bach evidently returned to Thuringia late in the summer of 1702, already a reasonably proficient organist and composer of keyboard and sacred music. By March 4, 1703, he was a member of the orchestra employed by Johann Ernst, duke of Weimar (and brother of Wilhelm Ernst, whose service Bach entered in 1708). When the new organ was completed at the Neue Kirche (New Church) in Arnstadt, on the northern edge of the Thuringian Forest, Bach helped test it, and in August 1703 he was appointed organist—at age 18.

## THE ARNSTADT PERIOD

At Arnstadt, where he remained until 1707, Bach devoted himself to keyboard music, for the organ in particular. In October 1705 he obtained a month's leave to walk to Lübeck (more than 200 miles [300 km]), with the specific intention of becoming acquainted with the spectacular organ playing and compositions of Dietrich Buxtehude. He did not return to Arnstadt until mid-January 1706.

During these early years, Bach inherited the musical culture of the Thuringian area, a thorough familiarity with the traditional forms and hymns (chorales) of the orthodox Lutheran service, and, in keyboard music, perhaps a bias toward the formalistic styles of the south. But he also learned eagerly from the northern rhapsodists, Buxtehude above all. By 1708 he had arrived at a first synthesis of northern and southern German styles.

Among the works that can be ascribed to these early years are the *Capriccio sopra la lontananza del suo fratello dilettissimo* (1704; *Capriccio on the Departure of His Most Beloved Brother*, BWV 992), the chorale prelude on *Wie schön leuchtet* (c. 1705; *How Brightly Shines*, BWV 739), and the fragmentary early version of the organ *Prelude and Fugue in G Minor* (before 1707, BWV 535a). (The "BWV" numbers provided are the standard catalog numbers of Bach's works as established in the *Bach-Werke-Verzeichnis*, prepared by the German musicologist Wolfgang Schmieder.)

## The Mühlhausen Period

In June 1707 Bach obtained a post at the Blasiuskirche in Mühlhausen in Thuringia. He moved there soon after and married his cousin Maria Barbara Bach at Dornheim on October 17. At Mühlhausen he produced several church cantatas; all of these works are cast in a conservative mold, based on biblical and chorale texts. The famous organ *Toccata and Fugue in D Minor* (BWV 565), written in the rhapsodic northern style, and the *Prelude and Fugue in D Major* (BWV 532) may also have been composed during the Mühlhausen period, as well as the organ *Passacaglia in C Minor* (BWV 582), an early example of Bach's instinct for large-scale organization. Cantata No. 71, *Gott ist mein König* (*God Is My King*), of Feb. 4, 1708, was the first of Bach's compositions to be published. Bach resigned from his post in Mühlhausen on June 25, 1708, and subsequently moved to Weimar, on the Ilm River.

## The Weimar Period

Bach was, from the outset, court organist at Weimar and a member of the orchestra. From Weimar, he occasionally visited Weissenfels, and in February 1713 he took part in a court celebration there that included a performance of his first secular cantata, *Was mir behagt*, also called the *Hunt Cantata* (BWV 208). On March 2, 1714, Bach became the concertmaster at Weimar; as such, he was charged with composing a cantata every month.

Bach's development cannot be traced in detail during the vital years 1708–14, when his style underwent a profound change. From the series of cantatas written in 1714–16, however, it is obvious that he had been decisively influenced by the new styles and forms of the contemporary Italian opera and by the innovations of such Italian concerto composers as Antonio Vivaldi. His favourite forms appropriated from the Italians were those based on refrain (ritornello) or da capo schemes in which wholesale repetition—literal or with modifications—of entire sections of a piece permitted him to create coherent musical forms with much larger dimensions than had hitherto been possible. These newly acquired techniques henceforth governed a host of Bach's arias and concerto movements, as well as many of his larger fugues; they also profoundly affected his treatment of chorales.

Among other works likely composed at Weimar are most of the *Orgelbüchlein* (*Little Organ Book*), all but the last of the so-called 18 "Great" chorale preludes, the earliest organ trios, and most of the organ preludes and fugues. The "Great" *Prelude and Fugue in G Major* for organ (BWV 541) was finally revised about 1715, and the *Toccata and Fugue in F Major* (BWV 540) may have been played at Weissenfels.

## THE KÖTHEN PERIOD

Late in 1717 Bach left Weimar to begin his new appointment as musical director to Prince Leopold of Köthen. In

Köthen, Bach was concerned chiefly with chamber and orchestral music, and it was there that the sonatas for violin and clavier and for viola da gamba and clavier and the works for unaccompanied violin and cello were put into something like their present form. The *Brandenburg Concertos* were finished by March 24, 1721. Bach also found time to complete several cantatas as well as compile pedagogical keyboard works, including the *Clavierbüchlein* for W.F. Bach (begun Jan. 22, 1720), some of the *French Suites*, the *Inventions* (1720), and the first book (1722) of *Das Wohltemperierte Klavier* (*The Well-Tempered Clavier*), a work that eventually consisted of two books, each of 24 preludes and fugues in all keys. The remarkable collection of "well-tempered" compositions systematically explores both the potentials of a newly established tuning procedure—which, for the first time in the history of keyboard music, made all the keys equally usable—and the possibilities for musical organization afforded by the system of "functional tonality," a kind of musical syntax consolidated in the music of the Italian concerto composers of the preceding generation and a system that was to prevail for the next 200 years. At the same time, *The Well-Tempered Clavier* is a compendium of the most popular forms and styles of the era: dance types, arias, motets, concerti, etc., presented within the unified aspect of a single compositional technique—the rigorously logical and venerable fugue.

Maria Barbara Bach died unexpectedly in 1720, and Bach married Anna Magdalena Wilcken, daughter of a trumpeter at Weissenfels, on Dec. 3, 1721. Apart from his first wife's death, Bach's first few years at Köthen were probably the happiest of his life, and he was on the best terms with the prince. But after the prince got married—to an apparently antimusical and demanding woman—Bach began to feel neglected. At the same time, he began to consider the education of his elder sons, born in 1710 and 1714, and his thoughts turned to Leipzig. On Feb. 7, 1723, Bach gave a trial performance in Leipzig in application for the position of cantor, which had been vacated some months earlier by the death of Johann Kuhnau. Bach received the appointment, was granted permission to leave Köthen, and was installed in his new position on May 13.

## YEARS AT LEIPZIG

As director of church music for the city of Leipzig, Bach had to supply performers for four churches: Peterskirche, Neue Kirche, Nikolaikirche, and Thomaskirche. His first official performance was on May 30, 1723 with Cantata No. 75, *Die Elenden sollen essen*. New works produced during this year include many cantatas and the *Magnificat* in its first version. The first half of 1724 saw the production of the *St. John Passion*, which was subsequently revised. The total number of cantatas produced during this ecclesiastical year was about 62, of which about 39 were new works.

On June 11, 1724, Bach began a fresh annual cycle of cantatas, and within the year he wrote 52 of the so-called chorale cantatas. Indeed, during his first two or three years at Leipzig, Bach produced a large number of new cantatas, sometimes at the rate of one a week. The hectic pace of production required Bach (and other Baroque composers) to invent or discover their ideas quickly; they could not rely on the unpredictable arrival of "inspiration." Consequently, the typical Baroque composer had to be a traditionalist who readily embraced the musical conventions and techniques of the time.

## SYMBOLISM

A repertoire of melody types existed, for example, that was generated by an explicit "doctrine of figures" that created musical equivalents for the figures of speech in the art of rhetoric. Closely related to these "figures" are such examples of pictorial symbolism in which the composer writes, say, a rising scale to match words that speak of rising from the dead or a descending chromatic scale (depicting a howl of pain) to sorrowful words. Pictorial symbolism of this kind occurs only in connection with words—in vocal music and in chorale preludes, where the words of the chorale are in the listener's mind. Number symbolism, another common device of the Baroque period, also is sometimes pictorial; in the *St. Matthew Passion*, for instance, it is reasonable that the question "Lord, is it I?" should be asked 11 times, once by each of the faithful disciples. The Baroque composer had at his disposal various other formulas for elaborating themes into complete compositions; skilled use of such formulas allowed the arias and choruses of a cantata to be spun out almost "automatically."

As a result of his intense activity in cantata production during his first three years in Leipzig, Bach had created a supply of church music to meet his future needs for the regular Sunday and feast day services. After 1726, therefore, he turned his attention to other projects. He did, however, produce the *St. Matthew Passion* in 1729, a work that inaugurated a renewed interest in the mid-1730s for vocal works on a larger scale than the cantata; the now-lost *St. Mark Passion* (1731); the *Christmas Oratorio*, BWV 248 (1734); and the *Ascension Oratorio* (Cantata No. 11, *Lobet Gott in seinen Reichen*; 1735).

## INSTRUMENTAL WORKS

In 1726, after he had completed the bulk of his cantata production, Bach began to publish the clavier *Partitas* singly, with a collected edition in 1731. The second part of the *Clavierübung*, containing the *Concerto in the Italian Style* and the *French Overture (Partita) in B Minor*, appeared in 1735. The third part, consisting of the *Organ Mass* with the *Prelude and Fugue ["St. Anne"] in E-flat Major* (BWV 552), appeared in 1739. From *c.* 1729 to 1736 Bach was honorary musical director to Weissenfels; and, from 1729 to 1737 and again from 1739 for a year or two, he directed the Leipzig Collegium Musicum. For these concerts, he adapted some of his earlier concerti as harpsichord concerti, thus becoming one of the first composers—if not the very first—of concerti for keyboard instrument and orchestra.

About 1733 Bach began to produce cantatas in honour of the elector of Saxony and his family, evidently with a view to the court appointment he secured in 1736; many of these secular movements were adapted to sacred words and reused in the *Christmas Oratorio*. The *Kyrie* and *Gloria* of the *Mass in B Minor*, written in 1733, were also dedicated to the elector, but the rest of the *Mass* was not put together until Bach's last years. On his visits to Dresden, Bach had won the regard of the Russian envoy, Hermann Karl, Reichsgraf (count) von Keyserlingk, who commissioned the so-called *Goldberg Variations*; these were published as part four of the *Clavierübung* about 1742, and Book Two of *Das Wohltemperierte Klavier* seems to have been compiled about the same time. In addition, he wrote a few cantatas, revised some of his Weimar organ works, and published the so-called *Schübler Chorale Preludes* in or after 1746.

## LAST YEARS

In May 1747 Bach visited his son (Carl Philipp) Emanuel at Potsdam and played before Frederick II the Great of Prussia. In July his improvisations, on a theme proposed by the king, took shape as *The Musical Offering*. In June 1747 he joined a Society of the Musical Sciences, to which he presented the canonic variations on the chorale *Vom Himmel hoch da komm' ich her* (*From Heaven Above to Earth I Come*).

Of Bach's last illness little is known except that it lasted several months and prevented him from finishing *The Art of the Fugue*; he succumbed to his illness on July 28, 1750, at Leipzig. Anna Magdalena was left badly off. Her stepsons apparently did nothing to help her, and her own sons were too young to do so. She died on Feb. 27, 1760, and was given a pauper's funeral. Unfinished as it was, *The Art of the Fugue* was published in 1751 and was reissued in 1752. Very few copies were sold, however.

## JOSEPH HAYDN

(b. March 31, 1732, Rohrau, Austria—d. May 31, 1809, Vienna)

Austrian composer Joseph Haydn was one of the most important figures in the development of the Classical style in music during the 18th century. He helped establish the forms and styles for the string quartet and the symphony.

### EARLY YEARS

Haydn's father was a wheelwright, his mother, before her marriage, a cook for the lords of the village. Haydn early revealed unusual musical gifts, and a cousin who was a school principal and choirmaster in the nearby city of Hainburg offered to take him into his home and train him.

Haydn, not yet six years old, left home, never to return to the parental cottage except for rare, brief visits.

The young Haydn sang in the church choir, learned to play various instruments, and obtained a good basic knowledge of music. His life changed decisively when he was eight years old, when the musical director of St. Stephen's Cathedral in Vienna invited him to serve as chorister at the Austrian capital's most important church. Thus, in 1740 Haydn moved to Vienna. He stayed at the choir school for nine years, acquiring an enormous practical knowledge of music by constant performances but receiving little instruction in music theory. When his voice changed, he was expelled from both the cathedral choir and the choir school.

With no money and few possessions, Haydn at 17 was left to his own devices. He eventually was introduced to the music-loving Austrian nobleman Karl Joseph von Fürnberg, in whose home he played chamber music and for whose instrumentalists he wrote his first string quartets. Through the recommendation of Fürnberg, Haydn was engaged in 1758 as musical director and chamber composer for the Bohemian count Ferdinand Maximilian von Morzin and was put in charge of an orchestra of about 16 musicians. For this ensemble he wrote his first symphony as well as numerous divertimenti for wind band or for wind instruments and strings.

## ESTERHÁZY PATRONAGE

Haydn stayed only briefly with von Morzin, and soon he was invited to enter the service of Prince Pál Antal Esterházy. The Esterházys were one of the wealthiest and most influential families of the Austrian empire and boasted a distinguished record of supporting music. Prince Pál Antal had an orchestra performing regularly in his castle at Eisenstadt, a small town some 30 miles (48 km) from Vienna, and he appointed the relatively unknown Haydn to be assistant conductor in 1761. While the music director oversaw church music, Haydn conducted the orchestra, coached the singers, composed most of the music, and served as chief of the musical personnel. Haydn worked well with the Esterházy family, and he remained in their service until his death.

In 1766 Haydn became musical director at the Esterházy court. He raised the quality and increased the size of the prince's musical ensembles by appointing many choice instrumentalists and singers. His ambitious plans were supported by Prince Miklós, who had become head of the Esterházy family in 1762. In addition to composing operas for the court, Haydn composed symphonies, string quartets, and other chamber music. The prince was a passionate performer on the baryton, and Haydn provided more than 120 compositions featuring this now-obsolete cellolike instrument.

Haydn served Prince Miklós for nearly 30 years. He frequently visited Vienna in the prince's retinue. On these visits he developed a close friendship with Wolfgang Amadeus Mozart. The two composers were inspired by each other's work.

The period from 1768 to about 1774 marks Haydn's maturity as a composer. The music written then, from the *Stabat Mater* (1767) to the large-scale *Missa Sancti Nicolai* (1772), would be sufficient to place him among the chief composers of the era. The many operas he wrote during these years did much to enhance his own reputation and that of the Esterházy court. Other important works from this period include the string quartets of Opus 20, the *Piano Sonata in C Minor*, and the turgid symphonies in minor keys, especially the so-called *Trauersymphonie in E*

*Minor*, No. 44 ("Mourning Symphony") and the *"Farewell"* *Symphony*, No. 45.

Haydn's operatic output continued to be strong until 1785, but his audience increasingly lay outside his employer's court. In 1775 he composed his first large-scale oratorio, *Il ritorno di Tobia*, for the Musicians' Society in Vienna, and the Viennese firm Artaria published his six Opus 33 quartets in the 1780s. These important quartets quickly set a new standard for the genre. In the mid-1780s a commission came from Paris to compose a set of symphonies. Also about this time, Haydn was commissioned to compose the *Seven Last Words of Our Saviour on the Cross*, one of his most admired works.

## ENGLISH PERIOD

When Prince Miklós died in 1790, he was succeeded by his son, Prince Antal, who did not care for music and dismissed most of the court musicians. Haydn was retained, however, and continued to receive his salary. At this point a violinist and concert manager, Johann Peter Salomon, arrived from England and commissioned from Haydn 6 new symphonies and 20 smaller compositions to be conducted by the composer himself in a series of orchestral concerts in London. Haydn gladly accepted this offer, and the two men set off for London in December 1790.

On New Year's Day 1791, Haydn arrived in England, and the following 18 months proved extremely rewarding. The 12 symphonies he wrote on his first and second visits to London represent the climax of his orchestral output. Their style and wit endeared the works to British audiences, and their popularity is reflected in the various nicknames bestowed on them—e.g., *The Surprise* (No. 94), *Military* (No. 100), *The Clock* (No. 101), and *Drumroll* (No. 103).

In June 1792 Haydn left London, ultimately for Vienna, where his return was only coolly received. This perhaps prompted him to make a second journey to England in January 1794. The principal compositions of his second visit to London were the second set of London (or Salomon) symphonies (Nos. 99–104) and the six Apponyi quartets (Nos. 54–59). While in London, Haydn reached even greater heights of inspiration, particularly in the last three symphonies he wrote (Nos. 102–104), of which the *Symphony No. 102 in B-flat Major* is especially impressive. Although King George III invited him to stay in England, Haydn returned to his native Austria to serve the new head of the Esterházy family, Prince Miklós II.

## THE LATE ESTERHÁZY AND VIENNESE PERIOD

While in London in 1791, Haydn had been deeply moved by the performance of George Frideric Handel's masterly oratorios. Deciding to compose further works in this genre, he obtained a suitable libretto, and, after settling in Vienna and resuming his duties for Prince Esterházy, he started work on the oratorio *The Creation*, the text of which had been translated into German by Baron Gottfried van Swieten. The work was planned and executed to enable performances in either German or English; it is believed to be the first musical work published with text underlay in two languages. The libretto was based on the epic poem *Paradise Lost* by John Milton and on the Genesis book of the Bible. *The Creation* was first publicly performed in 1798 and earned enormous popularity subsequently. Haydn then produced another oratorio, which absorbed him until 1801. An extended poem, *The Seasons*, by James Thomson, was chosen as the basis for the (much shorter) libretto, again adapted and translated by van Swieten so as to enable performance in either German or English. The oratorio achieved much success, both at the Austrian court and in public performances (although not in London).

Haydn's late creative output included six masses written for his patron Miklós II. He also continued to compose string quartets, notably the six Erdödy quartets known as Opus 76. In 1797 Haydn gave to the Austrian Empire the stirring song *Gott erhalte Franz den Kaiser* ("God Save Emperor Francis"). It was used for more than a century as the national anthem of the Austrian monarchy and as the patriotic song "Deutschland, Deutschland über alles" ("Germany, Germany Above All Else") in Germany, where it remains the national anthem as "Deutschlandlied." The song was so beloved that Haydn decided to use it as a theme for variations in one of his finest string quartets, the *Emperor Quartet* (Opus 76, No. 3).

After composing his last two masses in 1801 and 1802, Haydn undertook no more large-scale works. During the last years of his life, he was apparently incapable of further work. In 1809 Napoleon's forces besieged Vienna and in May entered the city. Haydn refused to leave his house and take refuge in the inner city. Napoleon placed a guard of honour outside Haydn's house, and on May 31 the enfeebled composer died peacefully; he was buried two days later.

## WOLFGANG AMADEUS MOZART

(b. Jan. 27, 1756, Salzburg, Archbishopric of Salzburg [Austria]—d. Dec. 5, 1791, Vienna)

Austrian composer Wolfgang Amadeus Mozart is widely recognized as one of the greatest composers in the history of Western music. With Haydn and Beethoven he brought to its height the achievement of the Viennese Classical school. Unlike any other composer in musical history, he wrote in all the musical genres of his day and

*The Mozart family: Wolfgang Amadeus Mozart* (seated at piano) *with his sister Maria Anna* (left) *and his parents, Leopold and Anna Maria* (in portrait); *oil on canvas by Johann Nepomuk della Croce, c. 1780–81; Mozart House, Salzburg, Austria.* © Photos.com/Jupiterimages

excelled in every one. His taste, his command of form, and his range of expression have made him seem the most universal of all composers.

## EARLY LIFE AND WORKS

Mozart's father, Leopold, was a composer, a well-known violinist, and the author of a celebrated theoretical treatise. From 1762 Leopold took young Mozart and his sister Maria Anna ("Nannerl"), who also was musically talented, on tours throughout Europe in which they performed as harpsichordists and pianists. Young Mozart performed as a violinist and organist and received numerous commissions. In Paris they met several German composers, and Mozart's first music was published (sonatas for keyboard and violin); in London they met, among others, Johann Christian Bach, and under his influence Mozart composed his first symphonies — three survive (K 16, K 19, and K 19a [K signifying the work's place in the catalog of Ludwig von Köchel]). Two more followed during a stay in The Hague on the return journey (K 22 and K 45a).

While the Mozarts were in Vienna in 1767–69 Mozart wrote a one-act German singspiel, *Bastien und Bastienne*, which was given privately. In 1769 his comic opera *La finta semplice* was performed in the archbishop's palace in Salzburg. Just a few months later, Mozart was appointed an honorary Konzertmeister at the Salzburg court.

## THE ITALIAN TOURS

Mastery of the Italian operatic style was a prerequisite for a successful international composing career, and Mozart accordingly visited Italy with his father. Their first tour, begun on Dec. 13, 1769, took them to all the main musical centres. In mid-October 1770 he reached Milan and began work on the new opera, *Mitridate, rè di Ponto* ("Mithradates, King of Pontus"), the premiere of which, on December 26, was a notable success.

The second Italian visit, between August and December 1771, saw the successful premiere of Mozart's opera *Ascanio in Alba*. Back in Salzburg in 1772, Mozart wrote eight symphonies, four divertimentos, several substantial sacred works, and an allegorical serenata, *Il sogno di Scipione*. The third and final Italian journey lasted from October 1772 until March 1773. The new opera *Lucio Silla* ("Lucius Sulla") was given on Dec. 26, 1772, and after a difficult premiere it proved highly successful.

The instrumental music of the period around the Italian journeys includes several symphonies (a few of them are done in a light, Italianate style), but others tread new ground in form, orchestration, and scale. There are also six string quartets and three divertimentos.

## EARLY MATURITY

Leopold took Mozart to Vienna in 1773, where the newest Viennese music had a considerable effect on the young composer; he produced a set of six string quartets showing fuller textures and a more intellectual approach to the medium. Soon after his return to Salzburg he wrote a group of symphonies, including, most notably, the "Little" G Minor (K 183) and the A Major (K 201).

The year 1774 saw the composition of more symphonies, concertos for bassoon and for two violins, serenades, and several sacred works. At the end of the year Mozart was commissioned to write an opera buffa, *La finta giardiniera* ("The Feigned Gardener Girl"), for the Munich carnival season, where it was duly successful.

A period of two and a half years (from March 1775) began in which Mozart worked steadily in his Salzburg post, now as a salaried Konzertmeister. During this period he wrote only one dramatic work, but he was productive in sacred and lighter instrumental music. His most impressive piece for the church was the *Litaniae de venerabili altaris sacramento* (K 243), which embraces a wide range of styles (fugues, choruses of considerable dramatic force, florid arias, and a plainchant setting). The instrumental works included divertimentos, concertos, and serenades, notably the *Haffner* (K 250).

## Mannheim and Paris

In 1777 he petitioned the archbishop for his release and, with his mother to watch over him, set out to find new opportunities. They went first to Munich, then to Augsburg. At the end of October they arrived at Mannheim, where they stayed for more than four months at the musically progressive court of the Elector Palatine. He became friendly with the Mannheim musicians, undertook some teaching and playing, and composed several piano sonatas, some with violin. Mozart and his mother reached Paris late in March 1778, and Mozart soon found work. His most important achievement there was the symphony (K 297), a brilliant D Major work.

By the time of the symphony's premiere, on June 18, his mother was seriously ill, and on July 3 she died. Soon after, Leopold negotiated a better post for Mozart in Salzburg, where he would be court organist and still nominally Konzertmeister, and Mozart reluctantly returned home in mid-January 1780.

## Salzburg and Munich

Much of Mozart's work after his return displayed his command of international styles, notably the symphonies K 318 in G Major and K 338 in C Major, as well as in the sinfonia concertante for violin and viola K 364. Also during this time, Mozart composed the two-piano concerto, the two-piano sonata, as well as a number of sacred works, including the best-known of his complete masses, the *Coronation Mass*.

But it was dramatic music that attracted Mozart above all, and in 1780 he received a commission to compose a serious Italian opera for Munich. The subject was to be

Idomeneus, king of Crete, and the librettist the local cleric Giambattista Varesco. In the resulting *Idomeneo, rè di Creta* Mozart depicted serious, heroic emotion with a richness unparalleled elsewhere in his operas. It includes plain recitative and bravura singing, and, though the texture is more continuous than in Mozart's earlier operas, its plan is essentially traditional. Given on Jan. 29, 1781, just after Mozart's 25th birthday, it met with due success.

## VIENNA: THE EARLY YEARS

Mozart was still in Munich in March 1781, when he was summoned to Vienna to join the celebration of the installation of the new archbishop, Joseph II. Mozart was treated poorly by the new archbishop, and, after only a few months of service, he requested his discharge and set about earning a living in Vienna. He also embarked on an opera, *Die Entführung aus dem Serail* (*The Abduction from the Seraglio*), and in December 1781 he married Constanze Weber, daughter of a music copyist, albeit without his father's blessing.

Musically, Mozart's main preoccupation was with *Die Entführung* in the early part of 1782. The opera reached the Burgtheater stage on July 16. Stylistically, the work has fuller textures, more elaboration, and longer arias than other German repertory. It uses accompanying figures and key relationships to embody meaning. Other noteworthy features include Turkish colouring, created by "exotic" turns of phrase and chromaticisms as well as janissary instruments; expressive and powerful arias for the heroine; and comic musical passages. The work enjoyed immediate and continuing success.

Later in the year Mozart worked on a set of three piano concertos and began a set of six string quartets. He also started work on a mass setting, in C Minor, of which only the first two sections, "Kyrie" and "Gloria," were completed. Among the influences on this music, besides the Austrian ecclesiastical tradition, was the music of the Baroque period, noticeable especially in the spare textures and austere lines of certain of the solo numbers. Mozart and his wife visited Salzburg in the summer and autumn of 1783, when the completed movements of the mass were performed.

## THE CENTRAL VIENNESE PERIOD

Back in Vienna Mozart entered on what was to be the most fruitful and successful period of his life. In 1782–83 he wrote three piano concertos (K 413–415), which he published in 1785 with string and optional wind parts. Six more followed in 1784, three each in 1785 and 1786 and one each in 1788 and 1791. With the 1784 group he established a new level of piano concerto writing; these concertos are at once symphonic, melodically rich, and orchestrally ingenious, and they also blend the virtuoso element effectively into the musical and formal texture of the work. After the 1784 group (K 449, 450, 451, 453, 456, and 459), all of which begin with themes stated first by the orchestra and later taken up by the piano, Mozart moved on in the concertos of 1785 (K 466, 467, and 482) to make the piano solo a reinterpretation of the opening theme. The 1786 group begins with the lyrical K 488, but then follow two concertos with a new level of symphonic unity and grandeur, that in C Minor (K 491), and the concerto in C Major (K 503).

Mozart's other important contributions of this time come in the fields of chamber and piano music. The outpouring of 1784 included the fine piano sonata K 457 and the piano and violin sonata K 454. He also wrote a quintet for piano and wind instruments (K 452), which he considered his finest work to date. The six string quartets on which he had embarked in 1782 were finished in the first days of 1785 and were published later that year.

## FROM *FIGARO* TO *DON GIOVANNI*

In spite of his success as a pianist and composer, Mozart had serious financial worries, and they worsened as the Viennese found other idols. Success in the court opera house was all-important. At Mozart's request, Lorenzo Da Ponte, an Italian of Jewish descent who was a talented poet and librettist of the court theatre, wrote a libretto, *Le nozze di Figaro*, based on Beaumarchais's revolutionary comedy, *Le Mariage de Figaro*. Both *Figaro* and the later opera *Don Giovanni* treat the traditional figure of the licentious nobleman. Perhaps the central achievement of *Figaro* lies in its ensembles, with their close link between music and dramatic meaning.

*Figaro* reached the stage on May 1, 1786, and was warmly received. The opera also enjoyed popularity in Prague, and at the end of the year Mozart was invited to go to the Bohemian capital; he went in January 1787 and gave a new symphony there, the *Prague* (K 504). He returned to Vienna in February 1787.

In May 1787 Mozart's father died. From this time Mozart's music includes the two string quintets K 515–516, as well as a number of short lieder and three instrumental works of note: the *Musikalischer Spass* (*Musical Joke*), a good-humoured parody of bad music; *Eine kleine Nachtmusik*, the much-loved serenade; and a piano and violin sonata, K 526.

But Mozart's chief occupation during 1787 was the composition of the comic opera *Don Giovanni*, commissioned for production in Prague; it was given on October 29 and was positively received. *Don Giovanni* was Mozart's second opera based on a libretto by Da Ponte.

## The Last Travels

On his return from Prague in mid-November 1787, Mozart was at last appointed to a court post, as *Kammermusicus*. The salary of 800 gulden seems to have done little to relieve the Mozarts' chronic financial troubles. Their debts, however, were never large; their anxieties were more a matter of whether they could live as they wished than whether they would starve. Nevertheless, Mozart was deeply depressed during the summer, writing of "black thoughts."

During the time of this depression Mozart was working on a series of three symphonies, K 543, K 550, and K 551 (the *Jupiter*; these, with the work written for Prague (K 504), represent the summa of his orchestral output.

The summer of 1789 saw the composition of the clarinet quintet, and thereafter Mozart concentrated on completing his next opera commission; the third of his Da Ponte operas, *Così fan tutte* was given on Jan. 26, 1790. This opera, the subtlest, most consistent, and most symmetrical of the three, was long reviled on account of its subject, female fickleness; but a more careful reading of it reveals that it is no frivolous piece but a penetrating essay on human feelings and their mature recognition. Features of the music of *Così fan tutte* — serenity, restraint, poise, irony — may be noted as markers of Mozart's late style. The remainder of the year was difficult and relatively unproductive.

## The Last Year

Music was flowing again in 1791: for a concert in March Mozart completed a piano concerto (K 595), reeled off numerous dances, and wrote two new string quintets. He also composed the score to Emanuel Schikaneder's *Die Zauberflöte* (*The Magic Flute*), and received another commission, for a requiem, to be composed under conditions of secrecy. In July Constanze gave birth to their sixth child, one of the two to survive. Mozart's letters to her show that he worked first on *Die Zauberflöte* before he left for Prague near the end of August. Pressure of work, however, was such that he took with him to Prague, along with Constanze, his pupil Franz Xaver Süssmayr, who almost certainly composed the plain recitatives for the new opera.

Mozart was back in Vienna by the middle of September; his clarinet concerto was finished by September 29, and the next day *Die Zauberflöte* had its premiere. The opera became the most loved of all of Mozart's works for the stage. Mozart had been ill during the weeks in Prague, but in October he managed to write a Masonic cantata and to work steadily on the commissioned requiem. Later in November he was ill and was confined to bed, and on December 5 he died of a severe fever. Constanze Mozart was anxious to have the requiem completed, as a fee was due. She handed it first to Joseph Eybler, who supplied some orchestration, and then to Süssmayr, who produced a complete version, writing several movements. This has remained the standard version of the work, if only because of its familiarity.

## LUDWIG VAN BEETHOVEN

(baptized Dec. 17, 1770, Bonn, archbishopric of Cologne [Germany]—d. March 26, 1827, Vienna, Austria)

As the creator of some of the most influential pieces of music ever written, German composer Ludwig van Beethoven bridged the 18th-century Classical period and the new beginnings of Romanticism. His greatest

breakthroughs in composition came in his instrumental
work, including his symphonies. Unlike his predecessor
Wolfgang Amadeus Mozart, for whom writing music
seemed to come easily, Beethoven always struggled to
perfect his work.

Beethoven's father and grandfather worked as court
musicians in Bonn. Ludwig's father, a singer, gave him
his early musical training. Although he had only meagre
academic schooling, he studied piano, violin, and French
horn, and before he was 12 years old he became a court
organist. Ludwig's first important teacher of composition
was Christian Gottlob Neefe. In 1787 he studied briefly
with Mozart, and five years later he left Bonn permanently
and went to Vienna to study with Joseph Haydn and later
with Antonio Salieri.

Beethoven's first public appearance in Vienna was on
March 29, 1795, as a soloist in one of his piano concerti. Even
before he left Bonn, he had developed a reputation for fine
improvisatory performances. In Vienna young Beethoven
soon accumulated a long list of aristocratic patrons.

## ONSET OF DEAFNESS AND ILL HEALTH

In the late 1700s Beethoven began to suffer from early
symptoms of deafness. Around the same time he developed
severe abdominal pain. By 1802 Beethoven was convinced
that his deafness not only was permanent, but was getting
progressively worse. He spent that summer in the country
and wrote what has become known as the "Heiligenstadt
Testament." In the document, apparently intended for his
two brothers, Beethoven expressed his humiliation and
despair. For the rest of his life he searched for a cure for
his ailments, but his abdominal distress persisted and by
1819 he had become completely deaf.

Beethoven never married. Although his friends were numerous, he was a rather lonely man, prone to irritability and dramatic mood swings. He continued to appear in public but increasingly focused his time on his compositions. Living near Vienna, he took long walks carrying sketchbooks, which became a repository of his musical ideas. These sketchbooks reveal the agonizingly protracted process by which Beethoven perfected his melodies, harmonies, and instrumentations.

## THREE PERIODS OF WORK

Most critics divide Beethoven's work into three general periods, omitting the earliest years of his apprenticeship in Bonn. The first period, from 1794 to about 1800, generally encompasses music whose most salient features are typical of the Classical era. The influence of such musicians as Mozart and Haydn is evident in Beethoven's early chamber music, as well as in his first two piano concerti and his first symphony. Although Beethoven added his own subtleties, including sudden changes of dynamics, the music was generally well constructed and congruent with the sensibilities of the Classical period.

The second period, from 1801 to 1814, includes much of Beethoven's improvisatory work. His *Symphony No. 3*, known as the "Eroica," and the *Fourth Piano Concerto* are fine examples of this period.

The final period, from 1814 to his death in 1827, is characterized by wider ranges of harmony and counterpoint. The last string quartets contain some of the composer's most vivid melodic and rhythmic material, while the form of the music is notably longer and more complex. In his symphonies and string quartets, he often replaced the minuet movement with a livelier scherzo. He also used improvisatory techniques, with surprise rhythmic accents and other unexpected elements.

Many critics and listeners regard Beethoven as the finest composer who ever lived. He elevated symphonic music to a new position of authority in the Western music tradition. He also made great strides with chamber music for piano, as well as for string quartets, trios, and sonatas. His works include nine symphonies, 32 piano sonatas, five piano concerti, 17 string quartets, ten sonatas for violin and piano, one opera (*Fidelio*), the *Mass in C Major*, *Missa Solemnis*, and other chamber music.

## STRUCTURAL INNOVATIONS

Beethoven remains the supreme exponent of what may be called the architectonic use of tonality. In his greatest sonata movements, such as the first allegro of the *Eroica*, the listener's subconscious mind remains oriented to E-flat major even in the most distant keys, so that when, long before the recapitulation, the music touches on the dominant (B-flat), this is immediately recognizable as being the dominant. Of his innovations in the symphony and quartet, the most notable is the replacement of the minuet by the more dynamic scherzo; he enriched both the orchestra and the quartet with a new range of sonority and variety of texture, and their forms are often greatly expanded. The same is true of the concerto, in which he introduced formal innovations that, though relatively few in number, would prove equally influential. In particular, the entry of a solo instrument before an orchestral ritornello in the *Fourth* and *Fifth* piano concerti (a device anticipated by Mozart but to quite different effect) reinforces the sense of the soloist as a protagonist, even a Romantic hero, an effect later composers would struggle to reproduce.

Although, in the finale of the *Ninth Symphony* and the *Missa Solemnis*, Beethoven shows himself a master of choral effects, the solo human voice gave him difficulty to the end. His many songs form perhaps the least important part of his output, although his song cycle *An die ferne Geliebte* would prove an important influence on later composers, especially Robert Schumann. His one opera, *Fidelio*, owes its preeminence to the excellence of the music rather than to any real understanding of the operatic medium. But even this lack of vocal sense could be made to bear fruit, in that it set his mind free in other directions. A composer such as Mozart or Haydn, whose conception of melody remained rooted in what could be sung, could never have written anything like the opening of the *Fifth Symphony*, in which the melody takes shape from three instrumental strands each giving way to the other. Richard Wagner was not far wrong when he hailed Beethoven as the discoverer of instrumental melody, even if his claim was based more narrowly on Beethoven's avoidance of cadential formulas.

Beethoven holds an important place in the history of the piano. In his day, the piano sonata was the most intimate form of chamber music that existed—far more so than the string quartet, which was often performed in public. For Beethoven, the piano sonata was the vehicle for his boldest and most inward thoughts. He did not anticipate the technical devices of such later composers as Frédéric Chopin and Franz Liszt, which were designed to counteract the percussiveness of the piano, partly because he himself had a pianistic ability that could make the most simply laid-out melody sing; partly, too, because the piano itself was still in a fairly early stage of development; and partly because he himself valued its percussive quality and could turn it to good account. Piano tone, caused by a hammer's striking a string, cannot move forward, as can the sustained, bowed tone of the violin, although careful phrasing on the player's part can make it seem to do so. Beethoven, however, is almost alone in writing melodies that accept this limitation, melodies of utter stillness in which each chord is like a stone dropped into a calm pool. And it is above all in the piano sonata that the most striking use of improvisatory techniques as an element of construction is found.

## An Enduring Mystery

Beethoven remained a subject of interest long after his death not only because of his music but also because of unresolved questions concerning his troubled life. An enduring topic of speculation was the cause of his debilitating illnesses and his erratic personality. In the "Heiligenstadt Testament," the composer recognized that this subject would long be a perplexing one: "After my death," he wrote, "if Dr. Schmidt is still alive, ask him in my name to discover my disease . . . so at least as much as is possible the world may be reconciled to me after my death."

Nearly two centuries later, a scientific analysis of strands of Beethoven's hair suggested a possible answer to this lingering question. Four years of study at Argonne National Laboratory in Argonne, Ill., and the McCrone Research Institute in Chicago led researchers to conclude in 2000 that Beethoven had lead poisoning, which may have caused his gastrointestinal distress, irritability, and depression and possibly contributed to his death. The cause of his deafness, however, remained more uncertain, as causal relationships between lead poisoning and the disability are rare.

# FRANZ SCHUBERT

(b. Jan. 31, 1797, Himmelpfortgrund, near Vienna [Austria]—d. Nov. 19, 1828, Vienna)

Franz Peter Schubert was an Austrian composer who bridged the worlds of Classical and Romantic music. Although especially noted for his songs (lieder) and chamber music, he also wrote symphonies, masses, and piano works.

## EARLY LIFE AND CAREER

Schubert's father was a schoolmaster, and his mother was in domestic service at the time of her marriage. Franz was their fourth surviving son, and he had a younger sister. The family was musical and cultivated string quartet playing in the home; Franz played the viola. He received the foundations of his musical education from his father and his brother Ignaz. In 1808 he won a scholarship that earned him a place in the imperial court chapel choir and an education at the Stadtkonvikt, the principal boarding school for commoners in Vienna, where his tutors included the composer Antonio Salieri, then at the height of his fame. Schubert played the violin in the students' orchestra and was quickly promoted to leader and sometime conductor.

Schubert's earliest works included a long *Fantasia for Piano Duet*, a song, several orchestral overtures, various pieces of chamber music, and three string quartets. An unfinished operetta on a text by August von Kotzebue, *Der Spiegelritter* (*The Looking-glass Knight*), also belongs to those years. Eventually Schubert's work came to the notice of Salieri; when his voice broke in 1812 and he left the college, he continued his studies privately with Salieri for at least another three years. During this time he entered a teachers' training college in Vienna and in 1814 became assistant in his father's school. Rejected for military service because of his short stature, he continued as a schoolmaster until 1818.

The numerous compositions he wrote between 1813 and 1815 are remarkable for their style, originality, and imagination. Besides five string quartets, there were three full-scale masses and three symphonies. His first full-length opera, *Des Teufels Lustschloss* (*The Devil's Palace of Desire*), was finished while he was at the training college. But at this period song composition was his chief interest. On Oct. 19, 1814, he first set to music a poem by Goethe, "Gretchen am Spinnrade" ("Gretchen at the Spinning Wheel"), from *Faust*; it was his 30th song, and in this masterpiece he created the German lied (art song). The following year brought the composition of more than 140 songs.

The many unfinished fragments and sketches of songs left by Schubert provide some insight into the working of his creative mind. The primary stimulus was melodic; the words of a poem engendered a tune. Harmony (chordal structure of a composition) and modulation (change of key) were then suggested by the contours of the melody. But the external details of the poet's scene—natural, domestic, or mythical—prompted such wonderfully graphic images in the accompaniments as the spinning wheel, the ripple of water, or the "shimmering robe" of spring. These features were fully present in the songs of 1815. During that year Schubert also was preoccupied with a number of ill-fated operas.

In 1816 Schubert took a leave of absence from his duties as school headmaster, and during his teaching hiatus he met the baritone Johann Michael Vogl. As a result of this meeting, Vogl's singing of Schubert's songs became the rage of the Viennese drawing rooms. But this period of freedom did not last, and in the autumn of 1817 Schubert returned to his teaching duties. The leave, however, had been particularly fruitful. Songs of this period include "Ganymed," "Der Wanderer," and the *Harper's Songs* from Goethe's novel *Wilhelm Meister*. There were two more symphonies: *No. 4 in C Minor*, which Schubert himself named the *Tragic* (1816), and the popular *No. 5 in B-flat Major* (1816). A fourth mass, in C major, was composed in 1816. The year 1817 is notable for the beginning of his masterly series of piano sonatas. Six were composed while staying at the home of life-long friend Franz von Schober, the finest being *No. 7 in E-flat Major* and *No. 11 in B Major*.

Schubert's years of schoolmastering ended in the summer of 1818. He had found the position frustrating, and in the spring of that year he had produced only one substantial work, the *Symphony No. 6 in C Major*. In the meantime his reputation was growing, however, and the first public performance of one of his works, the *Italian Overture in C Major*, took place on March 1, 1818, in Vienna. In June he took up the post of music master to the two daughters of Johann, Count Esterházy, in the family's summer residence at Zseliz, Hung. In the summer months Schubert completed the piano duets *Variations on a French Song* in E minor and the *Sonata in B-flat Major*, sets of dances, songs, and the *Deutsche Trauermesse* (*German Requiem*).

## MATURITY

On his return to Vienna he composed the operetta *Die Zwillingsbrüder* (*The Twin Brothers*), but the production of the work was postponed, and in June 1819 Schubert and Vogl set off for a protracted holiday in the singer's native district of upper Austria. There he composed the first of his widely known instrumental compositions, the *Piano Sonata in A Major*, D. 664, and the celebrated *Trout Quintet* for piano and strings. The close of 1819 saw him engrossed in songs to poems by his friend Johann Mayrhofer and by Goethe, who inspired "Prometheus."

In June 1820 *Die Zwillingsbrüder* was performed with moderate success in Vienna, Vogl doubling in the parts of the twin brothers. It was followed by the performance of incidental music for the play *Die Zauberharfe* (*The Magic Harp*), given in August of the same year. The melodious overture became famous as the *Rosamunde* overture. At the close of the year 1820, Schubert composed the *Quartettsatz* (*Quartet-Movement*) in C Minor, heralding the great string quartets of the middle 1820s, and another popular piece, the motet for female voices on the text of Psalm XXIII. In December 1820 he began the choral setting of Goethe's *Gesang der Geister über den Wassern* (*Song of the Spirits over the Water*) for male-voice octet with accompaniment for bass strings, D. 714, completed in February 1821.

During September and October 1821 Schubert worked on the three-act opera, *Alfonso und Estrell*. It was completed in February 1822 but was never performed. In July 1822, he produced the document called *Mein Traum* ("My Dream"), describing a quarrel between a music-loving youth and his father. The autumn of 1822 saw the beginning of the *Symphony in B Minor* (*Unfinished*). In November of the same year Schubert composed a piano fantasia and completed the *Mass in A-flat Major*.

At the close of 1822 Schubert contracted a venereal disease, and the following year was one of illness and retirement. He continued to write almost incessantly. In February 1823 he wrote the *Piano Sonata in A Minor*, and in April he made another attempt to gain success in Viennese theatres with the one-act operetta *Die Verschworenen* (*The Conspirators*), the title being changed later to *Der häusliche Krieg* (*Domestic Warfare*). The famous work of the year, however, was the song cycle *Die schöne Müllerin* ("The Fair Maid of the Mill"), representing the epitome of Schubert's lyrical art. Schubert spent part of the summer in the hospital and probably started work—while still a patient—on his most ambitious opera, *Fierrabras*. The year 1823 closed with Schubert's composition of the music for the play *Rosamunde*, performed at Vienna in December.

Schubert was ill, penniless, and plagued by a sense of failure early in 1824. Yet during this time he composed three masterly chamber works: the *String Quartet in A Minor*, a second string quartet in D Minor containing variations on his song *Der Tod und das Mädchen*, and the *Octet in F Major* for strings and wind instruments. In desperate need of money, he returned in the summer to his teaching post with the Esterházy family and in May 1824 went again to Zseliz. Once more his health and spirits revived. The period was marked by some piano duets, the *Piano Sonata in C Major* (*Grand Duo*), the *Variations on an Original Theme in A-flat Major*, and the *Divertissement à la hongroise* (*Hungarian Divertissement*).

During these years his songs were frequently performed. Publication proceeded rapidly, and his financial position, though still strained, was at any rate eased. This is the period of the *Lady of the Lake* songs, including the once popular but later neglected *Ave Maria*. Instrumental compositions are the piano sonatas in A Minor and in D Major, the latter composed at Badgastein. He sketched a symphony during the summer holiday, in all probability the beginnings of the *Symphony in C Major* (*Great*), completed in 1828.

## LAST YEARS

The resignation of Salieri as imperial *Kapellmeister* (musical director) in 1824 had led to the promotion of his deputy, Josef Eybler. In 1826 Schubert applied for the vacant post of deputy *Kapellmeister*, but in spite of strong support by several influential people he was unsuccessful. From then until his death two years later he seems to have let matters drift. Neither by application for professional posts nor submission of operatic work did he seek to establish himself.

The songs of 1826 include the settings of Shakespeare's "Hark! Hark! the Lark!" and "Who is Silvia?" Three fine instrumental works of this summer and autumn are the last: *String Quartet in G Major*, the *Piano Sonata in G Major*, and the beginning of the *Piano Trio in B Flat Major*. In 1827 he composed the first 12 songs of the cycle *Winterreise* (*Winter Journey*). Beethoven's death in 1827 undoubtedly had a profound effect on Schubert, for there is no denying that a more profound, more intellectual quality akin to that in Beethoven's music appears in his last instrumental works, especially the *Piano Trio in E-flat Major* (1827) and the *Piano Sonata in C Minor* (1828). In September 1827 Schubert spent a short holiday in Graz. On his return he composed the *Piano Trio in E-flat Major* and resumed work on Part II of the *Winterreise*. This is the period of his piano solos, the *Impromptus* and *Moments musicaux*.

A succession of masterpieces marks the last year of his life. Early in the year he composed the greatest of his piano duets, the *Fantasy in F Minor*. The *Great Symphony* was concluded in March, as was also the cantata *Miriams Siegesgesang* (*Miriam's Victory Song*). In June he worked at his sixth mass—in E-flat Major. A return to songwriting in August produced the series published together as the *Schwanengesang* (*Swan Song*). In September and early October the succession was concluded by the last three piano sonatas, in C Minor, A Major, and B-flat Major, and the great *String Quintet in C Major*—the swan song of the Classical era in music.

The only public concert Schubert gave took place on March 26, 1828. It was both artistically and financially a success, and the impecunious composer was at last able to buy himself a piano. At the end of August he moved into lodgings with his brother Ferdinand. Schubert's health, broken by the illness of 1823, had deteriorated, and his ceaseless work had exhausted him. In October he developed typhoid fever, and his last days were spent in the company of his brother and several close friends.

# FELIX MENDELSSOHN
(b. Feb. 3, 1809, Hamburg [Germany]—d. Nov. 4, 1847, Leipzig)

Jakob Ludwig Felix Mendelssohn-Bartholdy—or Felix Mendelssohn—was a German composer, pianist, musical conductor, and teacher who was among the most celebrated figures of the early Romantic period. In his music Mendelssohn largely observed Classical models and practices while initiating key aspects of Romanticism— the artistic movement that exalted feeling and the imagination above rigid forms and traditions. Among his most famous works are *Overture to A Midsummer Night's Dream* (1826), *Italian Symphony* (1833), a violin concerto (1844), two piano concerti (1831, 1837), the oratorio *Elijah* (1846), and several pieces of chamber music.

## EARLY LIFE AND WORKS

Felix was born of Jewish parents, Abraham and Lea Salomon Mendelssohn, from whom he took his first piano lessons. Though the Mendelssohns were proud of their ancestry, they considered it desirable, in accordance with 19th-century liberal ideas, to mark their emancipation from the ghetto by adopting the Christian faith. Accordingly Felix, together with his brother and two sisters, was baptized in his youth as a Lutheran Christian. The name Bartholdy, a

*The German composer, conductor, and musician Felix Mendelssohn, celebrated during the Romantic period for his accomplished works.* Getty Images/Redferns

family property on the river Spree, was held by a wealthy maternal uncle who had embraced Protestantism. When the fortune of this relative passed to the Mendelssohns, his name was adopted by them.

In 1811, during the French occupation of Hamburg, the family had moved to Berlin, where Mendelssohn studied the piano with Ludwig Berger and composition with K.F. Zelter, who, as a composer and teacher, exerted an enormous influence on his development. His personality was nourished by a broad knowledge of the arts and was also stimulated by learning and scholarship. He traveled with his sister to Paris, where he took further piano lessons and where he appears to have become acquainted with the music of Wolfgang Amadeus Mozart.

Mendelssohn was an extremely precocious musical composer. He wrote numerous compositions during his boyhood, among them 5 operas, 11 symphonies for string orchestra, concerti, sonatas, and fugues. He made his first public appearance in 1818 — at the age of nine — in Berlin.

In 1821 Mendelssohn was taken to Weimar to meet J.W. von Goethe, for whom he played works of J.S. Bach and Mozart and to whom he dedicated his *Piano Quartet No. 3. in B Minor* (1825). A remarkable friendship developed between the aging poet and the 12-year-old musician. The next year he reached his full stature as a composer with the *Overture to A Midsummer Night's Dream*.

Mendelssohn also became active as a conductor. On March 11, 1829, at the Singakademie, Berlin, he conducted the first performance since Bach's death of the *St. Matthew Passion*, thus inaugurating the Bach revival of the 19th and 20th centuries. Meanwhile he had visited Switzerland and had met Carl Maria von Weber, whose opera *Der Freischütz* encouraged him to develop a national character in music. Mendelssohn's great work of this period was the *String Octet in E-flat Major* (1825), displaying not only technical mastery and an almost unprecedented lightness of touch but great melodic and rhythmic originality. Mendelssohn developed in this work the genre of the swift-moving scherzo (a playful musical movement) that he would also use in the incidental music to *A Midsummer Night's Dream* (1842).

In the spring of 1829 Mendelssohn made his first journey to England, conducting his *Symphony No. 1 in C Minor* (1824) at the London Philharmonic Society. In the summer he went to Scotland, of which he gave many poetic accounts in his evocative letters. Describing, in a letter written from the Hebrides, the manner in which the waves break on the Scottish coast, he noted down, in the form of a musical symbol, the opening bars of the *Hebrides Overture* (1830–32; also known as *Fingal's Cave*). Between 1830 and 1832 he traveled in Germany, Austria, Italy, and Switzerland and, in 1832, returned to London, where he conducted the *Hebrides Overture* and where he published the first book of the piano music he called *Lieder ohne Worte* (*Songs Without Words*), completed in Venice in 1830. Gradually Mendelssohn's music was becoming the most popular of 19th-century composers in England.

Mendelssohn's *Symphony No. 3 in A Minor–Major*, or *Scottish Symphony*, as it is called, was dedicated to Queen Victoria. And he became endeared to the English musical public in other ways. The fashion for playing the "Wedding March" from his *A Midsummer Night's Dream* at bridal processions originates from a performance of this piece at the wedding of the Princess Royal after Mendelssohn's death, in 1858. In the meantime he had given the first performances in London of Ludwig van Beethoven's *Emperor* and *G Major* concerti. Later the popularity of his oratorio *Elijah*, first produced at Birmingham in 1846, established

Mendelssohn as a composer whose influence on English music equaled that of George Frideric Handel. Later generations of English composers, enamoured of Richard Wagner, Claude Debussy, or Igor Stravinsky, revolted against the domination of Mendelssohn and condemned the sentimentality of his lesser works.

In 1833 he was in London to conduct his *Italian Symphony* (*Symphony No. 4 in A Major–Minor*), and in the same year he became music director of Düsseldorf. At Düsseldorf, too, he began his first oratorio, *St. Paul*. In 1835 he became conductor of the celebrated Gewandhaus Orchestra at Leipzig, where he not only raised the standard of orchestral playing but made Leipzig the musical capital of Germany.

## MARRIAGE AND MATURITY

In 1835 Mendelssohn was overcome by the death of his father, Abraham, whose dearest wish had been that his son should complete *St. Paul*. He accordingly plunged into this work with renewed determination and the following year conducted it at Düsseldorf. The same year at Frankfurt he met Cécile Jeanrenaud, the daughter of a French Protestant clergyman. Though she was no more than 16, they became engaged and were married on March 28, 1837. Mendelssohn's sister Fanny, the member of his family who remained closest to him, spoke kindly of her sister-in-law. Indeed, Fanny was not only a composer in her own right—she had herself written some of the *Songs Without Words* attributed to her brother—but she seems to have exercised, by her sisterly companionship, a powerful influence on the development of his inner musical nature.

Works written over the following years include the *Variations sérieuses* (1841), for piano, the *Lobgesang* (1840; *Hymn of Praise*), *Psalm CXIV*, the *Piano Concerto No. 2 in D*

*Minor* (1837), and chamber works. In 1838 Mendelssohn began the *Violin Concerto in E Minor–Major*. Though he normally worked rapidly, this final expression of his lyrical genius compelled his arduous attention over the next six years. Later, in the 20th century, the *Violin Concerto* was still admired for its warmth of melody and for its vivacity, and it was also the work of Mendelssohn's that, for nostalgic listeners, enshrined the elegant musical language of the 19th century.

In 1843 Mendelssohn founded at Leipzig the conservatory of music where he taught composition. Visits to London and Birmingham followed, entailing an increasing number of engagements. These would hardly have affected his normal health; he had always lived on this feverish level. But at Frankfurt in May 1847 he was greatly saddened by the death of Fanny. His energies deserted him, and, following the rupture of a blood vessel, he soon died.

## FRÉDÉRIC CHOPIN

(b. March 1, 1810, Żelazow, near Warsaw, duchy of Warsaw [now in Poland]—d. Oct. 17, 1849, Paris, France)

Frédéric François Chopin, a Polish-French composer and pianist of the Romantic period, is best known for his solo pieces for piano and for his piano concerti. Although he wrote little but piano works, many of them brief, Chopin ranks as one of music's greatest tone poets by reason of his superfine imagination and fastidious craftsmanship. His works for solo piano include about 61 mazurkas, 16 polonaises, 26 preludes, 27 études, 21 nocturnes, 20 waltzes, 3 sonatas, 4 ballades, 4 scherzos, 4 impromptus, and many individual pieces—such as the *Barcarolle*, Opus 60 (1846); the *Fantasia*, Opus 49 (1841); and the *Berceuse*, Opus 57 (1845)—as well as 17 Polish songs.

## EARLY YEARS IN WARSAW AND VIENNA

Chopin's father, Nicholas, a French émigré in Poland, was employed as a tutor to various aristocratic families, including the Skarbeks, at Żelazowa Wola, one of whose poorer relations he married. When Frédéric was eight months old, Nicholas became a French teacher at the Warsaw lyceum. Chopin himself attended the lyceum from 1823 to 1826.

Chopin started piano lessons at age 7 with the 61-year-old Wojciech Zywny, an all-around musician with an astute sense of values. Zywny's simple instruction in piano playing was soon left behind by his pupil, who discovered for himself an original approach to the piano and was allowed to develop unhindered by academic rules and formal discipline. Chopin was soon invited to play at private soirées, and at age 8 he made his first public appearance at a charity concert. Three years later he performed in the presence of the Russian tsar Alexander I, who was in Warsaw to open Parliament. Playing was not alone responsible for his growing reputation as a child prodigy. At 7 he wrote a *Polonaise in G Minor*, which was printed, and soon afterward a march of his appealed to the Russian grand duke Constantine, who had it scored for his military band to play on parade. Other polonaises, mazurkas, variations, ecossaises, and a rondo followed, with the result that, when he was 16, his family enrolled him at the newly formed Warsaw Conservatory of Music. This school was directed by the Polish composer Joseph Elsner, with whom Chopin already had been studying musical theory.

Elsner realized that Chopin's individual imagination must never be checked by purely academic demands. Even before he came under Elsner's eye, Chopin had shown interest in the folk music of the Polish countryside and had received those impressions that later gave an unmistakable national colouring to his work. At the conservatory he was put through a solid course of instruction in harmony and composition; in piano playing he was allowed to develop a high degree of individuality.

Chopin made his performance debut in Vienna in 1829. A second concert confirmed his success, and on his return home he prepared himself for further achievements abroad by writing his *Piano Concerto No. 2 in F Minor* (1829) and his *Piano Concerto No. 1 in E Minor* (1830), as well as other works for piano and orchestra designed to exploit his brilliantly original piano style. His first études were also written at this time (1829–32) to enable him and others to master the technical difficulties in his new style of piano playing.

## YEARS IN PARIS

In March and October 1830 he presented his new works to the Warsaw public and then left Poland with the intention of visiting Germany and Italy for further study. He had gone no farther than Vienna when news reached him of the Polish revolt against Russian rule; this event, added to the disturbed state of Europe, caused him to remain profitlessly in Vienna until the following July, when he decided to make his way to Paris. Soon after his arrival in what was then the centre of European culture and in the midst of its own late-flowering Romantic movement, Chopin realized that he had found the milieu in which his genius could flourish. He quickly established ties with many Polish émigrés and with a younger generation of composers, including Franz Liszt and Hector Berlioz. Chopin decided to settle in Paris to pursue teaching and composing.

After his Paris concert debut in February 1832, Chopin realized that his extreme delicacy at the keyboard was not to everyone's taste in larger concert spaces. However, with his elegant manners, fastidious dress, and innate sensitivity, Chopin soon found himself a favourite in the great houses of Paris, both as a recitalist and as a teacher. His new piano works at this time included two books of études (1829–36), the *Ballade in G Minor* (1831–35), the *Fantaisie-Impromptu* (1835), and many smaller pieces, among them mazurkas and polonaises inspired by Chopin's strong nationalist feeling.

In 1836 Chopin met for the first time the novelist Aurore Dudevant, better known as George Sand; their liaison began in the summer of 1838. That autumn he set off with her and her children, Maurice and Solange, to winter on the island of Majorca. They rented a simple villa and were idyllically happy until the sunny weather broke and Chopin became ill. When rumours of tuberculosis reached the villa owner, they were ordered out and could find accommodations only in a monastery in the remote village of Valldemosa.

The cold and damp environment, malnutrition, peasant suspiciousness of their strange ménage, and the lack of a suitable concert piano hindered Chopin's artistic production and further weakened his precarious physical health. Sand realized that only immediate departure would save his life. They arrived at Marseille in early March 1839, and, thanks to a skilled physician, Chopin was sufficiently recovered after just under three months for them to start planning a return to Paris.

The summer of 1839 they spent at Nohant, Sand's country house about 180 miles (290 km) south of Paris. This period following the return from Majorca was to be the happiest and most productive of Chopin's life. For a regular source of income, he again turned to private teaching. There was also a growing demand for his new works, and, since he had become increasingly shrewd in his dealings with publishers, he could afford to live elegantly.

Health was a recurrent worry, and every summer Sand took him to Nohant for fresh air and relaxation. Chopin produced much of his most-searching music there, not only miniatures but also extended works, such as the *Fantaisie in F Minor* (composed 1840–41), the *Barcarolle* (1845–46), the *Polonaise-Fantaisie* (1845–46), the ballades in A-flat major (1840–41) and F minor (1842), and the *Sonata in B Minor* (1844). He seemed particularly anxious to develop his ideas into longer and more complex arguments, and he even sent to Paris for treatises by musicologists to strengthen his counterpoint. His harmonic vocabulary at this period also grew much more daring. He valued that quality throughout life as much as he abhorred descriptive titles or any hint of an underlying "program."

Family dissension arising from the marriage of Sand's daughter, Solange, caused Chopin's own relationship with Sand to become strained, and he grew increasingly moody and petulant. By 1848 the rift between him and Sand was complete, and pride prevented either from effecting the reconciliation they both actually desired. Thereafter Chopin seems to have given up his struggle with ill health.

Broken in spirit and depressed by the revolution that had broken out in Paris in February 1848, Chopin accepted an invitation to visit England and Scotland. His reception in London was enthusiastic, and he struggled through an exhausting round of lessons and appearances at fashionable parties. By now his health was deteriorating rapidly, and he made his last public appearance on a concert platform at the Guildhall in London on Nov. 16, 1848, when, in a final patriotic gesture, he played for the benefit of Polish refugees. He returned to Paris, where he died the following year.

## FRANZ LISZT

(b. Oct. 22, 1811, Raiding, Hung.—d. July 31, 1886, Bayreuth, Ger.)

Hungarian musician Franz Liszt was one of the greatest piano virtuosi of all time and also was a respected composer of the Romantic period. Among his many notable compositions are his 12 symphonic poems, two (completed) piano concerti, several sacred choral works, and a great variety of solo piano pieces.

### YOUTH AND EARLY TRAINING

Liszt's father, Ádám Liszt, was an official in the service of Prince Nicolas Esterházy, whose palace in Eisenstadt was frequented by many celebrated musicians. Ádám Liszt was a talented amateur musician who played the cello in the court concerts. By the time Franz was five years old he was already attracted to the piano and was soon given lessons by his father. He began to show interest in both church and Gypsy music. He developed into a religious child, also because of the influence of his father, who during his youth had spent two years in the Franciscan order.

Franz began to compose at the age of eight. When only nine he made his first public appearance as a concert pianist at Sopron and Pozsony (now Bratislava, Slovakia). His playing so impressed the local Hungarian magnates that they put up the money to pay for his musical education for the next six years. Ádám took Franz to Vienna, where he had piano lessons with Carl Czerny, a composer and pianist who had been a pupil of Ludwig van Beethoven, and studied composition with Antonio Salieri, the musical director at the Viennese court.

Liszt moved with his family to Paris in 1823, giving concerts in Germany on the way. Liszt's Paris debut on March 7, 1824, was sensational. Other concerts quickly followed, as well as a visit to London in June. He toured England again the following year, visiting Manchester, where his *New Grand Overture* was performed for the first time. This piece was used as the overture to his one-act opera *Don Sanche*, which was performed at the Paris Opéra on Oct. 17, 1825. In 1826 he toured France and Switzerland, returning to England again in the following year. Suffering from nervous exhaustion, Liszt went with his father to Boulogne to take seabaths to improve his health; there Ádám died of typhoid fever. Liszt returned to Paris and sent for his mother to join him; she had gone back to the Austrian province of Styria during his tours.

In 1828, while living mainly as a piano teacher in Paris, Liszt fell ill and subsequently underwent a long period of depression and doubt about his career. For more than a year he did not touch the piano. During this period Liszt took an active dislike to the career of a virtuoso. He made up for his previous lack of education by reading widely, and he came into contact with many of the leading artists of the day. With the July Revolution of 1830 resulting in the coronation of Louis-Philippe, he sketched out a *Revolutionary Symphony*.

Between 1830 and 1832 he met three men who were to have a great influence on his artistic life. At the end of 1830 he first met Hector Berlioz and heard the first performance of his *Symphonie fantastique*. From Berlioz he inherited the command of the Romantic orchestra and also the diabolic quality that remained in his work thereafter. He achieved the seemingly impossible feat of transcribing Berlioz's

*Symphonie fantastique* for the piano in 1833. In March 1831 he heard Niccolò Paganini play for the first time. He again became interested in virtuoso technique and resolved to transfer some of Paganini's fantastic violin effects to the piano, writing a fantasia on his *La campanella*. At this time he also met Frédéric Chopin, whose poetical style of music exerted a profound influence on Liszt.

## YEARS WITH MARIE D'AGOULT

In 1834 Liszt emerged as a mature composer with the solo piano piece *Harmonies poétiques et religieuses*, based on a collection of poems by Lamartine, and the set of three *Apparitions*. The lyrical style of these works is in marked contrast to his youthful compositions, which reflected the style of his teacher Czerny. In the same year, he met the novelist George Sand and also Marie de Flavigny, countess d'Agoult, with whom he began an affair. In 1835 she left her husband and family to join Liszt in Switzerland; their first daughter, Blandine, was born in Geneva on December 18. Liszt and Madame d'Agoult lived together for four years, mainly in Switzerland and Italy, though Liszt made occasional visits to Paris. He also taught at the newly founded Geneva Conservatory and published a series of essays, *On the Position of Artists*, in which he endeavoured to raise the status of the artist in society.

Liszt commemorated his years with Madame d'Agoult in the first two books of solo piano pieces collectively named *Années de pèlerinage* (1837–54; *Years of Pilgrimage*), which are poetical evocations of Swiss and Italian scenes. He also wrote the first mature version of the *Transcendental Études* (1838, 1851); these are works for solo piano based on his youthful *Étude en 48 exercices*, but here transformed into pieces of terrifying virtuosity. He transcribed for the piano six of Paganini's pieces—five studies and *La campanella*—and also three Beethoven symphonies, some songs by Franz Schubert, and further works of Berlioz.

His second daughter, Cosima, was born in 1837 and his son, Daniel, in 1839, but toward the end of that year his relations with Madame d'Agoult became strained and she returned to Paris with the children. Liszt then returned to his career as a virtuoso. For the next eight years Liszt traveled all over Europe, giving concerts in countries as far apart as Ireland, Portugal, Turkey, and Russia. He continued to spend his summer holidays with Madame d'Agoult and the children until 1844; then they finally parted, and Liszt took the children to Paris. Liszt's brilliance and success were at their peak during these years as a virtuoso, and he continued to compose, writing songs as well as piano works.

His visit to Hungary in 1839–40, the first since his boyhood, was an important event. His renewed interest in the music of the Gypsies laid the foundations for his *Hungarian Rhapsodies* and other piano pieces composed in the Hungarian style. He also wrote a cantata for the Beethoven Festival of 1845 and composed some smaller choral works.

## COMPOSITIONS AT WEIMAR

In February 1847 Liszt met the princess Carolyne Sayn-Wittgenstein at Kiev and later spent some time at her estate in Poland. She quickly persuaded him to give up his career as a virtuoso and to concentrate on composition. He gave his final concert at Yelizavetgrad (Kirovograd) in September of that year. Having been director of music extraordinary to the Weimar court in Germany since 1843, and having conducted concerts there since 1844, Liszt decided to settle there permanently in 1848. He was later joined by the princess, who had unsuccessfully tried to obtain a divorce from her husband. They resided together in Weimar, and this was the period of his greatest production: the first 12 symphonic poems, *A Faust Symphony* (1854; rev. 1857–61), *A Symphony to Dante's Divina Commedia* (1855–56), the *Piano Sonata in B Minor* (1852–53), the *Piano Concerto No. 1 in E-flat Major* (1849; rev. 1853 and 1856), and the Piano Concerto No. 2 in A Major (1839; rev. 1849–61). (A third piano concerto, in E-flat, composed in 1839, was not discovered until 1988.) During the period in Weimar Liszt also composed the *Totentanz* for piano and orchestra and revised the *Transcendental* and *Paganini Études* and the first two books of the *Années de pèlerinage*.

The grand duke who originally appointed Liszt in Weimar died in 1853, and his successor took little interest in music. Liszt resigned five years later, and, though he remained in Weimar until 1861, his position there became more and more difficult. His son, Daniel, had died in 1859 at the age of 20. Liszt was deeply distressed and wrote the oration for orchestra *Les Morts* in his son's memory. In May 1860 the princess had left Weimar for Rome in the hope of having her divorce sanctioned by the pope. He left Weimar in August of the following year, and, after traveling to Berlin and Paris, he arrived in Rome. He and the princess hoped to be married on his 50th birthday. At the last moment, however, the pope revoked his sanction of the princess's divorce; they both remained in Rome in separate establishments.

## EIGHT YEARS IN ROME

For the next eight years Liszt lived mainly in Rome and occupied himself more and more with religious music. He completed the oratorios *Die Legende von der heiligen Elisabeth* (1857–62) and *Christus* (1855–66) and a number of smaller works. He hoped to create a new kind of religious music that would be more direct and moving than the rather sentimental style popular at the time.

In 1862 his daughter Blandine died at the age of 26. Liszt wrote his variations on a theme from the J.S. Bach cantata *Weinen, Klagen* (*Weeping, Mourning*) ending with the chorale *Was Gott tut das ist wohlgetan* (*What God Does Is Well Done*), which must have been inspired by this event. The princess's husband died in 1864, but there was no more talk of marriage, and in 1865 Liszt took the four minor orders of the Roman Catholic church, though he never became a priest. In 1867 he wrote the *Hungarian Coronation Mass* for the coronation of the emperor Francis Joseph I of Austria as king of Hungary.

## LAST YEARS

In 1869 Liszt was invited to return to Weimar by the grand duke to give master classes in piano playing, and two years later he was asked to do the same in Budapest. From then until the end of his life he divided his time between Rome, Weimar, and Budapest. His music began to lose some of its brilliant quality and became starker, more introverted, and more experimental in style. His later works anticipate the styles of Claude Debussy, Béla Bartók, and even Arnold Schoenberg.

In 1886 Liszt left Rome for the last time. He attended concerts of his works in Budapest, Liège, and Paris and then went to London, where several concerts of his works were given. He then went on to Antwerp, Paris, and Weimar, and he played for the last time at a concert in Luxembourg on July 19. Two days later he arrived in Bayreuth for the annual Bayreuth festival. His health had not been good for some months, and he went to bed with a high fever, though he still managed to attend two performances. His final illness developed into pneumonia, and he died on July 31.

# RICHARD WAGNER

(b. May 22, 1813, Leipzig [Germany]—d. Feb. 13, 1883, Venice, Italy)

German dramatic composer and theorist Richard Wagner revolutionized the course of Western music through the harmonic and melodic intensity of his operatic works. Among his major works are *The Flying Dutchman* (1843), *Tannhäuser* (1845), *Lohengrin* (1850), *Tristan und Isolde* (1865), *Parsifal* (1882), and his great tetralogy, *The Ring of the Nibelung* (1869–76).

## EARLY LIFE

The artistic and theatrical background of Wagner's early years was a main formative influence. Impulsive and self-willed, he was a negligent scholar at the Kreuzschule, Dresden, and the Nicholaischule, Leipzig. He frequented concerts, however, taught himself the piano and composition, and read the plays of Shakespeare, Goethe, and Schiller.

Wagner enrolled at Leipzig University, where he applied himself earnestly to composition. His *Symphony in C Major* was performed at the Leipzig Gewandhaus concerts in 1833. On leaving the university that year, he spent the summer as operatic coach at Würzburg, where he composed his first opera, *Die Feen* (*The Fairies*), based on a fantastic tale by Carlo Gozzi. He failed to get the opera produced at Leipzig and became conductor to a provincial theatrical troupe from Magdeburg, having fallen in love with one of the actresses of the troupe, Wilhelmine (Minna) Planer, whom he married in 1836. The single performance of his second opera, *Das Liebesverbot* (*The Ban on Love*), after Shakespeare's *Measure for Measure*, was a disaster.

In 1839, fleeing from his creditors, he decided to put into operation his long-cherished plan to win renown in Paris, but his three years in Paris were calamitous. Living with a colony of poor German artists, he staved off starvation by means of musical journalism and hackwork. Nevertheless, in 1840 he completed *Rienzi* (after Bulwer-Lytton's novel), and in 1841 he composed his first representative opera, *Der fliegende Holländer* (*The Flying Dutchman*), based on the legend about a ship's captain condemned to sail forever.

In 1842, aged 29, he gladly returned to Dresden, where *Rienzi* was triumphantly performed on October 20. The next year *The Flying Dutchman* (produced at Dresden, Jan. 2, 1843) was less successful, since the audience was puzzled by the innovative way the new opera integrated the music with the dramatic content. But Wagner was appointed conductor of the court opera, a post that he held until 1849. On Oct. 19, 1845, *Tannhäuser* (based, like all his future works, on Germanic legends) was coolly received but soon proved a steady attraction.

The refusal of the court opera authorities in Dresden to stage his next opera, *Lohengrin*, was not based on artistic reasons; rather, they were alienated by Wagner's projected administrative and artistic reforms. His proposals would have taken control of the opera away from the court and created a national theatre whose productions would be chosen by a union of dramatists and composers. Preoccupied with ideas of social regeneration, he then became embroiled in the German revolution of 1848–49. He ultimately fled from Germany, unable to attend the first performance of *Lohengrin* at Weimar, given on Aug. 28, 1850.

## EXILE

For the next 15 years Wagner was not to present any further new works. Until 1858 he lived in Zürich, composing, writing treatises, and conducting. Having already studied the Siegfried legend and the Norse myths as a possible basis for an opera, and having written an operatic "poem," *Siegfrieds Tod* (*Siegfried's Death*), in which he conceived of Siegfried as the new type of man who would emerge after the successful revolution he hoped for, he now wrote a number of prose volumes on revolution, social and artistic. From 1849 to 1852 he produced his basic prose works: *Die Kunst und die Revolution* (*Art and Revolution*), *Das Kunstwerk der Zukunft* (*The Art Work of the Future*), *Eine Mitteilung an meine Freunde* (*A Communication to My Friends*), and *Oper und Drama* (*Opera and Drama*). The latter outlined a new, revolutionary type of musical stage work—the vast work, in fact, on which he was engaged. By 1852 he had added to the poem of *Siegfrieds Tod* three others to precede it, the whole being called *Der Ring des Nibelungen* (*The Ring of the Nibelung*) and providing the basis for a tetralogy of musical dramas: *Das Rheingold* (*The Rhine Gold*); *Die Walküre* (*The Valkyrie*); *Der junge Siegfried* (*Young Siegfried*), later called simply *Siegfried*; and *Siegfrieds Tod* (*Siegfried's Death*), later called *Götterdämmerung* (*The Twilight of the Gods*).

*The Ring* reveals Wagner's mature style and method, to which he had found his way at last during the period when his thought was devoted to social questions. He prophesied the disappearance of opera as artificial entertainment for an elite and the emergence of a new kind of musical stage work for the people, expressing the self-realization of free humanity. The new art form would be a poetic drama that should find full expression as a musical drama set to a continuous vocal-symphonic texture. This texture would be woven from basic thematic ideas, which Wagner called "motives," but which have since come to be known as "leading motives" (German *Leitmotive*, singular *Leitmotiv*). The leading motives would arise naturally as expressive vocal phrases sung by characters and would be developed by the orchestra as "reminiscences" to express the dramatic and psychological development.

This conception found full embodiment in *The Ring*, except that the leading motives did not always arise as vocal utterances but were often introduced by the orchestra to portray characters, emotions, or events in the drama. With his use of this method, Wagner rose immediately to his amazing full stature: his style became unified and deepened immeasurably, and he was able to fill his works from end to end with intensely characteristic music. By 1857 he had composed *Das Rhinegold, Die Walküre*, and two acts of *Siegfried*. But he now suspended work on *The Ring*: the impossibility of mounting this colossus within the foreseeable future was enforcing a stalemate on his career and led him to project a "normal" work capable of immediate production. Also, his optimistic social philosophy had yielded to a metaphysical, world-renouncing pessimism. The outcome was *Tristan und Isolde* (1857–59), of which the crystallizing agent was his hopeless love for Mathilde Wesendonk (the wife of a rich patron), which led to separation from his wife, Minna.

Wagner completed *Tristan* in Venice and in Lucerne, Switzerland. The work revealed a new subtlety in his use of leading motives, which in *Das Rhinegold* and *Die Walküre* he had used mainly to explain the action of the drama. The leading motives in *Tristan* ceased to remain neatly identifiable with their dramatic sources but worked with greater psychological complexity.

## RETURN FROM EXILE

In 1861 he went to Vienna and remained there about a year before traveling widely as a conductor while awaiting a projected production of *Tristan*. When this work was not produced because the artists were bewildered by its revolutionary stylistic innovations, Wagner began a second "normal" work, the comedy-opera *Die Meistersinger von*

*Nürnberg* (*The Meistersingers of Nürnberg*). By 1864, however, he had to flee from Vienna to avoid imprisonment for debt. He arrived in Stuttgart without a penny, a man of 51 without a future, almost at the end of his tether.

Something like a miracle saved him. In 1864 Louis II ascended the throne of Bavaria; he was a fanatical admirer of Wagner's art. Having read the poem of *The Ring*, Louis II invited Wagner to complete the work in Munich and set him up in a villa. During the next six years there were successful Munich productions of all of Wagner's representative works to date, including *Tristan* (1865), *Die Meistersinger* (1868), *Das Rhinegold* (1869), and *Die Walküre* (1870). During this time Wagner constantly ran into debt, and he also attempted to interfere in the government of the kingdom. In addition, he became the lover of the great Wagner conductor Hans von Bülow's wife, Cosima, the daughter of Liszt. She bore him three children—Isolde, Eva, and Siegfried—before her divorce in 1870 and her marriage to Wagner that year. For all these reasons, Wagner thought it advisable to leave Munich.

## Last Years in Bayreuth

In 1869 Wagner had resumed work on *The Ring*, which he now brought to its world-renouncing conclusion. It had been agreed with the king that the tetralogy should be first performed in its entirety at Munich, but Wagner broke the agreement, convinced that a new type of theatre must be built for the purpose. Having discovered a suitable site at the Bavarian town of Bayreuth, he toured Germany, conducting concerts to raise funds to support the plan, and in 1872 the foundation stone was laid. In 1874 Wagner moved into a house at Bayreuth that he called Wahnfried ("Peace from Illusion"). The whole vast project was eventually realized, in spite of enormous difficulties. *The Ring* received its triumphant first complete performance in the new Festspielhaus at Bayreuth on Aug. 13, 14, 16, and 17, 1876.

Wagner spent the rest of his life at Wahnfried, making a visit to London in 1877 to give a successful series of concerts and then making several to Italy. During these years he composed his last work, the sacred festival drama *Parsifal*, begun in 1877 and produced at Bayreuth in 1882. He died of heart failure, at the height of his fame, and was buried in the grounds of Wahnfried in the tomb he had himself prepared. Since then, except for interruptions caused by World Wars I and II, the Festspielhaus has staged yearly festivals of Wagner's works.

## GIUSEPPE VERDI

(b. Oct. 9/10, 1813, Roncole, near Busseto, duchy of Parma [Italy] — d. Jan. 27, 1901, Milan, Italy)

The leading Italian composer of opera in the 19th century, Giuseppe Fortunino Francesco Verdi is noted for operas such as *Rigoletto* (1851), *Il trovatore* (1853), *La traviata* (1853), *Don Carlos* (1867), *Aida* (1871), *Otello* (1887), and *Falstaff* (1893) and for his *Requiem Mass* (1874).

### EARLY YEARS

Born to a poor family, Verdi showed unusual musical talent at an early age. A local amateur musician named Antonio Barezzi helped him with his education. At Barezzi's expense Verdi was sent to Milan when he was 18. He stayed there for three years, then served as musical director in Busseto for two years before returning to Milan. By 1840, just as he had established a reputation and begun to make money, he was discouraged by personal tragedies. Within a three-year period his wife and both of his children died.

## Early Career

Verdi overcame his despair by composing *Nabucodonoser* (composed 1841, first performed 1842; known as *Nabucco*), based on the biblical Nebuchadnezzar (Nebuchadrezzar II). *Nabucco* succeeded sensationally, and Verdi at age 28 became the new hero of Italian music. The work sped across Italy and the whole world of opera; within a decade it had reached as far as St. Petersburg and Buenos Aires, Argentina.

There followed a period (1843–49) during which Verdi drove himself to produce nearly two operas a year. His aim was to make enough money for early retirement as a gentleman farmer at Sant'Agata, close to Roncole, where his forebears had settled. To "produce" an opera meant, at that time, to negotiate with an impresario, secure and edit (often heavily) a libretto, find or approve the singers, compose the music, supervise rehearsals, conduct the first three performances, deal with publishers, and more— all this while shuttling from one end of Italy to the other in the days before railroads.

Though masterpieces were unlikely to emerge from a schedule like this, Verdi's next two operas were wildly successful: *I Lombardi alla prima crociata* (1843; *The Lombards on the First Crusade*) and *Ernani* (1844). The latter became the only work of this period to gain a steady place in the opera repertory worldwide. His other operas had varying receptions. Verdi drew on a wide range of literature for his works of the 1840s, including Victor Hugo for *Ernani*, Lord Byron for *I due Foscari* (1844; *The Two Foscari*) and *Il corsaro* (1848; *The Corsair*), Friedrich von Schiller for *Giovanna d'Arco* (1845; *Joan of Arc*), *I masnadieri* (1847; *The Bandits*), and *Luisa Miller* (1849), Voltaire for *Alzira* (1845), and Zacharias Werner for *Attila* (1846). Only with *Macbeth* (1847), however, was Verdi inspired to fashion an opera that is as gripping as it is original and in many ways independent of tradition. Verdi knew the value of this work and revised it in 1865.

By that time he was receiving lucrative commissions from abroad—from London (*I masnadieri*) and Paris (*Jérusalem*, a thorough revision of *I Lombardi*, 1847). *La battaglia di Legnano* (1849; *The Battle of Legnano*), a tale of love and jealousy set against the Lombard League's victory over Frederick Barbarossa in 1176 CE, was Verdi's response to the Italian unification movement, or *Risorgimento*, which spilled over into open warfare in 1848, the year of revolutions.

## THE MIDDLE YEARS

The prima donna who created Abigaille in *Nabucco*, Giuseppina Strepponi, who also had helped Verdi as early as 1839 with *Oberto*, ultimately became his second wife. The new richness and depth of Verdi's musico-dramatic characterization in these years may have developed out of his relationship with Strepponi. She is often evoked in connection with the portrayal of Violetta in *La traviata* (*The Fallen Woman*). With Strepponi Verdi moved back to Busseto in 1849 and then to Sant'Agata.

In the meantime he had composed three operas that remain his best-known and best-loved: *Rigoletto* (1851), *Il trovatore* (1853; *The Troubadour*), and *La traviata* (1853). *Rigoletto* makes an important technical advance toward a coherent presentation of the drama in music, especially in the famous third act; there is less distinction between the recitatives (the parts of the score that carry the plot forward in imitation of speech), which tend toward *arioso* (melodic, lyric quality), and the arias, which are treated less formally and dovetailed into their surroundings, sometimes almost unobtrusively.

From 1855 to 1870 Verdi, who had become an international celebrity, devoted himself to providing works for the Opéra at Paris and other theatres conforming to the Parisian operatic standard, which demanded spectacular dramas on subjects of high seriousness in five acts with a ballet. His first essay in the new manner, *Les Vêpres siciliennes* (1855; *The Sicilian Vespers*), is a rather cold piece that had only lukewarm success from its premiere on. Two pieces for Italian theatres, *Simon Boccanegra* (1857) and *Un ballo in maschera* (1859; *A Masked Ball*), affected to a lesser extent by the impact of the grand operatic style, show the enrichment of Verdi's power as an interpreter of human character and as a master of orchestral colour. *Boccanegra* includes powerful scenes and creates a special windswept atmosphere appropriate to its Genoese pirate protagonist. Much more successful with the public was *Ballo*, a Romantic version of the assassination of Gustav III of Sweden.

In 1862 Verdi represented Italian musicians at the London Exhibition, for which he composed a cantata to words by the up-and-coming poet and composer Arrigo Boito. In opera the big money came from foreign commissions, and in the same year his next work, *La forza del destino* (*The Force of Destiny*), was produced at St. Petersburg. The epic-style *Forza*, includes the most extended religious scene in a Verdi opera and his first substantial comic role. *Don Carlos* (1867) is a setting of another play by Schiller in which religion is portrayed much more harshly, and much more in accordance with Verdi's lifelong strong anticlerical sentiments, than in *Forza*; it is regarded by some as Verdi's masterpiece.

Verdi felt that both operas with foreign commissions required revision for Italian theatres; this he accomplished for *Forza* in 1869 and *Don Carlo* (as it is now usually called) in 1884 and 1887. He needed none with the piece in which at last he fashioned a libretto exactly to his needs, *Aida*.

Commissioned by the khedive of Egypt to celebrate the opening of Cairo's new Opera House in 1869, *Aida* premiered there in 1871 and went on to receive worldwide acclaim.

## LATE YEARS

In 1873, while waiting in a Naples hotel for a production of *Aida*, Verdi wrote a string quartet, the only instrumental composition of his maturity. In the same year, he was moved by the death of the Italian patriot and poet Alessandro Manzoni to compose a requiem mass in his honour. One of the masterpieces in the oratorio tradition, the *Manzoni Requiem* is an impressive testimony to what Verdi could do outside the field of opera.

After 1873 the maestro considered himself retired, at long last, from that world of opera to which he had been bound for so many years. He settled in at Sant'Agata, where he became a major landholder and a very wealthy man. His unintended and unimagined return to the stage, many years after *Aida*, was entirely due to the initiative of his publisher, Giulio Ricordi, who proposed that Arrigo Boito should write a libretto based on Shakespeare's *Othello*. The Othello project then took shape, very slowly, on and off, until the opera finally opened at La Scala in 1887. In his 74th year, Verdi, stimulated by a libretto far superior to anything he had previously set, had produced his tragic masterpiece.

After a rapturous tour with *Otello* throughout Europe, Verdi once more retreated to Sant'Agata, declaring that he had composed his last opera. Yet Ricordi and Boito managed to intervene one more time. With infinite skill, Boito converted Shakespeare's *The Merry Wives of Windsor*, strengthened with passages adapted from the *Henry IV* plays, into the perfect comic libretto, *Falstaff*, which Verdi set to miraculously fresh and mercurial music. This, his last dramatic work, produced at La Scala in 1893, was a tremendous success.

Even after *Falstaff*, Verdi still interested himself in composition. His list of works ends with sacred music for chorus: a *Stabat Mater* and a *Te Deum* published, along with the somewhat earlier and slighter *Ave Maria* and *Laudi alla Vergine Maria*, under the title *Quattro pezzi sacri* (*Four Sacred Pieces*) in 1898. After a long decline, Verdi's wife Giuseppina died in 1897, and Verdi himself gradually grew weaker and died four years later.

## JOHANNES BRAHMS

(b. May 7, 1833, Hamburg [Germany] — d. April 3, 1897, Vienna, Austria-Hungary [now in Austria])

Johannes Brahms was a German composer and pianist of the Romantic period, who wrote symphonies, concerti, chamber music, piano works, choral compositions, and more than 200 songs. Brahms was the great master of symphonic and sonata style in the second half of the 19th century. He can be viewed as the defender of the Classical tradition of Joseph Haydn, Mozart, and Beethoven in a period when the standards of this tradition were being questioned or overturned by the Romantics.

### THE YOUNG PIANIST AND MUSIC DIRECTOR

The son of Jakob Brahms, an impecunious horn and double bass player, Johannes showed early promise as a pianist. He first studied music with his father. Between ages 14 and 16 Brahms earned money to help his family by playing in rough inns in the dock area of Hamburg and meanwhile composing and sometimes giving recitals. In 1850 he met Eduard Reményi, a Jewish Hungarian violinist, with whom he gave concerts and from whom he learned something of Roma (Gypsy) music—an influence that remained with him always.

The first turning point came in 1853, when he met the composer Robert Schumann, and an immediate friendship between the two composers resulted. Schumann wrote enthusiastically about Brahms in the periodical *Neue Zeitschrift für Musik*, praising his compositions. The article created a sensation. From this moment Brahms was a force in the world of music, though there were always factors that made difficulties for him.

Chief among these factors was the nature of Schumann's panegyric itself. There was already conflict between the "neo-German" school, dominated by Franz Liszt and Richard Wagner, and the more conservative elements, whose main spokesman was Schumann. The latter's praise of Brahms displeased the former, and Brahms himself, though kindly received by Liszt, did not conceal his lack of sympathy with the self-conscious modernists. He was therefore drawn into controversy, and most of the disturbances in his personal life arose from this situation. Gradually Brahms came to be on close terms with the Schumann household, and, when

*Johannes Brahms, 1853.* Encyclopædia Britannica, Inc.

Schumann was first taken mentally ill in 1854, Brahms assisted Clara Schumann in managing her family.

Between 1857 and 1860 Brahms moved between the court of Detmold—where he taught the piano and conducted a choral society—and Göttingen, while in 1859 he was appointed conductor of a women's choir in Hamburg. Such posts provided valuable practical experience and left him enough time for his own work. At this point Brahms's productivity increased, and, apart from the two *Serenades* for orchestra and the first *String Sextet in B-flat Major* (1858–60), he also completed his turbulent *Piano Concerto No. 1 in D Minor* (1854–58).

By 1861 he was back in Hamburg, and in the following year he made his first visit to Vienna, with some success; he settled in Vienna in 1863, assuming direction of the Singakademie, a fine choral society. There, despite a few failures and constant attacks by the Wagnerites, his music was established, and his reputation grew steadily. By 1872 he was principal conductor of the Society of Friends of Music (Gesellschaft der Musikfreunde), and for three seasons he directed the Vienna Philharmonic Orchestra.

In between these two appointments in Vienna, Brahms's work flourished and some of his most significant works were composed. The year 1868 witnessed the completion of his most famous choral work, *Ein deutsches Requiem* (*A German Requiem*), which had occupied him since Schumann's death. This work, based on biblical texts selected by the composer, made a strong impact at its first performance at Bremen on Good Friday, 1868. With the *Requiem*, which is still considered one of the most significant works of 19th-century choral music, Brahms moved into the front rank of German composers.

Brahms was also writing successful works in a lighter vein. In 1869 he offered two volumes of *Hungarian Dances* for piano duet; these were brilliant arrangements of Roma tunes he had collected in the course of the years. Their success was phenomenal, and they were played all over the world. In 1868–69 he composed his *Liebeslieder (Love Songs)* waltzes, which were for vocal quartet and four-hand piano accompaniment and incorporated Viennese dance tunes. Some of his greatest songs were also written at this time.

## MATURITY AND FAME

By the 1870s Brahms was writing significant chamber works and was moving with great deliberation along the path to purely orchestral composition. In 1873 he offered the masterly orchestral version of his *Variations on a Theme by Haydn*. After this successful experiment, he felt ready to embark on the completion of his *Symphony No. 1 in C Minor*. This magnificent work was completed in 1876 and first heard in the same year. Now that the composer had proved to himself his full command of the symphonic idiom, within the next year he produced his *Symphony No. 2 in D Major* (1877). He let six years elapse before his *Symphony No. 3 in F Major* (1883). In its first three movements this work appears to be a comparatively calm and serene composition—until the finale, which presents a gigantic conflict of elemental forces. Again after only one year, Brahms's last symphony, *No. 4 in E Minor* (1884–85), was begun. The symphony's most important movement is once more the finale. Brahms took a simple theme he found in J.S. Bach's *Cantata No. 150* and developed it in a set of 30 highly intricate variations.

Gradually Brahms's renown spread beyond Germany and Austria. Switzerland and The Netherlands showed true appreciation of his art, and Brahms's concert tours to these countries as well as to Hungary and Poland won great acclaim. The University of Breslau (now the University of Wrocław, Poland) conferred an honorary degree on him in

1879. The composer thanked the university by writing the *Academic Festival Overture* (1881) based on various German student songs. Among his other orchestral works at this time were the *Violin Concerto in D Major* (1878) and the *Piano Concerto No. 2 in B-flat Major* (1881).

By now Brahms's contemporaries were keenly aware of the significance of his works, and people spoke of the "three great Bs" (meaning Bach, Beethoven, and Brahms), to whom they accorded the same rank of eminence. Yet there was a sizable circle of musicians who did not admit Brahms's greatness. Fervent admirers of the avant-garde composers of the day, most notably Liszt and Wagner, looked down on Brahms's contributions as too old-fashioned and inexpressive.

Brahms remained in Vienna for the rest of his life. He resigned as director of the Society of Friends of Music in 1875, and from then on devoted his life almost solely to composition. When he went on concert tours, he conducted or performed (on the piano) only his own works. He maintained a few close personal friendships and remained a lifelong bachelor. During these years Brahms composed the *Double Concerto in A Minor* (1887) for violin and cello, the *Piano Trio No. 3 in C Minor* (1886), and the *Violin Sonata in D Minor* (1886–88). He also completed the first *String Quintet in F Major* (1882) and the second *String Quintet in G Major* (1890).

## FINAL YEARS

In 1891 Brahms was inspired to write chamber music for the clarinet. He consequently composed the *Trio for Clarinet, Cello, and Piano* (1891); the great *Quintet for Clarinet and Strings* (1891); and two *Sonatas for Clarinet and Piano* (1894). These works are beautifully adapted to the potentialities of the wind instrument.

In 1896 Brahms completed his *Vier ernste Gesänge* (*Four Serious Songs*), for bass voice and piano, on texts from both the Hebrew Bible and the New Testament, a pessimistic work dealing with the vanity of all earthly things and welcoming death as the healer of pain and weariness. The conception of this work arose from Brahms's thoughts of Clara Schumann, whose physical condition had gravely deteriorated. On May 20, 1896, Clara died, and soon afterward Brahms himself was compelled to seek medical treatment, in the course of which his liver was discovered to be seriously diseased. He appeared for the last time at a concert in March 1897, and in Vienna, in April 1897, he died of cancer.

## AIMS AND ACHIEVEMENTS

Brahms's music ultimately complemented and counteracted the rapid growth of Romantic individualism in the second half of the 19th century. He was a traditionalist in the sense that he greatly revered the subtlety and power of movement displayed by Haydn, Mozart, and Beethoven, with an added influence from Franz Schubert. The Romantic composers' preoccupation with the emotional moment had created new harmonic vistas, but it had two inescapable consequences. First, it had produced a tendency toward rhapsody that often resulted in a lack of structure. Second, it had slowed down the processes of music, so that Wagner had been able to discover a means of writing music that moved as slowly as his often-argumentative stage action. Many composers were thus decreasingly concerned to preserve the skill of taut, brilliant, and dramatic symphonic development that had so eminently distinguished the masters at the turn of the 18th and 19th centuries, culminating in Beethoven's chamber music and symphonies.

Brahms was acutely conscious of this loss, repudiated it, and set himself to compensate for it in order to keep alive a force he felt strongly was far from spent. But Brahms was desirous not of reproducing old styles but of infusing the language of his own time with constructive power. Thus his musical language actually bears little resemblance to Beethoven's or even Schubert's; harmonically it was much influenced by Schumann and even to some extent by Wagner. It is Brahms's supple and masterful control of rhythm and movement that indeed distinguishes him from all his contemporaries. This power of movement stems partly from his reverence for music of the distant past, specifically for the polyphonic school of the 16th century, elements of which he incorporated into his work.

In his orchestral works Brahms displays an unmistakable and highly distinctive deployment of tone colour, especially in his use of woodwind and brass instruments and in his string writing, but the important thing about it is that colour is deployed, rather than laid on for its own sake. A close relationship between orchestration and architecture dominates these works, with the orchestration contributing as much to the tonal colouring as do the harmonies and tonalities and the changing nature of the themes. Brahms was peculiarly adapted to the more subtle aspects of the relation between orchestra and soloist, and he set himself to recover the depth and grandeur of the concerto idea. He realized that the long introductory passage of the orchestra was the means of sharpening and deepening the complex relationship of orchestra to solo, especially when the time came for recapitulation, where an entirely new and often revelatory distribution of themes, keys, instrumentation, and tensions was possible.

Brahms also was a masterly miniaturist, not only in many of his fine and varied songs but also in his cunningly wrought late piano works. As a song composer, he ranged from the complex and highly organized to the extremely simple, strophic type. His late piano music, most of which is of small dimension, has a quiet and intense quality of its own that renders the occasional outburst of angry passion the more potent.

Brahms's musical range is finally attested by his choral music. *A German Requiem*, one of the choral masterpieces of its period, shows all his characteristics in this field together with an ability to integrate solo and tutti with the same kind of subtlety as in the concerti. The spaciousness and grandeur of this work's lines and the power of its construction place Brahms's underlying melancholy within the scope of a large, objective, nonreligious humane vision.

# SIR W. S. GILBERT AND SIR ARTHUR SULLIVAN

Respectively (b. Nov. 18, 1836, London, Eng.—d. May 29, 1911, Harrow Weald, Middlesex); (b. May 13, 1842, London, Eng.—d. Nov. 22, 1900, London)

English playwright and humorist Sir William Schwenk Gilbert and composer Sir Arthur (Seymour) Sullivan (commonly referred to as Gilbert and Sullivan) worked together to establish a distinctive English form of operetta. Gilbert's satire and verbal ingenuity were matched so well by Sullivan's unfailing melodiousness, resourceful musicianship, and sense of parody that the works of this unique partnership won lasting international acclaim.

Gilbert began to write in an age of rhymed couplets, puns, and travesty; his early work exhibits the facetiousness common to writers of extravaganza. But he turned away from this style and developed a genuinely artful style burlesquing contemporary behaviour. Many of his original targets are no longer topical—Pre-Raphaelite aesthetes in *Patience*; women's education (*Princess Ida*); Victorian plays about

Cornish pirates (*The Pirates of Penzance*); the long theatrical vogue of the "jolly jack tar" (*H.M.S. Pinafore*); bombastic melodrama (*Ruddigore*) — but Gilbert's burlesque is so good that it creates its own truth. As a librettist, Gilbert is outstanding not only because of his gift for handling words and casting them in musical shapes but also because through his words he offered the composer opportunities for burlesquing musical conventions.

Gilbert's early ambition was for a legal career, and a legacy in 1861 enabled him to leave the civil service to pursue it. He was called to the bar in November 1863. In 1861, however, he had begun to contribute comic verse to *Fun*, illustrated by himself and signed "Bab." These pieces were later collected as *The Bab Ballads* (1869), followed by *More Bab Ballads* (1873); the two collections, containing the germ of many of the later operas, were united in a volume with *Songs of a Savoyard* (1898).

Sullivan was the son of an Irish musician who became bandmaster at the Royal Military College; his mother was of Italian descent. He joined the choir of the Chapel Royal and later held the Mendelssohn Scholarship at the Royal Academy of Music, London, where he studied under Sir W. Sterndale Bennett and Sir John Goss. He continued his studies at the Leipzig Conservatory.

In 1861 he became organist of St. Michael's, London, and in the following year his music to *The Tempest* achieved great success at the Crystal Palace. Then followed his *Kenilworth* cantata (1864); a ballet, *L'Île enchantée*, produced at Covent Garden (where Sullivan was organist for a time); a symphony and a cello concerto; the *In Memoriam* and the *Overtura di Ballo* overtures; and numerous songs.

Gilbert's dramatic career began when a playwright, Thomas William Robertson, recommended him as someone who could produce a bright Christmas piece in only two weeks. Gilbert promptly wrote *Dulcamara, or the Little*

*Duck and the Great Quack*, a commercial success, and other commissions followed. Meanwhile, Sullivan's first comic opera was his setting of Sir Francis Cowley Burnand's *Cox and Box* (1867). An operetta, the *Contrabandista*, also on a libretto by Burnand, was produced in the same year. In 1870 Gilbert met Sullivan, and they started working together the following year. Together they created *Thespis, or the Gods Grown Old* (first performance 1871) and *Trial by Jury* (1875), a brilliant one-act piece that won instant popularity and ran for more than a year.

These early works were followed by four productions staged by then-manager of the Royalty Theatre, Richard D'Oyly Carte: *The Sorcerer* (1877), *H.M.S. Pinafore* (1878), *The Pirates of Penzance* (1879, New York; 1880, London), and *Patience, or Bunthorne's Bride* (1881). Carte built the Savoy Theatre in 1881 for productions of the partners' work, which collectively became known as the "Savoy Operas"; they included *Iolanthe, or the Peer and the Peri* (1882), *Princess Ida, or Castle Adamant* (1884), *The Mikado, or the Town of Titipu* (1885), *Ruddigore, or the Witch's Curse* (1887), *The Yeomen of the Guard* (1888), and *The Gondoliers* (1889).

By this time, however, relations between the partners had become strained, partly because Sullivan aimed higher than comic opera and because Gilbert was plagued by a jealous and petty nature when it came to financial matters. A rupture occurred, and the two were estranged until 1893, when they again collaborated, producing *Utopia Limited* and later *The Grand Duke* (1896).

Aside from his work with Sullivan, Gilbert wrote several popular burlesques for the dramatic stage: *Sweethearts* (1874), *Engaged* (1877), and *Rosencrantz and Guildenstern* (1891). He also created librettos for other composers; the music for his last opera, *Fallen Fairies, or the Wicked World* (1909), was by Edward German. His last play, *The Hooligan*, was performed in 1911. Gilbert was knighted in 1907.

After his split with Gilbert, Sullivan wrote the opera *Haddon Hall* (1892) to a libretto by Sydney Grundy. Sullivan also completed three other operettas: *The Chieftain* (1895), largely an adaptation of *Contrabandista*; *The Beauty Stone* (1898), with a libretto by Sir Arthur Wing Pinero and J. Comyns Carr; and *The Rose of Persia* (1889), with Basil Hood, who also wrote the libretto for *The Emerald Isle*, which was left unfinished by Sullivan and completed by Edward German.

In the course of his career, Sullivan independently composed a number of works in a more classical vein, including *The Prodigal Son* (1869), *The Light of the World* (1873), *The Martyr of Antioch* (1880), *The Golden Legend* (1886), and the "romantic opera" *Ivanhoe*. In addition, he wrote many hymn tunes, including "Onward! Christian Soldiers," and his song "The Lost Chord" attained great popularity. In 1876 Sullivan accepted the principalship of the National Training School for Music (later the Royal College of Music), which he held for five years; he was active as a conductor, particularly at the Leeds Festivals from 1880 to 1898. He was knighted in 1883.

## PYOTR ILYICH TCHAIKOVSKY

(b. April 25 [May 7, New Style], 1840, Votkinsk, Russia—d. Oct. 25 [Nov. 6], 1893, St. Petersburg)

Pyotr Ilyich Tchaikovsky is largely regarded as the most popular Russian composer of all time. His music has always had great appeal for the general public in virtue of its tuneful, open-hearted melodies, impressive harmonies, and colourful, picturesque orchestration, all of which evoke a profound emotional response. His oeuvre includes 7 symphonies, 11 operas, 3 ballets, 5 suites, 3 piano concertos, a violin concerto, 11 overtures (strictly speaking, 3 overtures and 8 single movement programmatic orchestral works),

4 cantatas, 20 choral works, 3 string quartets, a string sextet, and more than 100 songs and piano pieces.

## EARLY YEARS

Tchaikovsky was the second of six surviving children of Ilya Tchaikovsky, a manager of the Kamsko-Votkinsk metal works, and Alexandra Assier, a descendant of French émigrés. He manifested a clear interest in music from childhood, and his earliest musical impressions came from an orchestrina in the family home. At age four he made his first recorded attempt at composition, a song written with his younger sister Alexandra. In 1845 he began taking piano lessons with a local tutor, through which he became familiar with Frédéric Chopin's mazurkas and the piano pieces of Friedrich Kalkbrenner.

In 1850 Tchaikovsky entered the prestigious Imperial School of Jurisprudence in St. Petersburg, a boarding institution for young boys, where he spent nine years. He proved a diligent and successful student who was popular among his peers. At the same time Tchaikovsky formed in this all-male environment intense emotional ties with several of his schoolmates.

In 1854 his mother fell victim to cholera and died. During the boy's last years at the school, Tchaikovsky's father invited the professional teacher Rudolph Kündinger to give him piano lessons. At age 17 Tchaikovsky came under the influence of the Italian singing instructor Luigi Piccioli, and thereafter Tchaikovsky developed a lifelong passion for Italian music. Wolfgang Amadeus Mozart's *Don Giovanni* proved another revelation that deeply affected his musical taste. In the summer of 1861 he traveled outside Russia for the first time, visiting Germany, France, and England, and in October of that year he began attending music classes offered by the recently founded Russian

Musical Society. When St. Petersburg Conservatory opened the following fall, Tchaikovsky was among its first students.

Tchaikovsky spent nearly three years at St. Petersburg Conservatory, studying harmony and counterpoint with Nikolay Zaremba and composition and instrumentation with Anton Rubinstein. Among his earliest orchestral works was an overture entitled *The Storm* (composed 1864), a mature attempt at dramatic program music. The first public performance of any of his works took place in August 1865, when Johann Strauss the Younger conducted Tchaikovsky's *Characteristic Dances* at a concert in Pavlovsk, near St. Petersburg.

## MIDDLE YEARS

After graduating in December 1865, Tchaikovsky moved to Moscow to teach music theory at the Russian Musical Society, soon thereafter renamed the Moscow Conservatory. He found teaching difficult, but his friendship with the director, Nikolay Rubinstein, helped make it bearable. Within five years Tchaikovsky had produced his first symphony, *Symphony No. 1 in G Minor* (composed 1866; *Winter Daydreams*), and his first opera, *The Voyevoda* (1868).

In 1868 Tchaikovsky met a Belgian mezzo-soprano named Désirée Artôt, with whom he fleetingly contemplated a marriage, but their engagement ended in failure. The opera *The Voyevoda* was well received, even by the The Five, an influential group of nationalistic Russian composers who never appreciated the cosmopolitanism of Tchaikovsky's music. In 1869 Tchaikovsky completed *Romeo and Juliet*, an overture in which he subtly adapted sonata form to mirror the dramatic structure of Shakespeare's play. Nikolay Rubinstein conducted a successful performance of this work the following year, and it became the first of Tchaikovsky's compositions eventually to enter the standard international classical repertoire.

In March 1871 the audience at Moscow's Hall of Nobility witnessed the successful performance of Tchaikovsky's *String Quartet No. 1*, and in April 1872 he finished another opera, *The Oprichnik*. While spending the summer at his sister's estate in Ukraine, he began to work on his *Symphony No. 2 in C Minor*, later dubbed *The Little Russian*, which he completed later that year. *The Oprichnik* was first performed at the Maryinsky Theatre in St. Petersburg in April 1874. His next opera, *Vakula the Smith* (1874), later revised as *Cherevichki* (1885; *The Little Shoes*), was similarly judged. In his early operas the young composer experienced difficulty in striking a balance between creative fervour and his ability to assess critically the work in progress. However, his instrumental works began to earn him his reputation, and, at the end of 1874, Tchaikovsky wrote his *Piano Concerto No. 1 in B-flat Minor*, a work destined for fame despite its initial rejection by Rubinstein. The concerto premiered successfully in Boston in October 1875, with Hans von Bülow as the soloist. During the summer of 1875, Tchaikovsky composed *Symphony No. 3 in D Major*, which gained almost immediate acclaim in Russia.

## YEARS OF FAME

At the very end of 1875, Tchaikovsky left Russia to travel in Europe. He was powerfully impressed by a performance of Georges Bizet's *Carmen* at the Opéra-Comique in Paris; in contrast, the production of Richard Wagner's *Ring* cycle, which he attended in Bayreuth, Germany, during the summer of 1876, left him cold. In November 1876 he put the final touches on his symphonic fantasia *Francesca da Rimini*, a work with which he felt particularly pleased.

Earlier that year, Tchaikovsky had completed the composition of *Swan Lake*, which was the first in his famed trilogy of ballets. The ballet's premiere took place on Feb. 20, 1877, but it was not a success owing to poor staging and choreography.

The growing popularity of Tchaikovsky's music both within and outside of Russia inevitably resulted in public interest in him and his personal life. Although homosexuality was officially illegal in Russia, the authorities tolerated it among the upper classes. But social and familial pressures, as well as his discomfort with the fact that his younger brother Modest was exhibiting the same sexual tendencies, led to Tchaikovsky's hasty decision in the summer of 1877 to marry Antonina Milyukova, a young and naive music student who had declared her love for him. Tchaikovsky's homosexuality, combined with an almost complete lack of compatibility between the couple, resulted in matrimonial disaster—within weeks he fled abroad, never again to live with his wife. This experience forced Tchaikovsky to recognize that he could not find respectability through social conventions and that his sexual orientation could not be changed.

The year 1876 saw the beginning of the extraordinary relationship that developed between Tchaikovsky and Nadezhda von Meck, the widow of a wealthy railroad tycoon; it became an important component of their lives for the next 14 years. A great admirer of his work, she chose to become his patroness and eventually arranged for him a regular monthly allowance; this enabled him in 1878 to resign from the conservatory and devote his efforts to writing music. Thereafter he could afford to spend the winters in Europe and return to Russia each summer.

The period after Tchaikovsky's departure from Moscow proved creatively very productive. Early in 1878 he finished several of his most famous compositions—the opera

*Eugene Onegin*, the *Symphony No. 4 in F Minor*, and the *Violin Concerto in D Major*. From December 1878 to August 1879 he worked on the opera *The Maid of Orleans*, which was not particularly well received. Over the next 10 years Tchaikovsky produced his operas *Mazepa* (1883; based on Aleksandr Pushkin's *Poltava*) and *The Enchantress* (1887), as well as the masterly symphonies *Manfred* (1885) and *Symphony No. 5 in E Minor* (1888). His other major achievements of this period include *Serenade for Strings in C Major*, Opus 48 (1880), *Capriccio italien* (1880), and the *1812 Overture* (1880).

## FINAL YEARS

At the beginning of 1885, tired of his peregrinations, Tchaikovsky settled down in a rented country house near Klin, outside of Moscow. There he adopted a regular daily routine that included reading, walking in the forest, composing in the mornings and the afternoons, and playing piano duets with friends in the evenings. At the January 1887 premiere of his opera *Cherevichki*, he finally overcame his longstanding fear of conducting. Moreover, at the end of December he embarked upon his first European concert tour as a conductor, which included Leipzig, Berlin, Prague, Hamburg, Paris, and London. He met with great success and made a second tour in 1889. Between October 1888 and August 1889 he composed his second ballet, *The Sleeping Beauty*. During the winter of 1890, while staying in Florence, he concentrated on his third Pushkin opera, *The Queen of Spades*, which was written in just 44 days and is considered one of his finest. Later that year Tchaikovsky was informed by Nadezhda von Meck that she was close to ruin and could not continue his allowance. This was followed by the cessation of their correspondence, a circumstance that caused Tchaikovsky considerable anguish.

In the spring of 1891 Tchaikovsky was invited to visit the United States on the occasion of the inauguration of Carnegie Hall in New York City. He conducted before enthusiastic audiences in New York, Baltimore, and Philadelphia. Upon his return to Russia, he completed his last two compositions for the stage—the one-act opera *Iolanta* (1891) and a two-act ballet *Nutcracker* (1892). In February 1893 he began working on his *Symphony No. 6 in B Minor* (*Pathétique*), which was destined to become his most celebrated masterpiece. He dedicated it to his nephew Vladimir (Bob) Davydov, who in Tchaikovsky's late years became increasingly an object of his passionate love. His world stature was confirmed by his triumphant European and American tours and his acceptance in June 1893 of an honorary doctorate from the University of Cambridge.

On October 16 Tchaikovsky conducted his new symphony's premiere in St. Petersburg. The mixed reaction of the audience, however, did not affect the composer's belief that the symphony belonged among his best work. On October 21 he suddenly became ill and was diagnosed with cholera, an epidemic that was sweeping through St. Petersburg. Despite all medical efforts to save him, he died four days later from complications arising from the disease. Wild rumours circulated among his contemporaries concerning his possible suicide, which were revived in the late 20th century by some of his biographers, but these allegations cannot be supported by documentary evidence.

## GIACOMO PUCCINI

(b. Dec. 22, 1858, Lucca, Tuscany [Italy]—d. Nov. 29, 1924, Brussels, Belg.)

Italian composer Giacomo Puccini (in full, Giacomo Antonio Domenico Michele Secondo Maria Puccini) was one of the greatest exponents of operatic realism, who virtually brought the history of Italian opera to an end.

His mature operas include *La Bohème* (1896), *Tosca* (1900), *Madama Butterfly* (1904), and *Turandot*, left incomplete.

## EARLY LIFE AND MARRIAGE

Puccini was the last descendant of a family that for two centuries had provided the musical directors of the Cathedral of San Martino in Lucca. Puccini initially dedicated himself to music, therefore, not as a personal vocation but as a family profession. When Giacomo was five, his father died, and the municipality of Lucca supported the family with a small pension, keeping the position of cathedral organist open for the young Puccini until he came of age. He first studied music with two of his father's former pupils, and he played the organ in small local churches. A performance of Giuseppe Verdi's *Aida*, which he saw in Pisa in 1876, convinced him that his true vocation was opera. In the autumn of 1880 he went to study at the Milan Conservatory, where his principal teachers were Antonio Bazzini, a famous violinist and composer of chamber music, and Amilcare Ponchielli, the composer of the opera *La gioconda*. On July 16, 1883, he received his diploma and presented as his graduation composition *Capriccio sinfonico*, an instrumental work that attracted the attention of influential musical circles in Milan. In the same year, he entered *Le villi* in a competition for one-act operas. The judges did not think *Le villi* worthy of consideration, but a group of friends, led by the composer-librettist Arrigo Boito, subsidized its production, and its premiere took place with immense success at Milan's Verme Theatre on May 31, 1884. *Le villi* was remarkable for its dramatic power, its operatic melody, and, revealing the influence of Richard Wagner's works, the important role played by the orchestra. The music publisher Giulio Ricordi immediately acquired the copyright, with the stipulation that the opera be expanded to two acts. He also commissioned Puccini to write a new opera for La Scala and gave him a monthly stipend: thus began Puccini's lifelong association with Giulio Ricordi, who was to become a staunch friend and counselor.

After the death of his mother, Puccini fled from Lucca with a married woman, Elvira Gemignani. Finding in their passion the courage to defy the truly enormous scandal generated by their illegal union, they lived at first in Monza, near Milan, where a son, Antonio, was born. In 1890 they moved to Milan, and in 1891 to Torre del Lago, a fishing village on Lake Massaciuccoli in Tuscany. This home was to become Puccini's refuge from life, and he remained there until three years before his death, when he moved to Viareggio. The two were finally able to marry in 1904, after the death of Elvira's husband. Puccini's second opera, *Edgar*, based on a verse drama by the French writer Alfred de Musset, had been performed at La Scala in 1889, and it was a failure. Nevertheless, Ricordi continued to have faith in his protégé and sent him to Bayreuth in Germany to hear Wagner's *Die Meistersinger*.

## MATURE WORK AND FAME

Puccini returned from Bayreuth with the plan for *Manon Lescaut*, based, like the *Manon* of the French composer Jules Massenet, on the celebrated 18th-century novel by the Abbé Prévost. Beginning with this opera, Puccini carefully selected the subjects for his operas and spent considerable time on the preparation of the librettos. The psychology of the heroine in *Manon Lescaut*, as in succeeding works, dominates the dramatic nature of Puccini's operas. Meanwhile, the score of *Manon Lescaut*, dramatically alive, prefigures the operatic refinements achieved in his mature operas: *La Bohème*, *Tosca*, *Madama Butterfly*, and *La fanciulla del west* (1910; *The Girl of the Golden West*). These four mature works also tell a moving love story, one that centres entirely on the feminine protagonist and ends in a tragic resolution. All four speak the same refined and limpid musical language of the orchestra that creates the subtle play of thematic reminiscences. The music always emerges from the words, indissolubly bound to their meaning and to the images they evoke. In *Bohème*, *Tosca*, and *Butterfly*, he collaborated enthusiastically with the writers Giuseppe Giacosa and Luigi Illica. The first performance (Feb. 17, 1904) of *Madama Butterfly* was a fiasco, probably because the audience found the work too much like Puccini's preceding operas.

In 1908, having spent the summer in Cairo, the Puccinis returned to Torre del Lago, and Giacomo devoted himself to *Fanciulla*. Elvira unexpectedly became jealous of Doria Manfredi, a young servant from the village who had been employed for several years by the Puccinis. She drove Doria from the house threatening to kill her. Subsequently, the servant girl poisoned herself, and the Manfredis brought charges against Elvira Puccini for persecution and calumny, creating one of the most famous scandals of the time. Elvira was found guilty but was not sentenced, and Puccini paid damages to the Manfredis, who withdrew their accusations.

The premiere of *La fanciulla del west* took place at the Metropolitan in New York City on Dec. 10, 1910, with Arturo Toscanini conducting. It was a great triumph, and with it Puccini reached the end of his mature period. Puccini felt the new century advancing with problems no longer his own. He did not understand contemporary events, such as World War I. In 1917 at Monte-Carlo in Monaco, Puccini's opera *La rondine* was first performed and was quickly forgotten.

Always interested in contemporary operatic compositions, Puccini studied the works of Claude Debussy,

Richard Strauss, Arnold Schoenberg, and Igor Stravinsky. From this study emerged *Il trittico* (*The Triptych*; New York City, 1918), three stylistically individual one-act operas — the melodramatic *Il tabarro* (*The Cloak*), the sentimental *Suor Angelica*, and the comic *Gianni Schicchi*. His last opera, based on the fable of Turandot as told in the play *Turandot* by the 18th-century Italian dramatist Carlo Gozzi, is the only Italian opera in the Impressionistic style. Puccini did not complete *Turandot*, unable to write a final grand duet on the triumphant love between Turandot and Calaf. Suffering from cancer of the throat, he was ordered to Brussels for surgery, and a few days afterward he died with the incomplete score of *Turandot* in his hands.

*Turandot* was performed posthumously at La Scala on April 25, 1926, and Arturo Toscanini, who conducted the performance, concluded the opera at the point Puccini had reached before dying. Two final scenes were completed by Franco Alfano from Puccini's sketches.

Solemn funeral services were held for Puccini at La Scala in Milan, and his body was taken to Torre del Lago, which became the Puccini Pantheon. Shortly afterward, Elvira and Antonio were also buried there. The Puccini house became a museum and an archive.

## GUSTAV MAHLER

(b. July 7, 1860, Kaliště, Bohemia, Austrian Empire [Austria] — d. May 18, 1911, Vienna, Austria)

Austrian-Jewish composer and conductor Gustav Mahler is noted for his 10 symphonies and various songs with orchestra, which drew together many different strands of Romanticism. Although his music was largely ignored for 50 years after his death, Mahler was later regarded as an important forerunner of 20th-century techniques of composition and an acknowledged influence on such composers as Arnold Schoenberg, Dmitry Shostakovich, and Benjamin Britten.

## EARLY LIFE

Mahler was the second of 12 children of an Austrian-Jewish tavern keeper living in the Bohemian village of Kaliště (German: Kalischt), in the southwestern corner of the modern Czech Republic. Shortly after his birth the family moved to the nearby town of Jihlava (German: Iglau), where Mahler spent his childhood and youth. Mahler was afflicted by the tensions of being an "other" from the beginning of his life. As part of a German-speaking Austrian minority, he was an outsider among the indigenous Czech population and, as a Jew, an outsider among that Austrian minority; later, in Germany, he was an outsider as both an Austrian from Bohemia and a Jew.

Mahler's life was also complicated by the tension between his parents. His father had married a delicate woman from a cultured family, and, coming to resent her social superiority, he resorted to physically maltreating her. In consequence Mahler was alienated from his father and had a strong mother fixation. Furthermore, he inherited his mother's weak heart, which was to cause his death at the age of 50. This unsettling early background may explain the nervous tension, the irony and skepticism, the obsession with death, and the unremitting quest to discover some meaning in life that was to pervade Mahler's life and music.

Mahler's musical talent revealed itself early and significantly; around the age of four he began to reproduce military music and Czech folk music on the accordion and on the piano and began composing pieces of his own. The military and popular styles, together with the sounds of nature, became main sources of his mature inspiration. At 10 he made his debut as a pianist in Jihlava and at 15 was so proficient musically that he was accepted as a pupil at the Vienna Conservatory. After winning piano and composition prizes and leaving with a diploma, he supported himself by sporadic teaching while trying to win recognition as a composer. When he failed to win the Conservatory's Beethoven Prize for composition with his first significant work, the cantata *Das klagende Lied* (completed 1880; *The Song of Complaint*), he turned to conducting for a more secure livelihood.

## CAREER AS A CONDUCTOR

The next 17 years saw his ascent to the very top of his chosen profession. From conducting musical farces in Austria, he rose through various provincial opera houses to become artistic director of the Vienna Court Opera in 1897, at the age of 37. As a conductor he had won general acclaim, but as a composer, during this first creative period, he encountered the public's lack of comprehension that was to confront him for most of his career.

Since Mahler's conducting life centred in the traditional manner on the opera house, it is at first surprising that his whole mature output was entirely symphonic (his 40 songs are not true lieder but embryonic symphonic movements, some of which, in fact, provided a partial basis for the symphonies). But Mahler's unique aim, partially influenced by the school of Richard Wagner and Franz Liszt, was essentially autobiographical—the musical expression of a personal view of the world, particularly through song and symphony.

## MUSICAL WORKS: FIRST PERIOD

Each of Mahler's three creative periods produced a symphonic trilogy. The three symphonies of his first period were conceived on a programmatic basis (i.e., founded on a nonmusical story or idea), the actual programs (later discarded) being concerned with establishing some ultimate ground for existence in a world dominated by pain, death, doubt, and despair. To this end, he followed the example of Ludwig van Beethoven's *Symphony No. 6 in F Major* (*Pastoral*) and Hector Berlioz's *Symphonie fantastique* in building symphonies with more than the then-traditional four movements; that of Wagner's music-dramas in expanding the time span, enlarging the orchestral resources, and indulging in uninhibited emotional expression; that of Beethoven's *Symphony No. 9 in D Minor* (*Choral*) in introducing texts sung by soloists and chorus; and that of certain chamber works by Franz Schubert in introducing music from his own songs (settings of poems from the German folk anthology *Des Knaben Wunderhorn* [*The Youth's Magic Horn*] or of poems by himself in a folk style).

These procedures, together with Mahler's own tense and rhetorical style, phenomenally vivid orchestration, and ironic use of popular-style music, resulted in three symphonies of unprecedentedly wide contrasts but unified by his firm command of symphonic structure. The program of the purely orchestral *Symphony No. 1 in D Major* (1888) is autobiographical of his youth: the joy of life becomes clouded over by an obsession with death. The five-movement *Symphony No. 2* (1894; popular title *Resurrection*) begins with the death obsession and culminates in an avowal of the Christian belief in immortality, as projected in a huge finale portraying the Day of Judgment and involving soloists and chorus. The even vaster *Symphony No. 3 in D Major* (1896), also including a soloist and chorus, presents in six movements a Dionysiac vision of a great chain of being, moving from inanimate nature to human consciousness and the redeeming love of God.

The religious element in these works is highly significant. Mahler's disturbing early background, coupled with his lack of an inherited Jewish faith (his father was a freethinker), resulted in a state of metaphysical torment, which he resolved temporarily by identifying himself with Christianity. That this was a genuine impulse there can be no doubt, even if there was an element of expediency in his becoming baptized, early in 1897, because it made it easier for him to be appointed to the Vienna Opera post. The 10 years there represent his more balanced middle period. His newfound faith and his new high office brought a full and confident maturity, which was further stabilized by his marriage in 1902 to Alma Maria Schindler, who bore him two daughters, in 1902 and 1904.

## MUSICAL WORKS: MIDDLE PERIOD

As director of the Vienna Opera, Mahler achieved an unprecedented standard of interpretation and performance, and through a number of concert tours he also became famous over much of Europe as a conductor. He continued his recently acquired habit of devoting his summer vacations, in the Austrian Alps, to composing, and, since, in his case, this involved a ceaseless expenditure of spiritual and nervous energy, he placed an intolerable strain on his frail constitution.

Most of the works of this middle period reflect the fierce dynamism of Mahler's full maturity. An exception is *Symphony No. 4* (1900; popularly called *Ode to Heavenly Joy*), which has a song finale for soprano that evokes a naive peasant conception of the Christian heaven. At the same time, in dispensing with an explicit program and a chorus and coming near to the normal orchestral symphony, it does foreshadow the purely orchestral middle-period trilogy,

*Nos. 5, 6,* and *7. No. 5* (1902; popularly called *Giant*) and *No. 7* (1905; popularly called *Song of the Night*) move from darkness to light, though the light seems not the illumination of any afterlife but the sheer exhilaration of life on Earth. Between them stands the work Mahler regarded as his *Tragic Symphony*—the four-movement *No. 6 in A Minor* (1904), which moves out of darkness only with difficulty, and then back into total night. From these three symphonies onward, he ceased to adapt his songs as whole sections or movements, but in each he introduced subtle allusions, either to his *Wunderhorn* songs or to his settings of poems by Friedrich Rückert, including the cycle *Kindertotenlieder* (1901–04; *Songs on the Deaths of Children*).

At the end of this period he composed his monumental *Symphony No. 8 in E-flat Major* (1907) for eight soloists, double choir, and orchestra—a work known as the *Symphony of a Thousand*, owing to the large forces it requires, though Mahler gave it no such title; it constitutes the first continuously choral and orchestral symphony ever composed. The first of its two parts, equivalent to a symphonic first movement, is a setting of the medieval Catholic Pentecost hymn *Veni Creator Spiritus*; part two, amalgamating the three movement-types of the traditional symphony, has for its text the mystical closing scene of J.W. von Goethe's *Faust* drama (the scene of Faust's redemption). The work marked the climax of Mahler's confident maturity, since what followed was disaster—of which, he believed, he had had a premonition in composing his *Tragic Symphony, No. 6*. The finale originally contained three climactic blows with a large hammer, representing "the three blows of fate which fall on a hero, the last one felling him as a tree is felled" (he subsequently removed the final blow from the score). Afterward he identified these as presaging the three blows that fell on himself in 1907, the last of which portended his own death: his resignation was demanded at the Vienna Opera, his three-year-old daughter, Maria, died, and a doctor diagnosed his fatal heart disease.

## MUSICAL WORKS: LAST PERIOD

Thus began Mahler's last period, in which, at the age of 47, he became a wanderer again. He was obliged to make a new reputation for himself, as a conductor in the United States, directing performances at the Metropolitan Opera and becoming conductor of the Philharmonic Society of New York; yet he went back each summer to the Austrian countryside to compose his last works. He returned finally to Vienna, to die there, in 1911.

The three works constituting his last-period trilogy, none of which he ever heard, are *Das Lied von der Erde* (1908; *The Song of the Earth*), *Symphony No. 9* (1910), and *Symphony No. 10 in F Sharp Major*, left unfinished in the form of a comprehensive full-length sketch (though a full-length performing version has been made posthumously). Beginning as a song cycle, it grew into "A Symphony for Tenor, Baritone (or Contralto) and Orchestra." Yet, he would not call it "Symphony No. 9," believing, on the analogy of Beethoven and Bruckner, that a ninth symphony must be its composer's last. When he afterward began the actual *No. 9*, he said, half jokingly, that the danger was over, since it was "really the tenth"; but in fact, that symphony became his last, and *No. 10* remained in sketch form when he died.

This last-period trilogy marked an even more decisive break with the past than had the middle-period trilogy. It represents a threefold attempt to come to terms with modern man's fundamental problem—the reality of death, which in his case had effectively destroyed the religious faith he had opposed to death as an imagined event. *Das Lied von der Erde*—a six-movement "song-cycle symphony" *No. 8*—views the evanescence of all things human, finding sad consolation in the beauty of the Earth that endures after the individual is no longer alive to see it.

In the four-movement *No. 9*, purely orchestral, the confrontation with death becomes an anguished personal one, evoking horror and bitterness in Mahler's most modern and prophetic movement, the *Rondo-Burleske*, and culminating in a finale of heartbroken resignation. Growing familiarity with the sketch of *No. 10*, however, has suggested that he later broke through to a more positive attitude. The five movements of this symphony deal with the same conflict as the two preceding works, but the resignation attained at the end of the finale is entirely affirmative.

## CLAUDE DEBUSSY

(b. Aug. 22, 1862, Saint-Germain-en-Laye, France—d. March 25, 1918, Paris)

The works of French composer Claude Debussy (Achille-Claude Debussy) have been a seminal force in the music of the 20th century. Debussy developed a highly original system of harmony and musical structure that expressed in many respects the ideals to which the impressionist and symbolist painters and writers of his time aspired.

### EARLY PERIOD

Debussy showed a gift as a pianist by the age of nine. He was encouraged by Madame Mauté de Fleurville, who was associated with the Polish composer Frédéric Chopin, and in 1873 he entered the Paris Conservatory, where he studied the piano and composition, eventually winning in 1884 the Grand Prix de Rome with his cantata *L'Enfant prodigue* (*The Prodigal Child*).

While living with his parents in a poverty-stricken suburb of Paris, he unexpectedly came under the patronage of a Russian millionairess, Nadezhda Filaretovna von Meck, who engaged him to play duets with her and her children. He traveled with her to her palatial residences throughout Europe during the long summer vacations at the Conservatory. In Paris during this time he fell in love with a singer, Blanche Vasnier, the beautiful young wife of an architect; she inspired many of his early works.

This early style is well illustrated in one of Debussy's best-known compositions, *Clair de lune*. The title refers to a folk song that was the conventional accompaniment of scenes of the love-sick Pierrot in the French pantomime; and indeed the many Pierrot-like associations in Debussy's later music, notably in the orchestral work *Images* (1912) and the *Sonata for Cello and Piano* (1915; originally titled *Pierrot fâché avec la lune* ["Pierrot Vexed by the Moon"]), show his connections with the circus spirit that also appeared in works by other composers.

## MIDDLE PERIOD

As a holder of the Grand Prix de Rome, Debussy was given a three-year stay at the Villa Medici, in Rome, where, under what were supposed to be ideal conditions, he was to pursue his creative work. Debussy eventually fled from the Villa Medici after two years and returned to Blanche Vasnier in Paris. At this time Debussy lived a life of extreme indulgence. Once one of his mistresses, Gabrielle ("Gaby") Dupont, threatened suicide. His first wife, Rosalie ("Lily")

Texier, a dressmaker, whom he married in 1899, did in fact shoot herself, though not fatally, and, Debussy himself was haunted by thoughts of suicide.

The main musical influences on Debussy were the works of Richard Wagner and the Russian composers Aleksandr Borodin and Modest Mussorgsky. Wagner fulfilled the sensuous ambitions not only of composers but also of the symbolist poets and the impressionist painters. Wagner's conception of *Gesamtkunstwerk* ("total art work") encouraged artists to refine upon their emotional responses and to exteriorize their hidden dream states, often in a shadowy, incomplete form; hence the more tenuous nature of the work of Wagner's French disciples. It was in this spirit that Debussy wrote the symphonic poem *Prélude à l'après-midi d'un faune* (1894). Other early works by Debussy show his affinity with the English Pre-Raphaelite painters; the most notable of these works is *La Damoiselle élue* (1888), based on *The Blessed Damozel* (1850), a poem by the English poet and painter Dante Gabriel Rossetti. In the course of his career, however, which covered only 25 years, Debussy was constantly breaking new ground. His single completed opera, *Pelléas et Mélisande* (first performed in 1902), demonstrates how the Wagnerian technique could be adapted

*Claude Debussy.* © Photos.com/ Jupiterimages

to portray subjects like the dreamy nightmarish figures of this opera who were doomed to self-destruction. Debussy and his librettist, Maurice Maeterlinck, declared that they were haunted in this work by the terrifying nightmare tale of Edgar Allan Poe, *The Fall of the House of Usher*. The style of *Pelléas* was to be replaced by a bolder, more highly coloured manner. In his seascape *La Mer* (1905) he was inspired by the ideas of the English painter J. M.W. Turner and the French painter Claude Monet. In his work, as in his personal life, he was eager to gather experience from every region that the imaginative mind could explore.

## LATE PERIOD

In 1905 Debussy's illegitimate daughter, Claude-Emma, was born. He had divorced Lily Texier in 1904 and subsequently married his daughter's mother, Emma Bardac. For his daughter he wrote the piano suite *Children's Corner* (1908). Debussy's spontaneity and the sensitive nature of his perception facilitated his acute insight into the child mind, an insight noticeable particularly in *Children's Corner*; in the *Douze Préludes*, two books (1910, 1913; "Twelve Preludes"), for piano; and in the ballet *La Boîte à joujoux* (1st perf. 1919; *The Box of Toys*). In his later years, it is the pursuit of illusion that marks Debussy's instrumental writing, especially the strange, otherworldly *Cello Sonata*. This noble bass instrument takes on, in chameleon fashion, the character of a violin, a flute, and even a mandolin.

## EVOLUTION OF HIS WORK

Debussy's music marks the first of a series of attacks on the traditional language of the 19th century. He did not believe in the stereotyped harmonic procedures of the 19th century, and indeed it becomes clear from a study of mid-20th-century music that the earlier harmonic methods were being followed in an arbitrary, academic manner. Debussy's inquiring mind similarly challenged the traditional orchestral usage of instruments. He rejected the traditional dictum that string instruments should be predominantly lyrical. The pizzicato scherzo from his *String Quartet* (1893) and the symbolic writing for the violins in *La Mer*, conveying the rising storm waves, show a new conception of string colour. Similarly, he saw that woodwinds need not be employed for fireworks displays; they provide, like the human voice, wide varieties of colour. Debussy also used the brass in original colour transformations. In fact, in his music, the conventional orchestral construction, with its rigid woodwind, brass, and string departments, finds itself undermined or split up in the manner of the Impressionist painters. Ultimately, each instrument becomes almost a soloist, as in a vast chamber-music ensemble. Finally, Debussy applied an exploratory approach to the piano, the evocative instrument par excellence.

In his last works, the piano pieces *En blanc et noir* (1915; *In Black and White*) and in the *Douze Études* (1915; "Twelve Études"), Debussy had branched out into modes of composition later to be developed in the styles of Stravinsky and the Hungarian composer Béla Bartók. It is certain that he would have taken part in the leading movements in composition of the years following World War I. His life, however, was tragically cut short by cancer.

## SERGEY RACHMANINOFF

(b. March 20 [April 1, New Style], 1873, Oneg, near Semyonovo, Russia—d. March 28, 1943, Beverly Hills, Calif., U.S.)

Composer Sergey Vasilyevich Rachmaninoff was the last great figure of the tradition of Russian Romanticism and a leading piano virtuoso of his time. He is especially known for his piano concerti and the piece for piano and orchestra entitled *Rhapsody on a Theme of Paganini* (1954).

## EARLY LIFE

Rachmaninoff was born on an estate belonging to his grandparents, situated near Lake Ilmen in the Novgorod district. His father was a retired army officer and his mother the daughter of a general. The boy was destined to become an army officer until his father lost the entire family fortune through risky financial ventures and then deserted the family. Young Sergey's cousin Aleksandr Siloti, a well-known concert pianist and conductor, sensed the boy's abilities and suggested sending him to the noted teacher and pianist Nikolay Zverev in Moscow for his piano studies. It is to Zverev's strict disciplinarian treatment of the boy that musical history owes one of the great piano virtuosos of the 20th century. For his general education and theoretical subjects in music, Sergey became a pupil at the Moscow Conservatory.

At age 19 he graduated from the Conservatory, winning a gold medal for his one-act opera *Aleko* (after Aleksandr Pushkin's poem *Tsygany* ["The Gypsies"]). His fame and popularity, both as composer and concert pianist, were launched by two compositions: the *Prelude in C-sharp Minor*, played for the first time in public on Sept. 26, 1892, and his *Piano Concerto No. 2 in C Minor*, which had its first performance in Moscow on Oct. 27, 1901. The former piece, although it first brought Rachmaninoff to public attention, was to haunt him throughout his life—the prelude was constantly requested by his concert audiences. The concerto, his first major success, revived his hopes after a trying period of inactivity.

In his youth, Rachmaninoff was subject to emotional crises over the success or failure of his works as well as his personal relationships. Self-doubt and uncertainty carried him into deep depressions, one of the most severe of which followed the failure, on its first performance in March 1897, of his *Symphony No. 1 in D Minor*. The symphony was poorly performed, and the critics condemned it. During this period, while brooding over an unhappy love affair, he was taken to a psychiatrist, Nikolay Dahl, who is often credited with having restored the young composer's self-confidence, thus enabling him to write the *Piano Concerto No. 2* (which is dedicated to Dahl).

## MAJOR CREATIVE ACTIVITY

At the time of the Russian Revolution of 1905, Rachmaninoff was a conductor at the Bolshoi Theatre. Although more of an observer than a person politically involved in the revolution, he went with his family, in November 1906, to live in Dresden. There he wrote three of his major scores: the *Symphony No. 2 in E Minor* (1907), the symphonic poem *The Isle of the Dead* (1909), and the *Piano Concerto No. 3 in D Minor* (1909). The last was composed especially for his first concert tour of the United States, highlighting his much-acclaimed pianistic debut on Nov. 28, 1909, with the New York Symphony under Walter Damrosch. *Piano Concerto No. 3* requires great virtuosity from the pianist; its last movement is a bravura section as dazzling as any ever composed. In Philadelphia and Chicago he appeared with equal success in the role of conductor, interpreting his own symphonic compositions. Of these, the *Symphony No. 2* is the most significant: it is a work of deep emotion and haunting thematic material. While touring, he was invited to become permanent conductor of the Boston Symphony, but he declined the offer and returned to Russia in February 1910.

The one notable composition of Rachmaninoff's second period of residence in Moscow was his choral symphony *The Bells* (1913), based on Konstantin Balmont's Russian translation of the poem by Edgar Allan Poe. This work displays considerable ingenuity in the coupling of choral and orchestral resources to produce striking imitative and textural effects.

## LATER YEARS

After the Russian Revolution of 1917, Rachmaninoff went into his second self-imposed exile, dividing his time between residences in Switzerland and the United States. Although for the next 25 years he spent most of his time in an English-speaking country, he never mastered its language or thoroughly acclimatized himself. With his family and a small circle of friends, he lived a rather isolated life. He missed Russia and the Russian people—the sounding board for his music, as he said. And this alienation had a devastating effect on his formerly prolific creative ability. He produced little of real originality but rewrote some of his earlier work. Indeed, he devoted himself almost entirely to concertizing in the United States and Europe, a field in which he had few peers. His only substantial works from this period are the *Symphony No. 3 in A Minor* (1936), another expression of sombre, Slavic melancholy, and the *Rhapsody on a Theme of Paganini* for piano and orchestra, a set of variations on a violin caprice by Niccolò Paganini. Rachmaninoff's last major work, the *Symphonic Dances* for orchestra, was composed in 1940, about two years before his death.

# W. C. HANDY

(b. Nov. 16, 1873, Florence, Ala., U.S.—d. March 28, 1958, New York, N.Y.)

American composer William Christopher Handy, commonly known as W. C. Handy, changed the course of popular music by integrating the blues idiom into then-fashionable ragtime music. Among his best-known works is the classic "St. Louis Blues."

Handy was a son and grandson of African American Methodist ministers, and he was educated at Teachers Agricultural and Mechanical College in Huntsville, Ala. Going against family tradition, he began to cultivate his interest in music at a young age and learned to play several instruments, including the organ, piano, and guitar; he was a particularly skilled cornetist and trumpet player. Longing to experience the world beyond Florence, Handy left his hometown in 1892. He traveled throughout the Midwest, taking a variety of jobs with several musical groups. He also worked as a teacher in 1900–02. He conducted his own orchestra, the Knights of Pythias from Clarksdale, Miss., from 1903 to 1921. During the early years of this period of his life, Handy was steeped in the music of the Mississippi Delta and of Memphis, and he began to arrange some of those tunes for his band's performances. Unable to find a publisher for the songs he was beginning to write, Handy formed a partnership with Harry Pace and founded Pace & Handy Music Company (later Handy Brothers Music Company).

Handy worked during the period of transition from ragtime to jazz. Drawing on the vocal blues melodies of African American folklore, he added harmonizations to his orchestral arrangements. His work helped develop the conception of the blues as a harmonic framework within which to improvise. With his "Memphis Blues" (published 1912) and especially his "St. Louis Blues" (1914), he introduced a melancholic element, achieved chiefly by use of the "blue" or slightly flattened seventh tone of the scale, which was characteristic of African American folk music. Later he wrote other blues pieces ("Beale Street Blues," 1916; "Loveless Love") and several marches and symphonic compositions. He issued anthologies of African American spirituals and blues (*Blues: An Anthology*, 1926; *W.C. Handy's Collection of Negro Spirituals*, 1938; *A Treasury of the Blues*, 1949) and studies of black American musicians (*Negro Authors and Composers of the United States*, 1938; *Unsung Americans Sung*, 1944). His autobiography, *Father of the Blues*, was published in 1941.

## ARNOLD SCHOENBERG

(b. Sept. 13, 1874, Vienna, Austrian Empire [Austria] — d. July 13, 1951, Los Angeles, Calif., U.S.)

Austrian-American composer Arnold Franz Walter Schoenberg (also spelled Schönberg) created a new method of composition based on a row, or series, of 12 tones — a method described as atonality. He was also one of the most influential teachers of the 20th century, among his most significant pupils were Alban Berg and Anton Webern.

### EARLY LIFE

Schoenberg's father, Samuel, owned a small shoe shop in the Second, then predominantly Jewish, district, of Vienna. Neither Samuel nor his wife, Pauline (née Nachod), was particularly musical. There were, however, two professional singers in the family — Heinrich Schoenberg, the composer's brother, and Hans Nachod, his cousin.

Before he was nine years old, Schoenberg began composing little pieces for two violins, which he played with his teacher or with a cousin. A little later, when he acquired a viola-playing classmate, he advanced to the writing of string trios for two violins and viola. When he learned the cello, he promptly began composing quartets.

Schoenberg's father died in 1890. To help the family finances, the young man worked as a bank clerk until 1895. During this time he came to know Alexander von Zemlinsky, a rising young composer and conductor of the amateur orchestra Polyhymnia in which Schoenberg played cello. The two became close friends, and Zemlinsky gave Schoenberg instruction in harmony, counterpoint, and composition. This resulted in Schoenberg's first publicly performed work, the *String Quartet in D Major* (1897). Highly influenced by the style of Brahms, the quartet was well received by Viennese audiences during the 1897–98 and 1898–99 concert seasons.

## First Major Works

A great step forward took place in 1899, when Schoenberg composed the string sextet *Verklärte Nacht* (*Transfigured Night*), a highly romantic piece of program music (unified by a nonmusical story or image). Its programmatic nature and its harmonies outraged conservative program committees. Consequently, it was not performed until 1903, when it was violently rejected by the public.

In 1901 Schoenberg decided to move to Berlin, hoping to better his financial position. He married Mathilde von Zemlinsky, his friend's sister, and began working as musical director at the Überbrettl, an intimate artistic cabaret. He wrote many songs for this group, among them, "Nachtwandler" ("Sleepwalker") for soprano, piccolo, trumpet, snare drum, and piano (published 1969). With the encouragement of German composer Richard Strauss, Schoenberg composed his only symphonic poem for large orchestra, *Pelleas und Melisande* (1902–03), after the drama by the Belgian writer Maurice Maeterlinck. Back in Vienna in 1903, Schoenberg became acquainted with the Austrian composer Gustav Mahler, who became one of his strongest supporters.

Schoenberg's next major work was the *String Quartet No. 1 in D Minor*, Opus 7 (1904). The composition's high density of musical texture and its unusual form (one vast structure played without interruption for nearly 50 minutes) caused difficulties in comprehension at the work's premiere in 1907. A similar form was used in the more concise *Chamber Symphony in E Major* (1906), a work novel in its choice of instrumental ensemble: chamber-like group of 15 instruments.

During these years, Schoenberg's activity as a teacher became increasingly important. The young Austrian composers Alban Berg and Anton Webern began studying with him in 1904; both gained from him the impetus to their notable careers, and Schoenberg, in turn, benefitted greatly from the intellectual stimulation of his loyal disciples. Schoenberg's

*Austrian-American composer Arnold Schoenberg, who pioneered atonal music.* Fred Stein/Time & Life Pictures/Getty Images

textbooks include *Harmonielehre* ("Theory of Harmony"; 1911), *Models for Beginners in Composition* (1942), *Structural Functions of Harmony* (1954), *Preliminary Exercises in Counterpoint* (1963), and *Fundamentals of Musical Composition* (1967).

## EVOLUTION FROM TONALITY

Until this period all of Schoenberg's works had been strictly tonal; that is, each of them had been in a specific key, centred upon a specific tone. However, as his harmonies and melodies became more complex, tonality became of lesser importance. The process of "transcending" tonality can be observed at the beginning of the last movement of his *Second String Quartet* (1907–08).

On Feb. 19, 1909, Schoenberg finished his piano piece Opus 11, No. 1, the first composition ever to dispense completely with "tonal" means of organization. Such pieces, in which no one tonal centre exists and in which any harmonic or melodic combination of tones may be sounded without restrictions of any kind, are usually called atonal, although Schoenberg preferred "pantonal." Schoenberg's most important atonal compositions include *Five Orchestral Pieces*, Opus 16 (1909); the monodrama *Erwartung* (*Expectation*), a stage work for soprano and orchestra, Opus 17 (1924); *Pierrot Lunaire*, 21 recitations ("melodramas") with chamber accompaniment, Opus 21 (1912); *Die glückliche Hand* (*The Hand of Fate*), drama with music, Opus 18 (1924); and the unfinished oratorio *Die Jakobsleiter* (begun 1917).

Schoenberg's earlier music was by this time beginning to find recognition. On Feb. 23, 1913, his *Gurrelieder* (begun in 1900) was first performed in Vienna. This gigantic cantata, which calls for unusually large vocal and orchestral forces, represents a peak of the post-Romantic monumental style. The music was received with wild enthusiasm by the audience, but the embittered Schoenberg could no longer appreciate or acknowledge their response.

In 1911, unable to make a decent living in Vienna, he had moved to Berlin. He remained there until 1915, when, because of wartime emergency, he had to report to Vienna for military service. He spent brief periods in the Austrian Army in 1916 and 1917, until he was finally discharged on medical grounds. During the war years he did little composing, partly because of the demands of army service and partly because he was meditating on how to solve the vast structural problems that had been caused by his move away from tonality. Those meditations yielded a method of composition in which 12 tones related only to one another; Schoenberg's *Piano Suite*, Opus 25, was his first 12-tone piece.

In the 12-tone method, each composition is formed from a special row or series of 12 different tones. This row may be played in its original form, inverted (played upside down), played backward, or played backward *and* inverted. It may also be transposed up or down to any pitch level. All of it, or any part of it, may be sounded successively as a melody or simultaneously as a harmony. In fact, all harmonies and melodies in the piece must be drawn from this row. Although such a method might seem extremely restrictive, this did not prove to be the case. Using this technique, Schoenberg composed what many consider his greatest work, the opera *Moses und Aron* (begun in 1930).

For the rest of his life, Schoenberg continued to use the 12-tone method. Occasionally he returned to traditional tonality, in works such as the *Suite for String Orchestra* (1934); the *Variations on a Recitative for Organ*, Opus 40 (1940); and the *Theme and Variations for Band*, Opus 43A (1943).

After World War I Schoenberg's music won increasing acclaim, although his invention of the 12-tone method aroused considerable opposition. In 1923 his wife, Mathilde, died after a long illness, and a year later he married Gertrud Kolisch, the sister of the violinist Rudolf Kolisch. His success as a teacher continued to grow. In 1925 he was invited to direct the master class in musical composition at the Prussian Academy of Arts in Berlin.

Schoenberg's teaching was well received, and he was writing important works: the *Third String Quartet*, Opus 30 (1927); the opera *Von Heute auf Morgen* (*From Today to Tomorrow*), Opus 32 (1928–29, first performed in 1930); *Begleitmusik zu einer Lichtspielszene* (*Accompaniment to a Film Scene*), Opus 34 (1929–30). But political events proved his undoing. The rise of National Socialism in Germany in 1933 led to the extirpation of Jewish influence in all spheres of German cultural life. Schoenberg was dismissed from his post at the academy. He emigrated to the United States via Paris, and in November 1933 he took a position at the Malkin Conservatory in Boston. In 1934 he moved to California, where he spent the remainder of his life, becoming a citizen of the United States in 1941. He held major teaching positions at the University of Southern California (1935–36) and at the University of California at Los Angeles (1936–44).

Schoenberg's major American works show ever-increasing mastery and freedom in the handling of the 12-tone method. Some of the outstanding compositions of his American period are the *Violin Concerto*, Opus 36 (1934–36); the *Fourth String Quartet*, Opus 37 (1936); the *Piano Concerto*, Opus 42 (1942); and the *Fantasia* for violin with piano accompaniment, Opus 47 (1949). He also wrote a number of works of particular Jewish interest, including *Kol Nidre* for mixed chorus, speaker, and orchestra, Opus 39 (1938), and the *Prelude to the Genesis Suite* for orchestra and mixed chorus, Opus 44 (1945).

On July 2, 1951, Hermann Scherchen, the eminent conductor of 20th-century music, conducted the "Dance

Around the Gold Calf" from *Moses und Aron* at Darmstadt, W. Ger. The telegram telling of the great success of this performance was one of the last things to bring Schoenberg pleasure before his death 11 days later.

## CHARLES IVES

(b. Oct. 20, 1874, Danbury, Conn., U.S.—d. May 19, 1954, New York, N.Y.)

C harles Edward Ives was a significant American composer known for a number of innovations that anticipated most of the later musical developments of the 20th century.

Ives received his earliest musical instruction from his father, who was a bandleader, music teacher, and acoustician who experimented with the sound of quarter tones. At 12 Charles played organ in a local church, and two years later his first composition was played by the town band. In 1893 or 1894 he composed "Song for the Harvest Season," in which the four parts—for voice, trumpet, violin, and organ—were in different keys. That year he began studying at Yale University under Horatio Parker, then the foremost academic composer in the United States. His unconventionality disconcerted Parker, for whom Ives eventually turned out a series of "correct" compositions.

After graduation in 1898, Ives became an insurance clerk and part-time organist in New York City. In 1907 he founded the highly successful insurance partnership of Ives & Myrick, which he headed from 1916 to 1930. Nearly all his works were written before 1915, while operating his business, and many lay unpublished until his death. Indeed, his music became widely known only in the last years of his life. In 1947 he received the Pulitzer Prize for his *Third Symphony* (*The Camp Meeting*; composed 1904–11). His

*Second Symphony* (1897–1902) was first performed in its entirety 50 years after its composition.

Ives's music is intimately related to American culture and experience, especially that of New England. His compositions—with integrated quotations from popular tunes, revival hymns, barn dances, and classical European music—are frequently works of enormous complexity that freely employ sharp dissonance, polytonal harmonies, and polymetric constructions. He drew from European music what techniques he wished while experimenting with tone clusters, microtonal intervals, and elements of chance in music. (In one bassoon part he directs the player to play whatever he wants beyond a specific point.) Believing that all sound is potential music, he was somewhat of an iconoclast.

In *The Unanswered Question* (composed before 1908), a string quartet or string orchestra repeats simple harmonies; placed apart from them, a trumpet reiterates a question-like theme that is dissonantly and confusedly commented upon by flutes (optionally with an oboe or a clarinet). In the second movement of *Three Places in New England* (also titled *First Orchestral Set* and *A New England Symphony*; 1903–14), the music gives the effect of two bands approaching and passing each other, each playing its own melody in its own key, tempo, and rhythm. His monumental *Second Piano Sonata* (subtitled *Concord, Mass., 1840–60*), which was written from 1909 to 1915 and first performed in 1938, echoes the spirit of the New England Transcendentalists in its four sections, "Emerson," "Hawthorne," "The Alcotts," and "Thoreau." It contains tone clusters, quotes Beethoven, and includes a flute obbligato honouring Thoreau's wish to hear a flute over Walden. The mood of the sonata ranges from wild and dissonant to idyllic and mystical. It was published in 1920, together with Ives's pamphlet *Essays Before a Sonata*.

Ives conceived his *Second String Quartet* (1911–13; composition on second movement begun 1907) as a conversation, political argument, and reconciliation among four men; it is full of quotations from hymns, marches, and Beethoven, Brahms, and Tchaikovsky. His *Variations on America* (1891; additions before 1894) is the earliest polytonal piece known. In one of his piano and violin sonatas, he adds a passage for trumpet. His *114 Songs* (1919–24) for voice and piano vary from ballads to satire, hymns, protest songs, and romantic songs. In technique they range from highly complex (e.g., with tone clusters, polytonality, and atonality) to straightforward and simple.

Other compositions include *Central Park in the Dark* (1906), for chamber orchestra; *General William Booth Enters into Heaven* (1914; to Vachel Lindsay's poem), for soloist or choir and band but also performed in arrangements for chamber orchestra and for voice and piano; and the four-part symphony *A Symphony: New England Holidays* ("Washington's Birthday," 1909, rescored 1913; "Decoration Day," 1912; "Fourth of July," 1912–13; and "Thanksgiving and Forefathers' Day," 1904). The Ives manuscripts were given to the Library of the Yale School of Music by his wife, Harmony Ives, in 1955, and a temporary mimeographed catalog was compiled from 1954 to 1960 by pianist John Kirkpatrick.

## BÉLA BARTÓK

(b. March 25, 1881, Nagyszentmiklós, Hung., Austria-Hungary—d. Sept. 26, 1945, New York, N.Y., U.S.)

Hungarian composer, pianist, ethnomusicologist, and teacher Béla Bartók is known for the Hungarian flavour of his major musical compositions, which include orchestral works, string quartets, piano solos, several stage works, a cantata, and a number of settings of folk songs for voice and piano.

## CAREER IN HUNGARY

Bartók spent his childhood and youth in various provincial towns, studying the piano with his mother and later with a succession of teachers. He began to compose small dance pieces at age nine, and two years later he played in public for the first time, including a composition of his own in his program.

Bartók undertook his professional studies in Budapest, at the Royal Hungarian Academy of Music. He developed rapidly as a pianist but less so as a composer. His discovery in 1902 of the music of Richard Strauss stimulated his enthusiasm for composition. At the same time, a spirit of optimistic nationalism was sweeping Hungary, and the 22-year-old composer wrote a symphonic poem, *Kossuth* (1903); in a style reminiscent of Strauss, though with a Hungarian flavour, the work portrays the life of the great patriot Lajos Kossuth, who had led the revolution of 1848–49. Despite a scandal at the first performance, the work was received enthusiastically.

Shortly after Bartók completed his studies in 1903, he and the Hungarian composer Zoltán Kodály, who collaborated with Bartók, discovered that what they had considered Hungarian folk music and drawn upon for their compositions was instead the music of city-dwelling Roma (Gypsies). A vast reservoir of authentic Hungarian peasant music was subsequently made known by the research of the two composers. The initial collection was begun with the intention of revitalizing Hungarian music. Both composers not only transcribed many folk tunes for the piano and other media but also incorporated into their original music elements of rural music.

Bartók was appointed to the faculty of the Academy of Music in 1907 and retained that position until 1934, when he resigned to become a working member of the Academy of Sciences. His holidays were spent collecting folk material, and he soon began the publication of articles and monographs.

At the same time, Bartók was expanding the catalog of his compositions, with many new works for the piano, a substantial number for orchestra, and the beginning of a series of six string quartets that was to constitute one of his most impressive achievements. His first numbered quartet (1908) shows few traces of folk influence, but in the others that influence is omnipresent. The quartets parallel and illuminate Bartók's stylistic development: in the second quartet (1915–17) Berber elements reflect the composer's collecting trip to North Africa; in the third (1927) and fourth (1928) there is a more intensive use of dissonance; and in the fifth (1934) and sixth (1939) there is a reaffirmation of traditional tonality.

In 1911 Bartók wrote his only opera, *Duke Bluebeard's Castle*, an allegorical treatment of the legendary wife murderer with a score permeated by characteristics of traditional Hungarian folk songs, especially in the speech-like rhythms of the text setting. The technique is comparable to that used by the French composer Claude Debussy in his opera *Pelléas et Mélisande* (1902). A ballet, *The Wooden Prince* (1914–16), and a pantomime, *The Miraculous Mandarin* (1918–19), followed; thereafter he wrote no more for the stage.

Unable to travel during World War I, Bartók devoted himself to composition and the study of the collected folk music. During the short-lived proletarian dictatorship of the Hungarian Soviet Republic in 1919, he served as a member of the Music Council with Kodály and Dohnányi. Upon its overthrow Kodály was removed from his position at the Academy of Music; but Bartók, despite his defense of his colleague, was permitted to remain.

His most productive years were the two decades that followed the end of World War I in 1918, when his musical language was completely and expressively formulated. He had assimilated many disparate influences; in addition to those already mentioned—Strauss and Debussy—there were the 19th-century Hungarian composer Franz Liszt and the modernists Igor Stravinsky and Arnold Schoenberg. Bartók arrived at a vital and varied style, rhythmically animated, in which diatonic and chromatic elements are juxtaposed without incompatibility. Within these two creative decades, Bartók composed two concerti for piano and orchestra and one for violin; the *Cantata Profana* (1930), his only large-scale choral work; the *Music for Strings, Percussion, and Celesta* (1936) and other orchestral works; and several important chamber scores, including the *Sonata for Two Pianos and Percussion* (1937). The same period saw Bartók expanding his activities as a concert pianist, playing in most of the countries of western Europe, the United States, and the Soviet Union.

## U.S. Career

As Nazi Germany extended its sphere of influence in the late 1930s and Hungary appeared in imminent danger of capitulation, Bartók found it impossible to remain in his homeland. After a second concert tour of the United States in 1940, he immigrated there the same year. An appointment as research assistant in music at Columbia University, New York City, enabled him to continue working with folk music, transcribing and editing for publication a collection of Serbo-Croatian women's songs, a part of a much larger recorded collection of Yugoslav folk music. With his wife, the pianist Ditta Pásztory, he was able to give a few concerts. His health, however, had begun to deteriorate even before his arrival in the United States.

Bartók's last years were marked by the ravages of leukemia, which often prevented him from teaching, lecturing, or performing. Nonetheless, he was able to compose the *Concerto for Orchestra* (1943), the *Sonata for violin solo* (1944), and all but the last measures of the *Piano Concerto No. 3* (1945). When he died, his last composition, a viola concerto, was left an uncompleted mass of sketches (completed by Tibor Serly, 1945).

## IGOR STRAVINSKY

(b. June 5 [June 17, New Style], 1882, Oranienbaum [now Lomonosov], near St. Petersburg, Russia—d. April 6, 1971, New York, N.Y., U.S.)

Russian-born composer Igor Fyodorovich Stravinsky's works had a revolutionary impact on musical thought and sensibility just before and after World War I, and his compositions remained a touchstone of modernism for much of his long career.

### EARLY YEARS

Stravinsky's father was one of the leading Russian operatic basses of his day, and the mixture of the musical, theatrical, and literary spheres in the Stravinsky family household exerted a lasting influence on the composer. Nevertheless his own musical ability emerged quite slowly. As a boy he was given lessons in piano and music theory. But then he studied law and philosophy at St. Petersburg University (graduating in 1905), and only gradually did he become aware of his aptitude for musical composition. In 1902 he showed some of his early pieces to the composer Nikolay Rimsky-Korsakov, who was sufficiently impressed to take Stravinsky as a private pupil, while at the same time advising him not to enter the conservatory for conventional academic training.

Rimsky-Korsakov tutored Stravinsky mainly in orchestration and acted as the budding composer's mentor. He also used his influence to get his pupil's music performed. Several of Stravinsky's student works were performed in the weekly gatherings of Rimsky-Korsakov's class, and two of his works for orchestra—the *Symphony in E-flat Major* and *The Faun and the Shepherdess*, a song cycle with words by Aleksandr Pushkin—were played by the Court Orchestra in 1908, the year Rimsky-Korsakov died. In February 1909 a short but brilliant orchestral piece, the *Scherzo fantastique*, was performed in St. Petersburg at a concert attended by the impresario Serge Diaghilev, who was so impressed by Stravinsky's promise as a composer that he quickly commissioned some orchestral arrangements for the summer season of his Ballets Russes in Paris. For the 1910 ballet season Diaghilev approached Stravinsky again, this time commissioning the musical score for a new full-length ballet on the subject of the Firebird.

## RUSSIAN PERIOD

The premiere of *The Firebird* at the Paris Opéra on June 25, 1910, was a dazzling success that made Stravinsky known overnight as one of the most gifted of the younger generation of composers. *The Firebird* was the first of a series of spectacular collaborations between Stravinsky and Diaghilev's company. The following year saw the Ballets Russes' premiere on June 13, 1911, of the ballet *Petrushka*, with Vaslav Nijinsky dancing the title role to Stravinsky's musical score. Meanwhile, Stravinsky had conceived the idea of writing a kind of symphonic pagan ritual to be called *Great Sacrifice*. The result was *The Rite of Spring* (*Le Sacre du printemps*), the composition of which was spread over two years (1911–13). The first performance of *The Rite of Spring* at the Théâtre des Champs Élysées on May 29, 1913, provoked one of the more famous first-night riots in the history of musical theatre. Stirred by Nijinsky's unusual and suggestive choreography and Stravinsky's creative and daring music, the audience cheered, protested, and argued among themselves during the performance, creating such a clamour that the dancers could not hear the orchestra. This highly original composition, with its shifting and audacious rhythms and its unresolved dissonances, was an early modernist landmark. From this point on, Stravinsky was known as "the composer of *The Rite of Spring*" and the destructive modernist par excellence.

Stravinsky's successes in Paris with the Ballets Russes effectively uprooted him from St. Petersburg. He had married his cousin Catherine Nossenko in 1906, and, after the premiere of *The Firebird* in 1910, he brought her and their two children to France. The outbreak of World War I in 1914 seriously disrupted the Ballets Russes' activities in western Europe, however, and Stravinsky found he could no longer rely on that company as a regular outlet for his new compositions. The war also effectively marooned him in Switzerland, where he and his family had regularly spent their winters, and it was there that they spent most of the war. The Russian Revolution of October 1917 finally extinguished any hope Stravinsky may have had of returning to his native land.

By 1914 Stravinsky was exploring a more restrained and austere, though no less vibrantly rhythmic kind of musical composition. His musical production in the following years is dominated by sets of short instrumental and vocal pieces that are based variously on Russian folk texts and idioms and on ragtime and other style models from Western popular or dance music. He expanded some of these experiments into large-scale theatre pieces.

*The Wedding*, a ballet cantata begun by Stravinsky in 1914 and completed in 1923, is based on the texts of Russian village wedding songs. The "farmyard burlesque" *Renard* (1916) is similarly based on Russian folk idioms, while *The Soldier's Tale* (1918), a mixed-media piece using speech, mime, and dance accompanied by a seven-piece band, eclectically incorporates ragtime, tango, and other modern musical idioms in a series of highly infectious instrumental movements. After World War I the Russian style in Stravinsky's music began to fade, but not before it had produced another masterpiece in the *Symphonies of Wind Instruments* (1920).

## SHIFT TO NEOCLASSICISM

The compositions of Stravinsky's first maturity—from *The Rite of Spring* in 1913 to the *Symphonies of Wind Instruments* in 1920—make use of a modal idiom based on Russian sources and are characterized by a highly sophisticated feeling for irregular metres and syncopation and by brilliant orchestral mastery. But his voluntary exile from Russia prompted him to reconsider his aesthetic stance, and the result was an important change in his music—he abandoned the Russian features of his early style and instead adopted a Neoclassical idiom. Stravinsky's Neoclassical works of the next 30 years usually take some point of reference in past European music—a particular composer's work or the Baroque or some other historical style—as a starting point for a highly personal and unorthodox treatment that nevertheless seems to depend for its full effect on the listener's experience of the historical model from which Stravinsky borrowed.

The Stravinskys left Switzerland in 1920 and lived in France until 1939, and Stravinsky spent much of this time in Paris. (He took French citizenship in 1934.) Having lost his property in Russia during the revolution, Stravinsky was compelled to earn his living as a performer, and many of the works he composed during the 1920s and '30s were written for his own use as a concert pianist and conductor. His instrumental works of the early 1920s include the *Octet for Wind Instruments* (1923), *Concerto for Piano and Wind Instruments* (1924), *Piano Sonata* (1924), and the *Serenade in A* for piano (1925). These pieces combine a Neoclassical approach to style with what seems a self-conscious severity of line and texture. Though the starkness of this approach is softened in such later instrumental pieces as the *Violin Concerto in D Major* (1931), *Concerto for Two Solo Pianos* (1932–35), and the *Concerto in E-flat* (or *Dumbarton Oaks* concerto) for 16 wind instruments (1938), a certain cool detachment persists.

Though Stravinsky was raised in the Russian Orthodox Church, his parents were not highly observant. Nonetheless, in 1926 Stravinsky experienced a reconnection to the religion of his upbringing, which in turn had a notable effect on his stage and vocal music. A religious strain can be detected in such major works as the operatic oratorio *Oedipus Rex* (1927), which uses a libretto in Latin, and the cantata *Symphony of Psalms* (1930), an overtly sacred work that is based on biblical texts. Religious feeling is also evident in the ballets *Apollon musagète* (1928) and in *Persephone* (1934). The Russian element in Stravinsky's music occasionally reemerged during this period: the ballet *The Fairy's Kiss* (1928) is based on music by Pyotr Ilyich Tchaikovsky, and the *Symphony of Psalms* has some of the antique austerity of Russian Orthodox chant, despite its Latin text.

In the years following World War I, Stravinsky's ties with Diaghilev and the Ballets Russes had been renewed, but on a much looser basis. The only new ballet Diaghilev commissioned from Stravinsky was *Pulcinella* (1920). *Apollon musagète*, Stravinsky's last ballet to be mounted by Diaghilev, premiered in 1928, a year before Diaghilev's own death and the dissolution of his ballet company.

## Later Years in the United States

In 1938 Stravinsky's oldest daughter died of tuberculosis, and the deaths of his wife and mother followed in 1939, just months before World War II broke out. Early in 1940 he married Vera de Bosset, whom he had known for many years. In autumn 1939 Stravinsky had visited the United States to deliver the Charles Eliot Norton Lectures at Harvard University (later published as the *The Poetics of Music*, 1942), and in 1940 he and his new wife settled permanently in Hollywood, California. They became U.S. citizens in 1945.

During the years of World War II, Stravinsky composed two important symphonic works, the *Symphony in C* (1938–40) and the *Symphony in Three Movements* (1942–45). The *Symphony in C* represents a summation of Neo-classical principles in symphonic form, while the *Symphony in Three Movements* successfully combines the essential features of the concerto with the symphony. From 1948 to 1951 Stravinsky worked on his only full-length opera, *The Rake's Progress*, a Neoclassical work (with a libretto by W. H. Auden and the American writer Chester Kallman) based on a series of moralistic engravings by the 18th-century English artist William Hogarth. *The Rake's Progress* is a mock-serious pastiche of late 18th-century grand opera but is nevertheless typically Stravinskyan in its brilliance, wit, and refinement.

The success of these late works masked a creative crisis in Stravinsky's music, and his resolution of this crisis was to produce a remarkable body of late compositions. After World War II a new musical avant-garde had emerged in Europe that rejected neoclassicism and instead claimed allegiance to the serial, or 12-tone, compositional techniques of the Viennese composers Arnold Schoenberg, Alban Berg, and especially Anton von Webern. (Serial music is based on the repetition of a series of tones in an arbitrary but fixed pattern without regard for traditional tonality.) At first this sea change threw Stravinsky into a creative depression, but he eventually emerged from it, producing a series of cautiously experimental serial works (the *Cantata*, the *Septet*, *In Memoriam Dylan Thomas*), followed by a pair of intermittently serial masterpieces, the ballet *Agon* (completed 1957) and the choral work *Canticum Sacrum* (1955). These in turn led to the choral work *Threni* (1958), a setting of the biblical Lamentations of Jeremiah in which a strict 12-tone method of composition is applied to chantlike material whose underlying character recalls that of such earlier choral works as *The Wedding* and the *Symphony of Psalms*. In his *Movements* for piano and orchestra (1959) and his orchestral *Variations* (1964), Stravinsky refined his manner still further, pursuing a variety of arcane serial techniques to support a music of increasing density and economy and possessing a brittle, diamantine brilliance. Stravinsky's serial works are generally much briefer than his tonal works but have a denser musical content.

Though always in mediocre health, Stravinsky continued full-scale creative work until 1966. His last major work, *Requiem Canticles* (1966), is a profoundly moving adaptation of modern serial techniques to a personal imaginative vision that was deeply rooted in his Russian past. This piece is an amazing tribute to the creative vitality of a composer then in his middle 80s.

# LEADBELLY

(b. Jan. 21, 1885?, Jeter Plantation, near Mooringsport, La., U.S.—d. Dec. 6, 1949, New York, N.Y.)

In conjunction with his notoriously violent life, the ability of American folk-blues singer, songwriter, and guitarist Huddie William Ledbetter—better known as Leadbelly—to perform a vast repertoire of songs made him a legend.

Musical from childhood, Leadbelly played accordion, 6- and 12-string guitar, bass, and harmonica. He led a wandering life, learning songs by absorbing oral tradition. For a time he worked as an itinerant musician with Blind Lemon Jefferson. In 1918 he was imprisoned in Texas for murder. According to legend, he won his early release in 1925 by singing a song for the governor of Texas when he visited the prison. "Please Pardon Me," written and performed by a repentant Leadbelly, undoubtedly helped, but good behaviour throughout his sentence was certainly a factor as well.

Resuming a life of drifting, Leadbelly was imprisoned for attempted murder in 1930 in the Angola, La., prison farm. There he was "discovered" by the folklorists John Lomax and Alan Lomax, who were collecting songs for the Library of Congress. A campaign spearheaded by the Lomaxes secured his release in 1934, and he embarked on a concert tour of eastern colleges. Subsequently he published 48 songs and commentary (1936) about Depression-era conditions of blacks and recorded extensively. His first commercial recordings were made for the American Record Corporation, which did not take advantage of his huge folk repertory but rather encouraged him to sing blues. He settled in New York City in 1937, struggled to make enough money, and in 1939–40 he was jailed again, this time for assault. When he was released, he worked with Woody Guthrie, Sonny Terry, Brownie McGhee, and others as the Headline Singers, performed on radio, and, in 1945, appeared in a short film. In 1949, shortly before his death, he gave a concert in Paris.

Leadbelly died penniless, but within six months his song "Goodnight, Irene" had become a million-record hit for the singing group the Weavers; along with other pieces from his repertoire, among them "The Midnight Special" and "Rock Island Line," "Goodnight, Irene" became a standard.

Leadbelly's legacy is extraordinary. His recordings reveal his mastery of a great variety of song styles and his prodigious memory; his repertory included more than 500 songs. His rhythmic guitar playing and unique vocal accentuations make his body of work both instructive and compelling. Leadbelly's influence on later musicians — including Eric Clapton, Bob Dylan, Janis Joplin, and Kurt Cobain — was immense.

## CARTER FAMILY

The group consisted of Alvin Pleasant Carter, known as A.P. Carter (b. April 15, 1891, Maces Spring, Va., U.S. — d. Nov. 7, 1960, Kentucky), his wife, Sara, née Sara Dougherty (b. July 21, 1898, Flatwoods, Va., U.S. — d. Jan. 8, 1979, Lodi, Calif.), and his sister-in-law Maybelle Carter, née Maybelle Addington (b. May 10, 1909, Nickelsville, Va., U.S. — d. Oct. 23, 1978, Nashville, Tenn.).

The Carter Family was a singing group that was a leading force in the spread and popularization of the songs of the Appalachian Mountain region of the eastern United States.

The family's recording career began in 1927 in response to an advertisement placed in a local newspaper by a talent scout for Victor Records. Over the next 16 years, with two of Sara's children and three of Maybelle's (Helen, June, and Anita) also appearing, they recorded more than 300 songs for various labels, covering a significant cross section of the mountain music repertory, including old ballads and humorous songs, sentimental pieces from the 19th and early 20th centuries, and many religious pieces. They later performed extensively on radio, popularizing many songs that became standards of folk and country music, including "Jimmy Brown, the Newsboy," "Wabash Cannonball," "It Takes a Worried Man to Sing a Worried Song," and "Wildwood Flower."

The Carter Family was remarkable not only for its prolific recording but also for the musical accomplishment—and balance—of its members. A.P. was the group's songsmith. He was an avid collector of oral tradition, as well as an adept arranger of rural regional repertoire for consumption by a broader audience. A.P. also composed many new songs for the group, replicating the style of the traditional material. Sara, with her strong soprano voice, was typically the lead singer, supported by Maybelle's alto harmonies and A.P.'s bass and baritone interjections. The instrumental anchor of the Carter Family was Maybelle, a skilled performer on guitar, banjo, and autoharp. She also developed a unique finger-picking technique on guitar that continues to be emulated by many guitarists today.

In 1943 the Carter Family disbanded, its members subsequently forming various other groups. Maybelle ("Mother") Carter performed both with her daughters and as a soloist. In the 1950s the Carter Family re-formed and appeared intermittently, with a changing lineup. The original Carter Family was the first group admitted to the Country Music Hall of Fame.

Maybelle also sang periodically with her son-in-law Johnny Cash, whose gritty songs of social commentary had already propelled him to the top of the country-and-western music industry. Known for his black clothes and

Here the singing group, the Carter Family, poses with their instruments in Nashville, Tennessee, in the mid-1950s. Pictured from left to right are June, Maybelle, Anita, and Helen (sitting). Michael Ochs Archives/Getty Images

rebellious persona, Cash married June Carter in 1968 during a period of waning popularity, after she helped him combat his drug addiction. The signal event in Cash's turnaround was the album *Johnny Cash at Folsom Prison* (1968), recorded live at California's Folsom Prison. He won a new generation of fans in 1994 after the release of his acoustic album *American Recordings*. The recipient of numerous awards, Cash won 13 Grammy Awards, including a lifetime achievement award in 1999, and 9 Country Music Association Awards. Cash was elected to the Country Music Hall of Fame in 1980 and to the Rock and Roll Hall of Fame in 1992. In 1996 he received a Kennedy Center Honor.

## SERGEY PROKOFIEV

(b. April 23 [April 11, Old Style], 1891, Sontsovka, Ukraine, Russian Empire—d. March 5, 1953, Moscow, Russia, U.S.S.R.)

Twentieth-century Russian (and Soviet) composer Sergey Sergeyevich Prokofiev wrote in a wide range of musical genres, including symphonies, concerti, film music, operas, ballets, and program pieces.

### PREREVOLUTIONARY PERIOD

Prokofiev was born into a family of agriculturalists. Village life, with its peasant songs, left a permanent imprint on him. His mother, a good pianist, became the child's first mentor in music and arranged trips to the opera in Moscow. Meanwhile, the Russian composer Reinhold Glière twice went to Sontsovka in the summer months to train and prepare young Sergey for entrance into the conservatory at St. Petersburg. Prokofiev's years at the conservatory— 1904 to 1914—were a period of swift creative growth, and when he graduated he was awarded the Anton Rubinstein

Prize in piano for a brilliant performance of his own first large-scale work— the *Piano Concerto No. 1 in D-flat Major*.

Contacts with the then new currents in theatre, poetry, and painting played an important role in Prokofiev's development. He was attracted by the work of modernist Russian poets; by the paintings of the Russian followers of Paul Cézanne and Pablo Picasso; and by the theatrical ideas of Vsevolod Meyerhold. In 1914 Prokofiev became acquainted with the ballet impresario Serge Diaghilev, who became one of his most influential advisers for the next decade and a half.

The prerevolutionary period of Prokofiev's work was marked by intense exploration. The harmonic thought and design of his work grew more and more complicated. Prokofiev wrote the ballet *Ala and Lolli* (1914), on themes of ancient Slav mythology, for Diaghilev, who rejected it. Thereupon, Prokofiev reworked the music into the *Scythian Suite* for orchestra. Its premiere, in 1916, caused a scandal but was the culmination of his career in Petrograd (St. Petersburg). The ballet *The Tale of the Buffoon Who Outjested Seven Buffoons* (1915; reworked as *The Buffoon*, 1915–20), also commissioned by Diaghilev, was based on a folktale; it served as a stimulus for Prokofiev's searching experiments in the renewal of Russian music. Prokofiev also was active in the field of opera. In 1915–16 he composed *The Gambler*, a brilliant adaptation of the novella by Fyodor Dostoyevsky. Continuing the operatic tradition of Modest Mussorgsky, Prokofiev skillfully combined subtle lyricism, satiric malice, narrative precision, and dramatic impact. During this period, Prokofiev achieved great recognition for his first two piano concerti— the first the one-movement *Concerto in D-flat Major* (1911) and the second the dramatic four-movement *Concerto in G Minor* (1913).

The year 1917—during which there were two Russian revolutions—was astonishingly productive for Prokofiev.

As if inspired by feelings of social and national renewal, he wrote within one year an immense quantity of new music: he composed two sonatas, the *Violin Concerto No. 1 in D Major*, the *Classical Symphony*, and the choral work *Seven, They Are Seven*; he began the magnificent *Piano Concerto No. 3 in C Major*; and he planned a new opera, *The Love for Three Oranges*, after a comedy tale by the 18th-century Italian dramatist Carlo Gozzi, as translated and adapted by Meyerhold. In the summer of 1917 Prokofiev was included in the Council of Workers in the Arts, which led Russia's left wing of artistic activity. He later concluded that music had no place in the council's activities and decided to leave Russia temporarily to undertake a concert tour abroad.

## FOREIGN PERIOD

The next decade and a half are commonly called the foreign period of Prokofiev's work. For a number of reasons, chiefly the continued blockade of the Soviet Union, he could not return at once to his homeland. The first five years of Prokofiev's life abroad are usually characterized as the "years of wandering." In the summer of 1918, he gave several concerts in Japan, and in the United States his piano recitals in New York City evoked both delight and denunciation. In Chicago he was given a commission for a comic opera; *The Love for Three Oranges* was completed in 1919, though it was not produced until 1921.

In America, Prokofiev met a young singer of Spanish descent. Born Carlina Codina in Madrid and raised in New York, Lina Llubera eventually became his wife and the mother of two of his sons, Svyatoslav and Oleg. Not finding continuing support in the United States, the composer set out in the spring of 1920 for Paris for meetings with Diaghilev and the conductor Serge Koussevitzky. They

soon secured for him wide recognition in the most important western European musical centres. The production
of *The Buffoon* by Diaghilev's ballet troupe in Paris and
London in 1921 and the Paris premiere of the *Scythian Suite*
in 1921 and that of *Seven, They Are Seven* in 1924 consolidated
his reputation as a brilliant innovator. The successful performance of his *Piano Concerto No. 3* (1921) also marked one
of the peaks of Prokofiev's dynamic national style.

During 1922–23 Prokofiev spent more than a year and a
half in southern Germany, in the Bavarian town of Ettal.
There he prepared many of his compositions for the
printer and also continued work on the opera *The Flaming
Angel*, after a story by the contemporary Russian author
Valery Bryusov. The opera, which required many years of
work (1919–27), did not find a producer within Prokofiev's
lifetime.

In the autumn of 1923, Prokofiev settled in Paris, where
he was in close touch with progressive French musical
figures, such as the composers Francis Poulenc and Arthur
Honegger. Vexed by criticisms of his melodically lucid
*Violin Concerto No. 1*, which had its premiere in Paris in
1923, he addressed himself to a search for a more avant-garde
style. These tendencies appeared in several compositions
of the early 1920s, including the epic *Symphony No. 2 in D
Minor* and the *Symphony No. 3 in C Minor* (1928). In close
collaboration with Diaghilev, Prokofiev created new one-act
ballets, *Le Pas d'acier* (performed in 1927) and *The Prodigal
Son* (performed in 1929). *Le Pas d'acier* had a sensational
success in Paris and London, with its bold evocation of
images of Soviet Russia at the beginning of the 1920s. *The
Prodigal Son* had a lofty biblical theme and music that was
exquisitely lyrical. It reflects an emotional relaxation and
a clarification of style that are also seen in the *String Quartet
No. 1 in B Minor* (1930), in the *Sonata for Two Violins in C
Major* (1932), and in the ballet *On the Dnieper* (1932).

In 1927 Prokofiev toured the Soviet Union and was rapturously received by the Soviet public as a world-renowned Russian musician-revolutionary. During the 1920s and the early '30s, Prokofiev also toured with immense success as a pianist in the great musical centres of western Europe and the United States. His U.S. tours were attended with tumultuous success and brought him new commissions, such as the *Symphony No. 4 in C Major* (1930), for the 50th anniversary of the Boston Symphony, and the *String Quartet No. 1*, commissioned by the Library of Congress. His new piano concerti—*No. 4* (1931), for the left hand, and *No. 5 in G Major* (1932)—demonstrated anew his bent for virtuoso brilliance.

## SOVIET PERIOD

Although he enjoyed many aspects of life in the West, Prokofiev increasingly missed his homeland. Visits to the Soviet Union in 1927, 1929, and 1932 led him to return to Moscow permanently. From 1933 to 1935 the composer became a leading figure of Soviet culture. In the two decades constituting the Soviet period of Prokofiev's work—1933 to 1953—the realistic and epic traits of his art became more clearly defined. The synthesis of traditional tonal and melodic means with the stylistic innovations of 20th-century music was more fully realized.

In the years preceding World War II, Prokofiev created a number of classical masterpieces, including his *Violin Concerto No. 2 in G Minor* (1935) and the ballet *Romeo and Juliet* (1935–36). His work in theatre and the cinema gave rise to a number of programmatic suites, such as the *Lieutenant Kije* suite (1934), the *Egyptian Nights* suite (1934), and the symphonic children's tale *Peter and the Wolf* (1936). Turning to opera, he cast in the form of a contemporary drama of folk life his *Semyon Kotko*, depicting events of the civil war in the Ukraine (1939). The basis of the opéra bouffe *Betrothal in a Monastery* (composed in 1940, produced in 1946) was the play *The Duenna*, by the 18th-century British dramatist Richard Brinsley Sheridan. Testing his powers in other genres, he composed the monumental *Cantata for the 20th Anniversary of the October Revolution* (1937), on texts by Karl Marx, V.I. Lenin, and Joseph Stalin, and the cantata *The Toast* (1939), composed for Stalin's 60th birthday.

On his last trip abroad, in 1938, Prokofiev visited Hollywood, where he studied the technical problems of the sound film; he applied what he learned to the music for Sergey Eisenstein's film *Alexander Nevsky*, depicting the 13th-century heroic Russian struggle against the Teutonic Knights. The cantata *Alexander Nevsky* was based on the music of the film.

On the eve of World War II, he left his wife and sons for poet Mira Mendelssohn, who became his second (common-law) wife. Regardless of the difficulties of the war years, he composed with remarkable assiduity, even when the evacuation of Moscow in 1941 prevented him from returning to the city until 1944. From the first days of the war, his attention was centred on a very large-scale operatic project: an opera based on Leo Tolstoy's novel *War and Peace*. He was fascinated by the parallels between 1812, when Russia crushed Napoleon's invasion, and the then-current situation. Those who heard the work were struck both by its immensity of scale (13 scenes, more than 60 characters) and by its unique blend of epic narrative with lyrical scenes depicting the personal destinies of the major characters. His increasing predilection for national-epical imagery is manifested in the heroic majesty of the *Symphony No. 5 in B-flat Major* (1944) and in the music (composed 1942–45) for Eisenstein's two-part film *Ivan the Terrible* (Part I, 1944; Part II, 1948). Living in the Caucasus, in Central Asia, and in the Urals, the composer was everywhere interested in folklore, an interest that was reflected in the *String Quartet No. 2 in F Major* (1941), and in the projected comic opera *Khan Buzai* (never completed), on themes of Kazakh folktales.

Overwork was fatal to the composer's health, as was the stress he suffered in 1948, when he was censured by the Central Committee of the Soviet Communist Party for "formalism." During the last years of his life, Prokofiev seldom left his villa in a suburb of Moscow. His propensity for innovation, however, is still evident in such works as the *Symphony No. 6 in E-flat Minor* (1945–47), which is laden with reminiscence of the tragedies of the war just past; the *Sinfonia Concerto for Cello and Orchestra in E Minor* (1950–52), composed with consultation from the conductor and cellist Mstislav Rostropovich; and the *Violin Sonata in F Minor* (1938–46), dedicated to the violinist David Oistrakh, which is laden with Russian folk imagery. Just as in earlier years, the composer devoted the greatest part of his energy to musical theatre, as in the opera *The Story of a Real Man* (1947–48), the ballet *The Stone Flower* (1948–50), and the oratorio *On Guard for Peace* (1950). The lyrical *Symphony No. 7 in C-sharp Minor* (1951–52) was the composer's swan song.

In 1953 Prokofiev died suddenly of cerebral hemorrhage. On his worktable there remained a pile of unfinished compositions. The subsequent years saw a rapid growth of his popularity in the Soviet Union and abroad. In 1957 he was posthumously awarded the Soviet Union's highest honour, the Lenin Prize, for his *Symphony No. 7*.

## COLE PORTER

(b. June 9, 1891, Peru, Ind., U.S. — d. Oct. 15, 1964, Santa Monica, Calif.)

American composer and lyricist Cole Albert Porter brought a worldly élan to the American musical, embodying in his life the sophistication of his songs.

Porter was the grandson of a millionaire speculator, and the moderately affluent circumstances of his life probably contributed to the poise and urbanity of his musical style. He began violin study at the age of six and piano at eight; he composed an operetta in the style of Gilbert and Sullivan at 10 and saw his first composition, a waltz, published a year later. As a student at Yale University (B.A., 1913), he composed about 300 songs, including "Eli," "Bulldog," and "Bingo Eli Yale," and wrote college shows; later he studied at Harvard Law School (1914) and Harvard Graduate School of Arts and Sciences in music (1915–16). He made his Broadway debut with the musical comedy *See America First* (1916), which, however, closed after 15 performances.

In 1917, after the United States had entered World War I, Porter went to France. (He was not, as later reported, in French military service.) He became an itinerant playboy in Europe and, though rather openly homosexual, married a wealthy, older American divorcée, Linda Lee Thomas, on Dec. 18, 1919; they spent the next two decades in lively partying and social traveling, sometimes together, sometimes apart.

In 1928 Porter composed several songs for the Broadway success *Paris*, which led to a string of hit musical comedies, including *Fifty Million Frenchmen* (1929), *Gay Divorcée* (1932), *Anything Goes* (1934), *Red, Hot and Blue* (1934), *Jubilee* (1935), *Dubarry Was a Lady* (1939), *Panama Hattie* (1940), *Kiss Me, Kate* (1948, based on William Shakespeare's *The Taming of the Shrew*), *Can-Can* (1953), and *Silk Stockings* (1955). He concurrently worked on a number of motion pictures. Over the years he wrote such glittering songs and lyrics as "Night and Day," "I Get a Kick Out of You," "Begin the Beguine," "I've Got You Under My Skin," "In the Still of the Night," "Just One of Those Things," "Love for Sale," "My Heart Belongs to Daddy," "Too Darn Hot,"

*This photo of the great American songwriter and composer Cole Porter was taken in October of 1933, around the time he was working on his classic musical* Anything Goes. *Getty Images/Sasha*

"It's Delovely," "I Concentrate on You," "Always True to You in My Fashion," and "I Love Paris." He was especially adept at the catalog song, his best-known efforts being "Let's Do It" and "You're the Top."

Porter was one of the wittiest of all lyricists, with a subtlety of expression and a mastery of the interior rhyme. His work continues to stand as the epitome of sophisticated, civilized detachment in the popular song form. His large output might have been even more vast had not a horse-riding accident in 1937 left him a semi-invalid, necessitating 30 operations and the eventual amputation of a leg.

## JIMMIE RODGERS

(b. Sept. 8, 1897, Pine Springs Community, near Meridian, Miss., U.S.—d. May 26, 1933, New York City, N.Y.)

American singer, songwriter, and guitarist Jimmie Rodgers (byname of James Charles Rodgers) was one of the principal figures in the emergence of the country and western style of popular music.

Rodgers, whose mother died when he was a young boy, was the son of an itinerant railroad gang foreman, and his youth was spent in a variety of southern towns and cities. Having already run away with a medicine show by age 13, he left school for good at age 14. Rodgers began working on his father's railroad crews, initially as a water carrier, and during this time was likely exposed to the work songs and early blues of African American labourers. As a young man he held a number of jobs with the railroad, including those of baggage master, flagman, and brakeman, criss-crossing the Southwest but especially working the line between New Orleans and Meridian, Miss. Early on, Rodgers aspired to be an entertainer. He learned to play the guitar and banjo, honing what became his characteristic sound—a blend of traditional country, work, blues, hobo, and cowboy songs—that ultimately earned him the nick-name the "Singing Brakeman."

After contracting tuberculosis, Rodgers was forced to give up railroad work in 1924 or 1925 and began pursuing a performing career, playing everything from tent shows to street corners but with little success. He relocated to Asheville, N.C., and began appearing on local radio in 1927, backed by a string band. Following a disagreement with the band, Rodgers recorded as a guitar-playing solo artist. The popularity of his first recording, "Sleep, Baby, Sleep," sparked a long series of hits from among more than 110 recordings he would make in what proved to be a relatively short career (1928–33) that coincided with the beginning of the Great Depression. Rodgers toured widely in the South (also playing the vaudeville circuit) and, seeking a dry climate for his health, eventually settled in Texas.

Rodgers helped establish the template for country music and the model for country singers, infusing his per-formances and compositions with personality, humour, and heightened emotion, delivered in a unique vocal style at a time when "hillbilly music" consisted largely of old-time instrumentalists and singers who sounded much the same. Rodgers is perhaps best remembered for his distinctive blue yodel; it was popularized in "Blue Yodel No. 1" and was at the heart of some dozen other recorded versions. He was affectionately called "America's Blue Yodeler" by many of his fans. Most of Rodgers's original compositions were written with a variety of collaborators, the most prominent of whom was his sister-in-law, Elsie McWilliams. His hits, which span the emotional gauntlet and incorpo-rate elements of a wide variety of genres, include "Miss the Mississippi and You," "Daddy and Home," "Waiting for a Train," "Brakeman's Blues," and "Mississippi River Blues," among others. Rodgers recorded right up to his premature death, resting on a cot in the studio between takes during recording sessions. He was the first person inducted into the Country Music Hall of Fame.

## FLETCHER HENDERSON
(b. Dec. 18, 1897, Cuthbert, Ga., U.S.—d. Dec. 29, 1952, New York, N.Y.)

Fletcher Hamilton Henderson, Jr., (born James Fletcher Henderson) was an American musical arranger, bandleader, and pianist who was a leading pioneer in the sound, style, and instrumentation of big band jazz.

Henderson was born into a middle-class family; his father was a school principal and his mother a teacher. He changed his name (James was his grandfather's name, Fletcher Hamilton his father's) in 1916 when he entered Atlanta University, from which he graduated as a chemistry and math major. In 1920 he moved to New York, intending to work as a chemist while pursuing a graduate degree. Although he found a part-time laboratory job, he immediately began getting work as a pianist. Within months he was a full-time musician, and he began working for W.C. Handy's music publishing company as a song plugger (i.e., promoting songs to performers). In 1921 he took a position as musical factotum for Black Swan records, the first black-owned recording company, for which he organized small bands to provide backing for such singers as Ethel Waters. He played piano for leading black singers on more than 150 records between 1921 and 1923 and then began a full-time career as a bandleader.

Although Henderson had shown an interest in music from childhood, when his mother taught him piano, he knew little about jazz until he was in his 20s. His orchestra, made up of well-established New York musicians, at first played standard dance-band fare, with occasional ragtime and jazz inflections. The band became more jazz-oriented in 1924 when Henderson hired the young trumpeter Louis Armstrong. At about the same time, the band's musical director and alto saxophonist, Don Redman, conceived the arrangements and instrumentation that would become the standard for big bands. The rhythm section was established as piano, bass, guitar, and drums; and the trumpet, trombone, and reed sections composed the front line. Arrangements were constructed in the call-and-response manner (e.g., the brass section "calls," the reed section "responds"), and many tunes were based upon "riffs," identifiable musical passages repeated throughout the song.

Henderson was a superb arranger but a poor businessman. Although the band had played major venues and been heard on the radio and in recordings, the band's finances were frequently in disarray, and musicians often left without notice to join other bands. He nevertheless managed to keep his band going until the mid-1930s, at which time he sold many of his arrangements to Benny Goodman, who used them to define the sound of his new band. "King Porter Stomp," "Down South Camp Meetin'," "Bugle Call Rag," "Sometimes I'm Happy," and "Wrappin' It Up" are among the Henderson arrangements that became Goodman hits.

Through the Goodman band, Henderson's arrangements became a blueprint for the sound of the swing era. Henderson arranged for Goodman for several years and formed a short-lived band of his own in 1936. That year, Henderson issued "Christopher Columbus," which became the biggest hit released under his own name. Henderson had little success in his subsequent attempts to organize bands and spent most of the 1940s arranging for Goodman, Count Basie, and others. He formed a sextet in 1950 that became the house band at New York's Cafe Society, but he suffered a stroke soon thereafter and was forced to retire.

## BESSIE SMITH

(b. April 15, 1898?, Chattanooga, Tenn., U.S.—d. Sept. 26, 1937, Clarksdale, Miss.)

American singer Bessie Smith was one of the greatest of blues vocalists.

Smith grew up in poverty and obscurity. She may have made a first public appearance at the age of eight or nine at the Ivory Theatre in her hometown. About 1919 she was discovered by Gertrude "Ma" Rainey, one of the first of the great blues singers, from whom she received some training. For several years Smith traveled through the South singing in tent shows and bars and theatres in small towns. After 1920 she made her home in Philadelphia, and it was there that she was first heard by a representative of Columbia Records. In February 1923 she made her first recordings, including the classic "Down Hearted Blues," which became an enormous success, selling more than two million copies. She made 160 recordings in all, in many of which she was accompanied by some of the great jazz musicians of the time, including Fletcher Henderson, Benny Goodman, and Louis Armstrong.

Bessie Smith's subject matter was the classic material of the blues: poverty and oppression, love—betrayed or unrequited—and stoic acceptance of defeat at the hands of a cruel and indifferent world. The great tragedy of her career was that she outlived the topicality of her idiom. In the late 1920s her record sales and her fame diminished as social forces changed the face of popular music and bowdlerized the earthy realism of the sentiments she expressed in her music. Her gradually increasing alcoholism caused managements to become wary of engaging her.

Known in her lifetime as the "Empress of the Blues," Smith was a bold, supremely confident artist who often disdained the use of a microphone. Her art expressed the frustrations and hopes of a whole generation of black Americans. She died from injuries sustained in a road accident.

## GEORGE GERSHWIN

(b. Sept. 26, 1898, Brooklyn, N.Y., U.S.—d. July 11, 1937, Hollywood, Calif.)

George Gershwin, born Jacob Gershvin, was one of the most significant and popular American composers of all time. He wrote primarily for the Broadway musical theatre, but important as well are his orchestral and piano compositions in which he blended, in varying degrees, the techniques and forms of classical music with the stylistic nuances and techniques of popular music and jazz.

### EARLY CAREER AND INFLUENCES

Gershwin was the son of Russian-Jewish immigrants. Although his family and friends were not musically inclined, Gershwin developed an early interest in music through his exposure to the popular and classical compositions he heard at school and in penny arcades. He began his musical education at age 11, when his family bought a second-hand upright piano, ostensibly so that George's older sibling, Ira, could learn the instrument. When George surprised everyone with his fluid playing of a popular song, which he had taught himself by following the keys on a neighbour's player piano, his parents decided that George would be the family member to receive lessons.

Gershwin continued to broaden his musical knowledge and compositional technique throughout his career with various mentors. After dropping out of school at age 15, he earned an income by making piano rolls for player pianos and by playing in New York nightclubs. His most important job in this period was his stint as a song plugger, working very long hours demonstrating sheet music for the Jerome Remick music-publishing company. Although Gershwin's burgeoning creativity was hampered by his three-year stint in "plugger's purgatory," it was nevertheless an experience that greatly improved his dexterity and increased his skills at improvisation and transposing. While still in his teens, Gershwin worked as an accompanist for popular singers and as a rehearsal pianist for Broadway musicals. In 1916 he composed his first published song, "When You Want 'Em You Can't Get 'Em (When You've Got 'Em You Don't Want 'Em)," as well as his first solo piano composition, "Rialto Ripples." He began to attract the attention of Broadway luminaries.

These early experiences greatly increased Gershwin's knowledge of jazz and popular music. He enjoyed especially the songs of Irving Berlin and Jerome Kern and he was inspired by their work to compose for the Broadway stage. In 1919 entertainer Al Jolson performed the Gershwin song "Swanee" in the musical *Sinbad*; it became an enormous success, selling more than two million recordings and a million copies of sheet music, and making Gershwin an overnight celebrity. Also in 1919, Gershwin composed his first "serious" work, the *Lullaby* for string quartet.

## RHAPSODY IN BLUE

During the next few years, Gershwin contributed songs to various Broadway shows and revues. From 1920 to 1924 he composed scores for the annual productions of George White's *Scandals*, the popular variety revue. For the *Scandals* production of 1922, Gershwin convinced producer White to incorporate a one-act jazz opera. This work, *Blue Monday*

*In this photo, circa 1925, the popular American composer George Gershwin, sits at a piano ready to play.* Getty Images/Hulton Archive.

was poorly received and was removed from the show after one performance. Bandleader Paul Whiteman, who had conducted the pit orchestra for the show, was nevertheless impressed by the piece. He and Gershwin shared the common goal of bringing respectability to jazz music. To this end, in late 1923 Whiteman asked Gershwin to compose a piece for an upcoming concert. Legend has it that Gershwin forgot about the request until early January 1924, when he read a newspaper article announcing that the Whiteman concert on February 12 would feature a major new Gershwin composition. Writing at a furious pace in order to meet the deadline, Gershwin composed *Rhapsody in Blue*, perhaps his best-known work, in three weeks' time.

Owing to the haste in which it was written, *Rhapsody in Blue* was somewhat unfinished at its premiere. Gershwin improvised much of the piano solo during the performance, and conductor Whiteman had to rely on a nod from Gershwin to cue the orchestra at the end of the solo. Nevertheless, the piece was a resounding success and brought Gershwin worldwide fame. The revolutionary work incorporated trademarks of the jazz idiom (blue notes, syncopated rhythms, onomatopoeic instrumental effects) into a symphonic context. Arranged by Ferde Grofé (composer of the *Grand Canyon Suite*) for either symphony orchestra or jazz band, the work is perhaps the most-performed and most-recorded orchestral composition of the 20th century.

## POPULAR SONGS

For the remainder of his career, Gershwin devoted himself to both popular songs and orchestral compositions. His Broadway shows from the 1920s and '30s featured numerous songs that became standards, including: "Fascinating

Rhythm," "Oh, Lady Be Good," "Sweet and Low-Down," "Someone to Watch over Me," "Strike Up the Band," "The Man I Love," "'S Wonderful," "Embraceable You," and "But Not for Me." He also composed several songs for Hollywood films, such as "Let's Call the Whole Thing Off," "They All Laughed," "A Foggy Day," "Nice Work If You Can Get It," and "Love Walked In." His lyricist for nearly all of these tunes was his older brother, Ira, whose glib, witty lyrics—often punctuated with slang, puns, and wordplay—received nearly as much acclaim as George's compositions. The Gershwin brothers comprised a somewhat unique songwriting partnership in that George's melodies usually came first—a reverse of the process employed by most composing teams.

One of the Gershwins' best-known collaborations, "I Got Rhythm," was introduced by Ethel Merman in the musical *Girl Crazy* (1930). The following year, Gershwin scored a lengthy, elaborate piano arrangement of the song, and in late 1933 he arranged the piece into a set of variations for piano and orchestra; *"I Got Rhythm" Variations* has since become one of Gershwin's most-performed orchestral works. Gershwin's piano score for "I Got Rhythm" was part of a larger project begun in 1931, *George Gershwin's Songbook*, a collection of Gershwin's personal favourite hit tunes, adapted "for the above-average pianist."

## OTHER WORKS FOR ORCHESTRA

In 1925 Gershwin was commissioned by the Symphony Society of New York to write a concerto. The resulting work, *Concerto in F* (1925), Gershwin's lengthiest composition, was divided into three traditional concerto movements. The first movement loosely follows a sonata structure of exposition, development, and recapitulation. The second movement is a slow, meditative adaptation of blues progressions, and the third movement introduces new themes and returns, rondo-like, to the themes of the first. Although not as well received at the time as *Rhapsody in Blue*, the *Concerto in F* eventually came to be regarded as one of Gershwin's most important works.

*An American in Paris* (1928), Gershwin's second-most famous orchestral composition, was inspired by the composer's trips to Paris throughout the 1920s. His stated intention with the work was to "portray the impressions of an American visitor in Paris as he strolls about the city, listens to various street noises, and absorbs the French atmosphere." It is this piece that perhaps best represents Gershwin's employment of both jazz and classical forms. The harmonic structure of *An American in Paris* is rooted in blues traditions, and soloists are often required to bend, slide, and growl certain notes and passages, in the style of jazz musicians of the 1920s.

Gershwin's other major orchestral compositions have grown in stature and popularity throughout the years. His *Second Rhapsody* (1931) was featured, in embryonic form, as incidental music in the film *Delicious* (1931). Gershwin's *Cuban Overture* (1932), employed rhumba rhythms and such percussion instruments as claves, maracas, bongo drums, and gourds, all of which were generally unknown at the time in the United States.

## PORGY AND BESS

Throughout his career, Gershwin had major successes on Broadway with shows such as *Lady, Be Good!* (1924), *Strike Up the Band* (1930), and, especially, the political satire *Of Thee I Sing* (1931), for which Ira and librettists George S. Kaufman and Morrie Ryskind shared a Pulitzer Prize. These shows, smash hits in their time, are (save for Gershwin's music) largely forgotten today; ironically, his most enduring and respected Broadway work, *Porgy and Bess*, was lukewarmly received upon its premiere in 1935. Gershwin's "American Folk Opera" was inspired by the DuBose Heyward novel *Porgy* (1925) and featured a libretto and lyrics by Ira and the husband-wife team of DuBose and Dorothy Heyward. Theatre critics received the premiere production enthusiastically, but highbrow music critics were derisive, distressed that "lowly" popular music should be incorporated into an opera structure. Black audiences throughout the years have criticized the work for its condescending depiction of stereotyped characters and for Gershwin's inauthentic appropriation of black musical forms. Nevertheless, Gershwin's music—including such standards as "Summertime," "It Ain't Necessarily So," "Bess, You Is My Woman Now," and "I Got Plenty O' Nuttin"—transcended early criticism to attain a revered niche in the musical world, largely because it successfully amalgamates various musical cultures to evoke something uniquely American and wholly Gershwin.

## Aftermath

Gershwin was known as a gregarious man whose huge ego was tempered by a genuinely magnetic personality. He loved his work and approached every assignment with enthusiasm, never suffering from "composer's block." Throughout the first half of 1937, Gershwin began experiencing severe headaches and brief memory blackouts, although medical tests showed him to be in good health. By July, Gershwin exhibited impaired motor skills and drastic weight loss, and he required assistance in walking. He lapsed into a coma on July 9, and a spinal tap revealed the presence of a brain tumour. Gershwin never regained consciousness and died during surgery two days later.

# DUKE ELLINGTON

(b. April 29, 1899, Washington, D.C., U.S.—d. May 24, 1974, New York, N.Y.)

American pianist Duke Ellington (born Edward Kennedy Ellington) was one of the most influential jazz composers and bandleaders of the 20th century. One of the originators of big-band jazz, Ellington led his band for more than 50 years, composed thousands of scores, and created one of the most distinctive ensemble sounds in all of Western music.

Ellington grew up in a secure, middle-class family in Washington, D.C. His family encouraged his interests in the fine arts, and he began studying piano at age seven. Inspired by ragtime performers, he began to perform professionally at age 17. On July 2, 1918, a 19-year-old Ellington married Edna Thompson, who had grown up across the street from him. Their son Mercer was born March 11, 1919. (Another child, born the following year, died in infancy.) Ellington first played in New York City in 1923. Later that year he moved there and, in Broadway nightclubs, led a sextet that grew in time into a 10-piece ensemble. The singular blues-based melodies, the harsh, vocalized sounds of his trumpeter, Bubber Miley (who used a plunger ["wa-wa"] mute), and the sonorities of the distinctive trombonist Joe ("Tricky Sam") Nanton (who played muted "growl" sounds) all influenced Ellington's early "jungle style," as seen in such masterpieces as "East St. Louis Toodle-oo" (1926) and "Black and Tan Fantasy" (1927).

Extended residencies at the Cotton Club in Harlem (1927–32, 1937–38) stimulated Ellington to enlarge his band to 14 musicians and to expand his compositional scope. He selected his musicians for their expressive individuality, and several members of his ensemble—including trumpeter Cootie Williams (who replaced Miley), cornetist Rex Stewart, trombonist Lawrence Brown, baritone saxophonist Harry

Carney, alto saxophonist Johnny Hodges, and clarinetist Barney Bigard—were themselves important jazz artists. (With these exceptional musicians, who remained with him throughout the 1930s, Ellington made hundreds of recordings, appeared in films and on radio, and toured Europe in 1933 and 1939.

The expertise of this ensemble allowed Ellington to use new harmonies to blend his musicians' individual sounds. He illuminated subtle moods with ingenious combinations of instruments; among the most famous examples is "Mood Indigo" in his 1930 setting for muted trumpet, unmuted trombone, and low-register clarinet. In 1931 Ellington began to create extended works, including such pieces as *Creole Rhapsody, Reminiscing in Tempo*, and *Diminuendo in Blue/Crescendo in Blue*. He composed a series of works to highlight the special talents of his soloists. Williams, for example, demonstrated his versatility in Ellington's miniature concertos *Echoes of Harlem* and *Concerto for Cootie*. Some of Ellington's numbers—notably "Caravan" and "Perdido" by trombonist Juan Tizol—were cowritten or entirely composed by sidemen.

A high point in Ellington's career came in the early 1940s, when he composed several masterworks—including the above-mentioned *Concerto for Cootie*, his fast-tempo showpieces "Cotton Tail" and "Ko-Ko," and the uniquely structured, compressed panoramas "Main Stem" and "Harlem Air Shaft"—in which successions of soloists are accompanied by diverse ensemble colours. The variety and ingenuity of these works are extraordinary, as are their unique forms, which range from logically flowing expositions to juxtapositions of line and mood. By then, Billy Strayhorn, composer of what would become the band's theme song, "Take the 'A' Train," had become Ellington's composing-arranging partner.

Not limiting himself to jazz innovation, Ellington also wrote such great popular songs as "Sophisticated Lady,"

*This 1958 photo catches the legendary big band leader and jazz pianist, Duke Ellington, adjusting his bow tie, probably before a show.* Getty Images/ Evening Standard

"Rocks in My Bed," and "Satin Doll." In other songs, such as "Don't Get Around Much Any More," "Prelude to a Kiss," and "I Let a Song Go out of My Heart," he made wide interval leaps an Ellington trademark. A number of these hits were introduced by Ivy Anderson, who was the band's female vocalist in the 1930s.

During these years Ellington became intrigued with the possibilities of composing jazz within classical forms. His musical suite *Black, Brown and Beige* (1943), a portrayal of African American history, was the first in a series of suites he composed, usually consisting of pieces linked by subject matter. It was followed by, among others, *Liberian Suite* (1947); *A Drum Is a Woman* (1956), created for a television production; *Such Sweet Thunder* (1957), impressions of William Shakespeare's scenes and characters; a recomposed, reorchestrated version of *Nutcracker Suite* (1960; after Peter Tchaikovsky); *Far East Suite* (1964); and *Togo Brava Suite* (1971). Ellington's symphonic *A Rhapsody of Negro Life* was the basis for the film short *Symphony in Black* (1935). Ellington wrote motion-picture scores for *The Asphalt Jungle* (1950) and *Anatomy of a Murder* (1959) and composed for the ballet and theatre—including, at the height of the civil rights movement, the show *My People* (1964), a celebration of African American life. In his last decade he composed several pieces of sacred music.

Although Ellington's compositional interests and ambitions changed over the decades, his melodic, harmonic, and rhythmic characteristics were for the most part fixed by the late 1930s, when he was a star of the swing era. Ellington's stylistic qualities were shared by Strayhorn, who increasingly participated in composing and orchestrating music for the Ellington band. During 1939–67 Strayhorn collaborated so closely with Ellington that jazz scholars may never determine how much the gifted deputy influenced or even composed works attributed to Ellington.

The Ellington band toured Europe often after World War II; it also played in Asia (1963–64, 1970), West Africa (1966), South America (1968), and Australia (1970) and frequently toured North America. Despite this grueling schedule, some of Ellington's musicians stayed with him for decades; Carney, for example, was a band member for 47 years. For the most part, later replacements fit into roles that had been created by their distinguished predecessors.

Not least of the band's musicians was Ellington himself, a pianist whose style originated in ragtime and the stride piano idiom of James P. Johnson and Willie "The Lion" Smith. He adapted his style for orchestral purposes, accompanying with vivid harmonic colours and, especially in later years, offering swinging solos with angular melodies. An elegant man, Ellington maintained a regal manner as he led the band and charmed audiences with his suave humour. His career spanned more than half a century— most of the documented history of jazz. He continued to lead the band until shortly before his death in 1974.

## KURT WEILL

(b. March 2, 1900, Dessau, Ger.—d. April 3, 1950, New York, N.Y., U.S.)

German-born American composer Kurt Julian Weill created a revolutionary kind of opera of sharp social satire in collaboration with the writer Bertolt Brecht.

Weill studied privately with Albert Bing and at the Staatliche Hochschule für Musik in Berlin with Engelbert Humperdinck. He gained some experience as an opera coach and conductor in Dessau and Lüdenscheid (1919–20). Settling in Berlin, he studied (1921–24) under Ferruccio Busoni, beginning as a composer of instrumental works. His early music was expressionistic, experimental, and abstract. His first two operas, *Der Protagonist* (one act, libretto by Georg Kaiser, 1926) and *Royal Palace* (1927), established his position, with Ernst Krenek and Paul Hindemith, as among Germany's most promising young opera composers.

Weill's first collaboration as composer with Bertolt Brecht was on the singspiel (or "songspiel," as he called it) *Mahagonny* (1927), which was a succès de scandale at the Baden-Baden (Germany) Festival in 1927. This work sharply satirizes life in an imaginary America that is also Germany. Weill then wrote the music and Brecht provided the libretto for *Die Dreigroschenoper* (1928; *The Threepenny Opera*), which was a transposition of John Gay's *Beggar's Opera* (1728) with the 18th-century thieves, highwaymen, jailers, and their women turned into typical characters in the Berlin under- world of the 1920s. This work established both the topical opera and the reputations of the composer and librettist. Weill's music for it was in turn harsh, mordant, jazzy, and hauntingly melancholy. *Mahagonny* was elaborated as a full-length opera, *Aufstieg und Fall der Stadt Mahagonny* (composed 1927–29; "Rise and Fall of the City of Mahagonny"), and first presented in Leipzig in 1930. Widely considered Weill's masterpiece, the opera's music showed a skillful synthesis of American popular music, ragtime, and jazz.

Weill's wife, the actress Lotte Lenya (married 1926), sang for the first time in *Mahagonny* and was a great success in it and in *Die Dreigroschenoper*. These works aroused much controversy, as did the students' opera *Der Jasager* (1930; "The Yea-Sayer," with Brecht) and the cantata *Der Lindberghflug* (1928; "Lindbergh's Flight," with Brecht and Hindemith). After the production of the opera *Die Bürgschaft* (1932; "Trust," libretto by Caspar Neher), Weill's political and musical ideas and his Jewish birth made him persona non grata to the Nazis, and he left Berlin for Paris and then for London. His music was banned in Germany until after World War II.

Weill and his wife divorced in 1933 but remarried in 1937 in New York City, where he resumed his career. He wrote music for plays, including Paul Green's *Johnny Johnson* (1936) and Franz Werfel's *Eternal Road* (1937). His operetta *Knickerbocker Holiday* appeared in 1938 with a libretto by Maxwell Anderson, followed by the musical play *Lady in the Dark* (1941; libretto and lyrics by Moss Hart and Ira Gershwin), the musical comedy *One Touch of Venus* (1943; with S.J. Perelman and Ogden Nash), the musical version of Elmer Rice's *Street Scene* (1947), and the musical tragedy *Lost in the Stars* (1949; with Maxwell Anderson). Weill's American folk opera *Down in the Valley* (1948) was much performed. Two of his songs, the "Morität" ("Mack the Knife") from *Die Dreigroschenoper* and "September Song" from *Knickerbocker Holiday*, have remained popular. Weill's *Concerto for violin, woodwinds, double bass, and percussion* (1924), *Symphony No. 1* (1921; "Berliner Sinfonie"), and *Symphony No. 2* (1934; "Pariser Symphonie"), works praised for their qualities of invention and compositional skill, were revived after his death.

## AARON COPLAND

(b. Nov. 14, 1900, Brooklyn, N.Y., U.S.—d. Dec. 2, 1990, North Tarrytown [now Sleepy Hollow], N.Y.)

American composer Aaron Copland achieved a distinctive musical characterization of American themes in an expressive modern style.

Copland, the son of Russian-Jewish immigrants, was born in New York City and attended public schools there. An older sister taught him to play the piano, and by the time he was 15 he had decided to become a composer. In the summer of 1921 Copland attended the newly founded school for Americans at Fontainebleau, where he came under the influence of Nadia Boulanger, a brilliant teacher who shaped the outlook of an entire generation of American musicians. He decided to stay on in Paris, where he became Boulanger's first American student in composition. After three years in Paris, Copland returned to New York City with an important commission: Nadia Boulanger had asked him to write an organ concerto for her American appearances. Copland composed the piece while working as the pianist of a hotel trio at a summer resort in Pennsylvania. That season the *Symphony for Organ and Orchestra* had its premiere in Carnegie Hall with the New York Symphony.

In his growth as a composer Copland mirrored the important trends of his time. After his return from Paris, he worked with jazz rhythms in *Music for the Theater* (1925) and the *Piano Concerto* (1926). There followed a period during which he was strongly influenced by Igor Stravinsky's neoclassicism, turning toward an abstract style he described as "more spare in sonority, more lean in texture." This outlook prevailed in the *Piano Variations* (1930), *Short Symphony* (1933), and *Statements for Orchestra* (1933–35). After this last work, there occurred a change of direction that was to usher in the most productive phase of Copland's career. He realized that a new public for modern music was being created by the new media of radio, phonograph, and film scores: "It made no sense to ignore them and to continue writing as if they did not exist. I felt that it was worth the effort to see if I couldn't say what I had to say in the simplest possible terms." Copland therefore was led to what became a most significant development after the 1930s: the attempt to simplify the new music in order that it would have meaning for a large public.

The decade that followed saw the production of the scores that spread Copland's fame throughout the world. Most important of these were the three ballets based on American folk material: *Billy the Kid* (1938), *Rodeo* (1942), and *Appalachian Spring* (1944; commissioned by dancer Martha Graham). To this group belonged also *El salón México* (1936), an orchestral piece based on Mexican melodies and rhythms; two works for high-school students—the "play opera" *The Second Hurricane* (1937) and *An Outdoor Overture* (1938); and a series of film scores, of which the best known are *Of Mice and Men* (1939), *Our Town* (1940), *The Red Pony* (1948), and *The Heiress* (1948). Typical too of the Copland style are two major works that were written in time of war— *Lincoln Portrait* (1942), for speaker and chorus, on a text drawn from Lincoln's speeches, and *Letter from Home* (1944), as well as the melodious *Third Symphony* (1946).

In his later years Copland refined his treatment of Americana: "I no longer feel the need of seeking out conscious Americanism. Because we live here and work here, we can be certain that when our music is mature it will also be American in quality." His later works include an opera, *The Tender Land* (1954); *Twelve Poems of Emily Dickinson* (1950), for voice and piano; and the delightful *Nonet* (1960). During these years Copland also produced a number of works in which he showed himself increasingly receptive to the serial techniques of the so-called 12-tone school of composer Arnold Schoenberg. Notable among such works are the stark and dissonant *Piano Fantasy* (1957); *Connotations* (1962), which was commissioned for the opening of Lincoln Center for the Performing Arts in New York City; and *Inscape* (1967). The 12-tone works were not generally well received; after 1970 Copland virtually stopped composing, though he continued to lecture and to conduct through the mid-1980s.

*American composer Aaron Copland created a large volume of work building on different styles throughout the 20th century.* Getty Images/Erich Auerbach

For the better part of four decades, as composer (of operas, ballets, orchestral music, band music, chamber music, choral music, and film scores), teacher, writer of books and articles on music, organizer of musical events, and a much sought-after conductor, Copland expressed "the deepest reactions of the American consciousness to the American scene." He received more than 30 honorary degrees and many additional awards. He also wrote a number of books on music.

A private man not given to making public statements about his personal life, Copland nonetheless made no efforts to hide his homosexuality, traveling openly with younger lovers. And though blacklisted during the McCarthy era, the government-led censure had no lasting effect on Copland's work and career.

## LOUIS ARMSTRONG
(b. Aug. 4, 1901, New Orleans, La., U.S. — d. July 6, 1971, New York, N.Y.)

Louis Armstrong, or Satchmo (a truncation of "Satchel Mouth"), was the leading trumpeter and one of the most influential artists in jazz history.

Armstrong grew up in dire poverty in New Orleans, La., when jazz was very young. As a child he worked at odd jobs and sang in a boys' quartet. In 1913 he was sent to the Colored Waifs Home as a juvenile delinquent. There he learned to play cornet in the home's band, and playing music quickly became a passion. Armstrong developed rapidly: he played in marching and jazz bands, becoming skillful enough to replace New Orleans jazz cornetist King Oliver in the important Kid Ory band in about 1918, and in the early 1920s he played in Mississippi riverboat dance bands.

Fame beckoned in 1922 when Oliver, then leading a band in Chicago, sent for Armstrong to play second cornet. Oliver's Creole Jazz Band was the apex of the early, contrapuntal New Orleans ensemble style, and it included musicians such as the brothers Johnny and Baby Dodds and pianist Lil Hardin, who married Armstrong in 1924. The young Armstrong became popular through his ingenious ensemble lead and second cornet lines, his cornet duet passages (called "breaks") with Oliver, and his solos. He recorded his first solos as a member of the Oliver band in such pieces as "Chimes Blues" and "Tears."

Encouraged by his wife, Armstrong quit Oliver's band to seek further fame. He played for a year in New York City in Fletcher Henderson's band and on many recordings with others before returning to Chicago and playing in large orchestras. There he created his most important early works, the Armstrong Hot Five and Hot Seven recordings of 1925–28, on which he emerged as the first great jazz soloist. By then the New Orleans ensemble style, which allowed few solo opportunities, could no longer contain his explosive creativity. He retained vestiges of the style in such masterpieces as "Hotter Than That," "Struttin' with Some Barbecue," "Wild Man Blues," and "Potato Head Blues" but largely abandoned it while accompanied by pianist Earl Hines ("West End Blues" and "Weather Bird"). By that time Armstrong was playing trumpet, and his technique was superior to that of all competitors. Altogether, his immensely compelling swing, his brilliant technique, his sophisticated, daring sense of harmony, his ever-mobile, expressive attack, timbre, and inflections, his gift for creating vital melodies; his dramatic, often complex sense of solo design, and his outsized musical energy and genius made these recordings major innovations in jazz.

Armstrong was a famous musician by 1929, when he moved from Chicago to New York City and performed in the theatre review *Hot Chocolates*. He toured America and

Europe as a trumpet soloist accompanied by big bands; for several years beginning in 1935, Luis Russell's big band served as the Louis Armstrong band. During this time he abandoned much of the material of his earlier years for popular songs by such composers as Hoagy Carmichael, Irving Berlin, and Duke Ellington. With his new repertoire came a new, simplified style: he created melodic paraphrases and variations as well as chord-change-based improvisations on these songs. His trumpet range continued to expand, as demonstrated in the high-note showpieces in his repertoire. His beautiful tone and bravura solos with brilliant high-note climaxes led to such masterworks as "That's My Home," "Body and Soul," and "Star Dust." One of the inventors of scat singing, he began to sing lyrics on most of his recordings, varying melodies or decorating with scat phrases in a gravel voice that was immediately identifiable. Although he sang such humorous songs as "Hobo, You Can't Ride This Train," he also sang many standard songs, often with an intensity and creativity that equaled those of his trumpet playing.

Louis and Lil Armstrong separated in 1931. From 1935 to the end of his life, Armstrong's career was managed by Joe Glaser, who hired Armstrong's bands and guided his film career (beginning with *Pennies from Heaven*, 1936) and radio appearances. Armstrong was the dominant influence on the swing era, when most trumpeters attempted to emulate his inclination to dramatic structure, melody, or technical virtuosity. Trombonists, too, appropriated Armstrong's phrasing, and saxophonists as different as Coleman Hawkins and Bud Freeman modeled their styles on different aspects of Armstrong's. Above all else, his swing-style trumpet playing influenced virtually all jazz horn players who followed him, and the swing of his vocal style was an important influence on singers from Billie Holiday to Bing Crosby.

In most of Armstrong's movie, radio, and television appearances, he was featured as a good-humoured entertainer. He played a rare dramatic role in the film *New Orleans* (1947), in which he also performed in a Dixieland band. This prompted the formation of Louis Armstrong's All-Stars, a Dixieland band that at first included such other jazz greats as Hines and trombonist Jack Teagarden. For most of the rest of Armstrong's life, he toured the world with changing All-Stars sextets. It was the period of his greatest popularity; he produced hit recordings such as "Mack the Knife" and "Hello, Dolly!" and outstanding albums such as his tributes to W.C. Handy and Fats Waller. In his last years ill health curtailed his trumpet playing, but he continued as a singer. His last film appearance was in *Hello, Dolly!* (1969), but his most memorable film role may well be as narrator of and bandleader in the 1956 hit musical *High Society*, also starring Frank Sinatra, Bing Crosby, and Grace Kelly.

More than a great trumpeter, Armstrong was a bandleader, singer, soloist, film star, and comedian. One of his most remarkable feats was his frequent conquest of the popular market. He nonetheless made his greatest impact on the evolution of jazz itself, which at the start of his career was popularly considered to be little more than a novelty. With his great sensitivity, technique, and capacity to express emotion, Armstrong not only ensured the survival of jazz but led in its development into a fine art.

## UMM KULTHŪM

(b. May 4, 1904?, Tummāy al-Zahāyrah, Egypt—d. Feb. 3, 1975, Cairo)

E gyptian singer Umm Kulthūm mesmerized Arab audiences from the Persian Gulf to Morocco for half a century. She was one of the most famous Arab singers and public personalities in the 20th century.

Umm Kulthūm's father was a village imam who sang traditional religious songs at weddings and holidays to make ends meet. She learned to sing from him, and, when he noticed the strength of her voice, he began taking her with him, dressed as a boy to avoid the opprobrium of displaying a young daughter onstage. Egyptian society during Umm Kulthūm's youth held singing—even of the religious variety—to be a disreputable occupation, especially for a female. Umm Kulthūm made a name for herself singing in the towns and villages of the Egyptian delta (an area throughout which she retained a great following). By the time she was a teenager, she had become the family star.

Sometime about 1923 the family moved to Cairo, a major centre of the lucrative world of entertainment and emerging mass media production in the Middle East. There they were perceived as old-fashioned and countrified. To improve her image and acquire sophistication, Umm Kulthūm studied music and poetry from accomplished performers and literati and copied the manners of the ladies of wealthy homes in which she was invited to sing. She soon made a name in the homes and salons of the wealthy as well as in public venues such as theatres and cabarets. By the mid-1920s she had made her first recordings and had achieved a more polished and sophisticated musical and personal style. By the end of the 1920s, she had become a sought-after performer and was one of the best-paid musicians in Cairo. Her extremely successful career in commercial recording eventually extended to radio, film, and television. In 1936 she made her first motion picture, *Wedad*, in which she played the title role. It was the first of six motion pictures in which she was to act.

Beginning in 1937, she regularly gave a performance on the first Thursday (which in most Islamic countries is the last day of the workweek) of every month. By this time she had moved from singing religious songs to performing popular tunes—often in the colloquial dialect and accompanied by a small traditional orchestra—and she became known for her emotive, passionate renditions of arrangements by the best composers, poets, and songwriters of the day. These included the poets Aḥmad Shawqī and Bayrām al-Tūnisī (who wrote many of the singer's colloquial Egyptian songs) and, later, the noted composer Muḥammad ʿAbd al-Wahhāb, with whom she collaborated on 10 songs. The first of these tunes, "Inta ʿUmrī" ("You Are My Life"), remains a modern classic. Her strong and nuanced voice and her ability to fashion multiple iterations of single lines of text drew audiences into the emotion and meaning of the poetic lyrics and extended for hours what often had been written as relatively short compositions.

Known sometimes as Kawkab al-Sharq ("Star of the East"), Umm Kulthūm had an immense repertoire, which included religious, sentimental, and nationalistic songs. In the midst of the turmoil created by two world wars, the Great Depression of the 1930s, and the 1952 Egyptian revolution, she cultivated a public persona as a patriotic Egyptian and a devout Muslim. She sang songs in support of Egyptian independence ("Nashīd al-Jāmiʿah" ["The University Anthem"], "Saʿalu Qalbī" ["Ask My Heart"]) and in the 1950s sang many songs in support of Egyptian leader Gamal Abdel Nasser, with whom she developed a close friendship. One of her songs associated with Nasser—"Wallāhi Zamān, Yā Silāḥī" ("It's Been a Long Time, O Weapon of Mine")—was adopted as the Egyptian national anthem from 1960 to 1979. She served as president of the Musician's Union for seven years and held positions on numerous government commissions on the arts. Her popularity was further enhanced by her generous donations to Arab causes. After Egypt's defeat in the Six-Day War of June 1967, she toured

Egypt and the broader Arab world, donating the proceeds of her concerts to the Egyptian government.

Health problems plagued the singer most of her life. During the late 1940s and early '50s, she worked only on a limited basis, and on a number of occasions throughout her life she traveled to Europe and the United States for treatment of a variety of ailments. Most obviously, problems with her eyes (purportedly from years spent in front of stage lights) forced her to wear heavy sunglasses, which became a hallmark during her later life. Such was her popularity that news of her death provoked a spontaneous outpouring of hysterical grief, and millions of admirers lined the streets for her funeral procession. She remained one of the Arab world's best-selling singers even decades after her death. In 2001 the Egyptian government established the Kawkab al-Sharq Museum in Cairo to celebrate the singer's life and accomplishments.

## COUNT BASIE

(b. Aug. 21, 1904, Red Bank, N.J., U.S.—d. April 26, 1984, Hollywood, Fla.)

American jazz musician William Basie, popularly known as "Count," was noted for his spare, economical piano style and for his leadership of influential and widely heralded big bands.

Basie studied music with his mother and was later influenced by the Harlem pianists James P. Johnson and Fats Waller, receiving informal tutelage on the organ from the latter. He began his professional career as an accompanist on the vaudeville circuit. Stranded in Kansas City, Mo., in 1927, Basie remained there and in 1935 assumed the leadership of a nine-piece band composed of former members of the Walter Page and Bennie Moten orchestras. One night, while the band was broadcasting on a shortwave radio station in Kansas City, he was dubbed "Count" Basie by a radio announcer who wanted to indicate his standing in a class with aristocrats of jazz such as Duke Ellington. Jazz critic and record producer John Hammond heard the broadcasts and promptly launched the band on its career. Though rooted in the riff style of the 1930s swing-era big bands, the Basie orchestra played with the forceful drive and carefree swing of a small combo. They were considered a model for ensemble rhythmic conception and tonal balance—this despite the fact that most of Basie's sidemen in the 1930s were poor sight readers; mostly, the band relied on "head" arrangements (so called because the band had collectively composed and memorized them, rather than using sheet music).

The early Basie band was also noted for its legendary soloists and outstanding rhythm section. It featured such jazzmen as tenor saxophonists Lester Young and Herschel Evans, trumpeters Buck Clayton and Harry "Sweets" Edison, and trombonists Benny Morton and Dicky Wells. The legendary Billie Holiday was a vocalist with Basie for a short stint (1937–38), although she was unable to record with the band because of her contract with another record label; mostly, vocals were handled by Jimmy Rushing. The rhythm unit for the band—pianist Basie, guitarist Freddie Green (who joined the Basie band in 1937 and stayed for 50 years), bassist Walter Page, and drummer Jo Jones—was unique in its lightness, precision, and relaxation, becoming the precursor for modern jazz accompanying styles. Basie began his career as a stride pianist, reflecting the influence of Johnson and Waller, but the style most strongly associated with him was characterized by spareness and precision. Whereas other pianists were noted for technical flash and dazzling dexterity, Basie was known for his use of silence and for reducing his solo passages to the minimum amount of notes required for maximum emotional and rhythmic effect.

The Basie orchestra had several hit recordings during the late 1930s and early '40s, among them "Jumpin' at the Woodside," "Every Tub," "Lester Leaps In," "Super Chief," "Taxi War Dance," "Miss Thing," "Shorty George," and "One O'Clock Jump," the band's biggest hit and theme song. It had continued success throughout the war years, but, like all big bands, it had declined in popularity by the end of the 1940s. During 1950 and '51, economy forced Basie to front an octet, the only period in his career in which he did not lead a big band. In 1952 increased demand for personal appearances allowed Basie to form a new orchestra that in many ways was as highly praised as his bands of the 1930s and '40s. (Fans distinguish the two major eras in Basie bands as the "Old Testament" and "New Testament.") The Basie orchestra of the 1950s was a slick, professional unit that was expert at sight reading demanding arrangements. Outstanding soloists such as tenor saxophonists Lucky Thompson, Paul Quinichette, and Eddie "Lockjaw" Davis and trumpeters Clark Terry and Charlie Shavers, figured prominently. Singer Joe Williams, whose authoritative, blues-influenced vocals can be heard on hit recordings such as "Every Day I Have the Blues" and "Alright, Okay, You Win," was also a major component in the band's success. Arrangers Neal Hefti, Buster Harding, and Ernie Wilkins defined the new band's sound on recordings such as "Li'l Darlin'," "The Kid from Red Bank," "Cute," and "April in Paris" and on celebrated albums such as *The Atomic Mr. Basie* (1957).

The 1950s band showcased the sound and style Basie was to employ for the remainder of his career, although there were to be occasional—and successful—experiments such as *Afrique* (1970), an album of African rhythms and avant-garde compositions that still managed to remain faithful to the overall Basie sound. Throughout the 1960s, Basie's recordings were often unremarkable, but he remained an exceptional concert performer and made fine records with singers Ella Fitzgerald, Sarah Vaughan, and Frank Sinatra. When jazz record producer Norman Granz formed his Pablo label in the 1970s, several established jazz artists, including Basie, signed on in order to record unfettered by commercial demands. Basie benefited greatly from his association with Granz and made several recordings during the '70s that rank among his best work. He recorded less often with his big band during this era (although when he did, the results were outstanding), concentrating instead on small-group and piano-duet recordings. Especially noteworthy were the albums featuring the duo of Basie and Oscar Peterson, with Basie's economy and Peterson's dexterous virtuosity proving an effective study in contrasts. Many of Basie's albums of the '70s were Grammy Award winners or nominees.

Suffering from diabetes and chronic arthritis during his later years, Basie continued to front his big band until a month before his death in 1984. The band itself carried on into the next century, with Thad Jones, Frank Foster, and Grover Mitchell each assuming leadership for various intervals. Basie's autobiography, *Good Morning Blues*, written with Albert Murray, was published posthumously in 1985. Along with Duke Ellington, Count Basie is regarded as one of the two most important and influential bandleaders in the history of jazz.

## DMITRY SHOSTAKOVICH

(b. Sept. 12 [Sept. 25, New Style], 1906, St. Petersburg, Russia—d. Aug. 9, 1975, Moscow, Russia, U.S.S.R.)

Russian composer Dmitry Dmitriyevich Shostakovich was renowned particularly for his 15 symphonies, numerous chamber works, and concerti, many of them written under the pressures of government-imposed standards of Soviet art.

## EARLY LIFE AND WORKS

Shostakovich was the son of an engineer. He entered the Petrograd (formerly St. Petersburg, subsequently Leningrad) Conservatory in 1919, where he studied piano with Leonid Nikolayev until 1923 and composition until 1925 with Aleksandr Glazunov and Maksimilian Steinberg. Even before his keyboard success in Warsaw, he had had a far greater success as a composer with the *Symphony No. 1* (1924–25), which quickly achieved worldwide currency. The symphony's stylistic roots were numerous; the influence of composers as diverse as Tchaikovsky and Paul Hindemith is clearly discernible. In the music Shostakovich wrote in the next few years he submitted to an even wider range of influences, and Shostakovich openly experimented with avant-garde trends. His satiric opera *The Nose* (composed 1927–28), based on Nikolay Gogol's story *Nos*, displayed a comprehensive awareness of what was new in Western music, although already it seems as if the satire is extended to the styles themselves, for the avant-garde sounds are contorted with wry humour. Not surprisingly, Shostakovich's finer second opera, *Lady Macbeth of the Mtsensk District* (composed 1930–32; revised and retitled *Katerina Izmaylova*), marked a stylistic retreat. Yet even this more accessible musical language was too radical for the Soviet authorities.

From 1928, when Joseph Stalin inaugurated his First Five-Year Plan, a direct and popular style was demanded in music. Avant-garde music and jazz were officially banned in 1932. Shostakovich did not experience immediate official displeasure, but when it came it was devastating. A performance of *Lady Macbeth of the Mtsensk District* in 1936 precipitated the official condemnation of the opera and of its creator.

Shostakovich was bitterly attacked in the official press, and both the opera and the still-unperformed *Symphony No. 4* (1935–36) were withdrawn. The composer responded with his next major work, *Symphony No. 5* (1937). Compounded largely of serious, even sombre and elegiac music and presented with a compelling directness, the symphony scored an immediate success with both the public and the authorities.

With his *Symphony No. 5*, Shostakovich forged the style that he used in his subsequent compositions. Gustav Mahler was a clear progenitor of both *Symphony No. 4* and *Symphony No. 5*, but the latter represented a drastic shift in technique. Whereas the earlier symphony had been a sprawling work, founded upon a free proliferation of melodic ideas, the first movement of *Symphony No. 5* was marked by melodic concentration and Classical form. Indeed, Shostakovich had an almost obsessive concern with the working out of a single expressive character, which can also be seen in the recurrence in his mature music of certain thematic ideas, notably various permutations founded upon the juxtaposition of the major and minor third, and the four-note cell D-E♭-C-B derived from the composer's initials in their German equivalent (D. Sch.), interpreted according to the labels of German musical notation (in which "S," spoken as "Es," equals E♭ and "h" equals B).

In 1937 Shostakovich became a teacher of composition in the Leningrad Conservatory, and the German attack on the Soviet Union in 1941 found him still in that city. He composed his *Symphony No. 7* (1941) in beleaguered Leningrad during the latter part of that year and finished it in Kuybyshev (now Samara), to which he and his family had been evacuated. The work achieved a quick fame, as much because of the quasi-romantic circumstances of its composition as because of its musical quality. In 1943 Shostakovich settled in Moscow as a teacher of composition at the conservatory, and from 1945 he taught also at the Leningrad Conservatory.

## LATER LIFE AND WORKS

Shostakovich's works written during the mid-1940s contain some of his best music, especially the *Symphony No. 8* (1943), the *Piano Trio* (1944), and the *Violin Concerto No. 1* (1947–48). Their prevailing seriousness, even grimness, was to contribute to Shostakovich's second fall from official grace. When the Cold War began, the Soviet authorities sought to impose a firmer ideological control, demanding a more accessible musical language than some composers were currently using. In Moscow in 1948, at a now notorious conference, the leading figures of Soviet music—including Shostakovich—were attacked and disgraced. As a result, the quality of Soviet composition slumped in the next few years, and his teaching activities at both the Moscow and Leningrad conservatories were terminated. Yet he was not completely intimidated, and, in his *String Quartet No. 4* (1949) and especially his *Quartet No. 5* (1951), he offered a splendid rejoinder to those who would have had him renounce completely his style and musical integrity. His *Symphony No. 10*, composed in 1953, the year of Stalin's death, flew in the face of his official detractors, yet, like his *Symphony No. 5*, compelled acceptance by sheer quality and directness.

From that time on, Shostakovich's biography is essentially a catalog of his works. He was left to pursue his creative career largely unhampered by official interference. The composer had visited the United States in 1949, and in 1958 he made an extended tour of western Europe, where he received a number of honours for his music. After Prokofiev's death in 1953, he was the undisputed head of Russian music. Since his own death his music has been the subject of furious contention between those upholding the Soviet view of the composer as a sincere Communist and those who view him as a closet dissident.

## BILL MONROE

(b. Sept. 13, 1911, Rosine, Ky., U.S.—d. Sept. 9, 1996, Springfield, near Nashville, Tenn.)

Creation of the bluegrass style of country music is credited to American singer, songwriter, and mandolin player William ("Bill") Smith Monroe.

The youngest of eight children of a Kentucky farmer and entrepreneur, Monroe was exposed early to traditional folk music by his mother. Another important early musical influence on the young Monroe was Arnold Schultz, a local African American miner who also was an accomplished fiddler and guitarist and who played both blues and country music. Monroe began playing the mandolin professionally in 1927 in a band led by his older brothers Birch and Charlie. In 1930 they moved to Indiana, and in 1932 they joined a barn-dance touring show; their reputation grew, but, because Birch did not like to travel, Bill and Charlie maintained the Monroe Brothers as a duo, touring widely from Nebraska to South Carolina. In 1936 they made their first recordings on the RCA Victor label, recording 60 songs for Victor over the next two years. In 1938 Bill and Charlie decided to form separate bands. Bill's second band, the Blue Grass Boys (his first, called the Kentuckians, played together for only three months), auditioned for the Grand Ole Opry on radio station WSM in Nashville, Tenn., and became regular performers on that program in 1939.

Monroe's signature sound emerged fully in 1945, when banjoist Earl Scruggs and guitarist Lester Flatt joined his band. Scruggs was among the first banjoists in country music whose principal role was musical rather than comical; Monroe's original banjoist David ("Stringbean") Akeman had provided a humorous touch to the proceedings. The Blue Grass Boys established the classic makeup of a blue-grass group—with mandolin, fiddle, guitar, banjo, and upright bass—and ultimately bequeathed the band's name to the genre itself. Bluegrass is characterized by acoustic instruments; a driving syncopated rhythm; tight, complex harmonies; and the use of higher keys—B-flat, B, and E rather than the customary G, C, and D. The band played traditional folk songs and Monroe's own compositions, the most famous of which were "Blue Moon of Kentucky" (later famously covered and transformed by a young Elvis Presley), "Uncle Pen" (a tribute to another early influence on Monroe, his fiddle-playing uncle Pendleton Vandiver), and "Raw Hide." Although Monroe had sung only har-mony as a member of the Monroe Brothers, his high, mournful tenor (both as lead and backing voice) estab-lished the convention of bluegrass music's "high lonesome" vocals, and his breakneck-tempo mandolin playing set the standard for other bluegrass performers.

The Blue Grass Boys enjoyed wide popularity, but Scruggs and Flatt quit in 1948 in order to form their own influential bluegrass band, the Foggy Mountain Boys. Soon other bands playing this style of music began to appear, many of them led by former members of Monroe's band, such as Sonny Osborne (the Osborne Brothers), Carter Stanley (who with his brother Ralph formed the Stanley Brothers), Don Reno, Jimmy Martin, and Mac Wiseman. Bluegrass was promoted at numerous annual festivals, such as the one founded by Monroe in 1967 at Bean Blossom, Ind. He continued to perform until shortly before his death.

## MAHALIA JACKSON

(b. Oct. 26, 1911, New Orleans, La., U.S.—d. Jan. 27, 1972, Evergreen Park, near Chicago, Ill.)

American gospel music singer Mahalia Jackson is known as the "Queen of Gospel Song."

Jackson was brought up in a strict religious atmosphere. Her father's family included several entertainers, but she was forced to confine her own musical activities to singing in the church choir and listening—surreptitiously—to recordings of Bessie Smith and Ida Cox as well as of Enrico Caruso. When she was 16 she went to Chicago and joined the Greater Salem Baptist Church choir, where her remarkable contralto voice soon led to her selection as a soloist.

Jackson first came to wide public attention in the 1930s, when she participated in a cross-country gospel tour singing such songs as "He's Got the Whole World in His Hands" and "I Can Put My Trust in Jesus." In 1934 her first recording, "God Gonna Separate the Wheat from the Tares," was a success, leading to a series of other recordings. Jackson's first great hit, "Move on Up a Little Higher," appeared in 1945; it was especially important for its use of the "vamp," an indefinitely repeated phrase (or chord pattern) that provides a foundation for solo improvisation. All the songs with which she was identified—including "I Believe," "Just over the Hill," "When I Wake Up in Glory," and "Just a Little While to Stay Here"—were gospel songs, with texts drawn from biblical themes and strongly influenced by the harmonies, rhythms, and emotional force of blues. Jackson refused to sing any but religious songs or indeed to sing at all in surroundings that she considered inappropriate. But she sang on the radio and on television and, starting in 1950, performed to overflow audiences in

*The great American gospel singer Mahalia Jackson is seen here in 1971 singing at the Imperial Palace in Tokyo for the Emperor Hirohito's 70th birthday.* Getty Images/Keystone

annual concerts at Carnegie Hall in New York City. Eight of Jackson's records sold more than a million copies each.

Jackson was enormously popular abroad; her version of "Silent Night," for example, was one of the all-time best-selling records in Denmark. She made a notable appearance at the Newport (Rhode Island) Jazz Festival in 1957—in a program devoted entirely, at her request, to gospel songs—and she sang at the inauguration of President John F. Kennedy in January 1961. In the 1950s and '60s she was active in the civil rights movement; in 1963 she sang the old African American spiritual "I Been 'Buked and I Been Scorned" for a crowd of more than 200,000 in Washington, D.C., just before Civil Rights leader Martin Luther King, Jr., delivered his famous "I Have a Dream" speech.

## ROBERT JOHNSON

(b. c. 1911, Hazlehurst, Miss., U.S.—d. Aug. 16, 1938, near Greenwood, Miss.)

R obert Johnson was an American blues composer, guitarist, and singer whose eerie falsetto singing voice and masterful, rhythmic slide guitar influenced both his contemporaries and many later blues and rock musicians.

Johnson was the product of a confusing childhood, with three men serving as his father before he reached age seven. Little is known about his biological father (Noah Johnson, whom his mother never married), and the boy and his mother lived on various plantations in the Mississippi Delta region before settling briefly in Memphis, Tenn., with her first husband (Robert Dodds, who had changed his surname to Spencer). The bulk of Johnson's youth, however, was spent in Robinsonville, Miss., with his mother and her second husband (Dusty Willis). There Johnson learned to play the Jew's harp and harmonica before taking up the guitar. In 1929 he married

16-year-old Virginia Travis, whose death in childbirth (along with that of their baby) in April 1930 devastated Johnson.

In Robinsonville he came in contact with well-known Mississippi Delta bluesmen Willie Brown, Charley Patton, and Son House—all of whom influenced his playing and none of whom was particularly impressed by his talent. They were dazzled by his musical ability, however, when he returned to town after spending as much as a year away. That time away is central to Johnson's mythic status. According to legend, during that period Johnson made a deal with Satan at a crossroads, acquiring his prodigious talent as a guitarist, singer, and songwriter in exchange for the stipulation that he would have only eight more years to live. (A similar story circulated in regard to another Mississippi bluesman, Tommy Johnson.) Music historian Robert Palmer, in his highly regarded book *Deep Blues* (1981), instead ascribes Robert Johnson's remarkable musical attainments to the time he had to hone his skills as a guitarist under the instruction of Ike Zinneman as a result of the financial support he received from the older woman he married near Hazlehurst, Miss. (Johnson's birthplace), and to the wide variety of music to which he was exposed during his hiatus from Robinsonville, including the single-string picking styles of Lonnie Johnson and Scrapper Blackwell.

After returning briefly to Robinsonville, Johnson settled in Helena, Ark., where he played with Elmore James, Robert Nighthawk, and Howlin' Wolf, among others. He also became involved with Estella Coleman and informally adopted her son, Robert Lockwood, Jr., who later became a notable blues musician under the name Robert Jr. Lockwood. Johnson traveled widely throughout Mississippi, Arkansas, Texas, and Tennessee and as far north as Chicago and New York, playing at house parties, juke joints, and lumber camps and on the street. In 1936–37 he made a series of recordings in a hotel room in San Antonio, Texas, and a warehouse in Dallas. His repertoire included several blues songs by House and others, but Johnson's original numbers, such as "Me and the Devil Blues," "Hellhound on My Trail," "Sweet Home Chicago," "I Believe I'll Dust My Broom," "Ramblin' on My Mind," and "Love in Vain" are his most compelling pieces. Unlike the songs of many of his contemporaries—which tended to unspool loosely, employing combinations of traditional and improvised lyrics—Johnson's songs were tightly composed, and his song structure and lyrics were praised by Bob Dylan. Despite the limited number of his recordings, Johnson had a major impact on other musicians, including Muddy Waters, Elmore James, Eric Clapton, and the Rolling Stones. Johnson died of poisoning after drinking strychnine-laced whiskey in a juke joint.

## WOODY GUTHRIE

(b. July 14, 1912, Okemah, Okla., U.S.—d. Oct. 3, 1967, New York, N.Y.)

The songs of prolific American folksinger and songwriter Woodrow ("Woody") Wilson Guthrie chronicled the plight of common people, especially during the Great Depression.

Guthrie, the third of five children, was the son of a onetime cowboy, land speculator, and local Democratic politician who named him after Pres. Woodrow Wilson. His mother, who introduced her children to a wide variety of music, was thought to be mentally ill and was institutionalized when Guthrie was a teenager. Her erratic behaviour was actually caused by Huntington's disease, a hereditary neurological disorder about which little was known at the time and which would later afflict Guthrie too. The family lived near the relocated Creek nation in Okemah, Okla., a small agricultural and railroad town that boomed in the 1920s when oil was discovered in the area. The effect on the town and its people of the decline that followed the boom sensitized the young Guthrie to others' suffering, which he had also experienced firsthand through the calamities that befell his splintering family. (Guthrie paid particular attention to this period of his life in his auto-biographical novel *Bound for Glory* [1943].)

Soon after his mother's institutionalization, Guthrie began "rambling" for the first time, coming to love life on the road. Though he often left Okemah to travel during his teens, he always returned to continue his high school education. At age 19 he relocated to Pampa, Texas, where he married Mary Jennings, with whom he had three children. When the Great Depression deepened and drought turned a large section of the Great Plains into the Dust Bowl, making it impossible for Guthrie to support his family, he again took to the road. Like so many other dis-placed people from the region (collectively called "Okies" regardless of whether they were Oklahomans), he headed for California, playing his guitar and harmonica and sing-ing in taverns, taking odd jobs, and visiting hobo camps as he traveled by freight train, hitchhiked, or simply walked westward. In Los Angeles in 1937, he landed a spot per-forming on the radio, first with his cousin, Jack Guthrie, then with Maxine Crissman, who called herself Lefty Lou. At that time Guthrie began songwriting in earnest, giving voice to the struggles of the dispossessed and downtrodden while celebrating their indomitable spirit in songs such as "Do Re Mi," "Pretty Boy Floyd," and "Dust Bowl Refugee."

Guthrie's politics became increasingly leftist, and by the time he moved to New York City in 1940 he had become an important musical spokesman for labour and populist sentiments, embraced by left-leaning intellectuals and courted by communists. In New York, to which he had brought his family, Guthrie became one of the principal songwriters for the Almanac Singers, a group of activist performers—including Leadbelly, Pete Seeger, Sonny Terry, Brownie McGhee, and Cisco Houston—who used their music to attack fascism and support humanitarian and leftist causes.

In 1941 Guthrie made his first recordings, with folklorist Alan Lomax, and traveled to the Pacific Northwest, where a commission to write songs in support of federal dam building and electrification projects produced such well-known compositions as "Grand Coulee Dam" and "Roll On Columbia." Back in New York after serving as a merchant marine during World War II, his first marriage having ended in divorce, Guthrie married Marjorie (Greenblatt) Mazia, a Martha Graham Dance Company dancer with whom he would have four children (including son Arlo, who would become an important singer-songwriter in his own right in the 1960s).

As the political tide in the United States turned conservative and then reactionary during the 1950s, Guthrie and his folksinger friends in New York kept alive the flame of activist music making. He continued writing and performing politically charged songs that inspired the American folk revival of the 1960s, at the head of which were performers such as Bob Dylan, Joan Baez, and Phil Ochs, who came to pay homage to Guthrie in his hospital room in New Jersey, to which he was confined beginning in 1954, after his increasingly erratic actions were finally and correctly diagnosed as the result of Huntington's disease. Among the more than 1,000 songs that Guthrie wrote were a number of remarkable children's songs written in the language and from the perspective of childhood, as well as some of the most lasting and influential songs in the canon of American music, not least "So Long (It's Been Good to Know Yuh)", "Hard Traveling," "Blowing Down This Old

*Woody Guthrie, an American folksinger and songwriter, seen here singing and playing his guitar on a New York City street.* Eric Schaal/Time & Life Pictures/Getty Images

Dusty Road," "Union Maid," and (inspired by John Steinbeck's The Grapes of Wrath) "Tom Joad." Probably the most famous of his works is "This Land Is Your Land," which became a pillar of the Civil Rights movement of the 1960s.

At the time of his death in 1967, Guthrie had already begun to assume legendary stature as a folk figure, and his influence on such pivotal singer-songwriters as Bob Dylan and Bruce Springsteen was immense. A film version of his book *Bound for Glory* appeared in 1976, and in 1998 Billy Bragg and alternative rockers Wilco released the critically acclaimed *Mermaid Avenue*, a collection of previously unrecorded lyrics by Guthrie that they had set to music; *Mermaid Avenue Vol. II* followed in 2000.

## JOHN CAGE

(b. Sept. 5, 1912, Los Angeles, Calif., U.S.—d. Aug. 12, 1992, New York, N.Y.)

Music of the mid-20th century was profoundly influenced by the inventive compositions and unorthodox ideas of American avant-garde composer John Milton Cage, Jr.

The son of an inventor, Cage briefly attended Pomona College and then traveled in Europe for a time. Returning to the United States in 1931, he studied music with Richard Buhlig, Arnold Schoenberg, Adolph Weiss, and Henry Cowell. While teaching in Seattle (1936–38), he began organizing percussion ensembles to perform his compositions, and he began experimenting with works for dance in collaboration with his longtime friend, the choreographer and dancer Merce Cunningham.

Cage's early compositions were written in the 12-tone method of his teacher Schoenberg, but by 1939 he had begun to experiment with increasingly unorthodox instruments such as the "prepared piano" (a piano modified by objects placed between its strings in order to produce percussive and otherworldly sound effects). Cage also experimented with tape recorders, record players, and radios in his effort to step outside the bounds of conventional Western music and its concepts of meaningful sound. The concert he gave with his percussion ensemble at the Museum of Modern Art in New York City in 1943 marked the first step in his emergence as a leader of the American musical avant-garde.

In the following years, Cage turned to Zen Buddhism and other Eastern philosophies, concluding that all the activities that make up music must be seen as part of a single natural process. He came to regard all kinds of sounds as potentially musical, and he encouraged audiences to take note of all sonic phenomena, rather than only those elements selected by a composer. To this end he cultivated the principle of indeterminism in his music. He used a number of devices to ensure randomness and thus eliminate any element of personal taste on the part of the performer: unspecified instruments and numbers of performers, freedom of duration of sounds and entire pieces, inexact notation, and sequences of events determined by random means such as by consultation with the Chinese *Yijing* (*I Ching*). In his later works he extended these freedoms over other media, so that a performance of *HPSCHD* (completed 1969) might include a light show, slide projections, and costumed performers, as well as the 7 harpsichord soloists and 51 tape machines for which it was scored.

Among Cage's best-known works are *4'33"* (*Four Minutes and Thirty-three Seconds*, 1952), a piece in which the performer or performers remain utterly silent onstage for that amount of time (although the amount of time is left to the determination of the performer); *Imaginary Landscape No. 4* (1951), for 12 randomly tuned radios, 24 performers, and conductor; the *Sonatas and Interludes* (1946–48) for prepared piano; *Fontana Mix* (1958), a piece based on a series of programmed transparent cards that, when superimposed, give a graph for the random selection of electronic sounds; *Cheap Imitation* (1969), an "impression" of the music of Erik Satie; and *Roaratorio* (1979), an electronic composition utilizing thousands of words found in James Joyce's novel *Finnegans Wake*.

Cage published several books, including *Silence* (1961) and *M: Writings '67–'72* (1973). His influence extended to such established composers as Earle Brown, Lejaren Hiller, Morton Feldman, and Christian Wolff.

## MUDDY WATERS

(b. April 4, 1915, Rolling Fork, Miss., U.S.—d. April 30, 1983,
Westmont, Ill.)

Dynamic American blues guitarist and singer McKinley
Morganfield, better known as Muddy Waters, played a
major role in creating the post–World War II electric blues.

Waters, whose nickname came from his proclivity for
playing in a creek as a boy, grew up in the cotton country
of the Mississippi Delta, where he was raised principally
by his grandmother on the Stovall plantation near
Clarksdale, Miss. He taught himself to play harmonica as
a child and took up guitar at age 17. He eagerly absorbed
the classic Delta blues styles of Robert Johnson, Son
House, and others while developing a style of his own. As
a young man, he drove a tractor on the sharecropped
plantation, and on weekends he operated the cabin in
which he lived as a "juke house," where visitors could party
and imbibe moonshine whiskey made by Waters. He performed both on his own and in a band, occasionally earning
a little money playing at house parties. He was first
recorded in 1941, for the U.S. Library of Congress by
archivist Alan Lomax, who had come to Mississippi in
search of Johnson (who had already died by that time).

In 1943 Waters—like millions of other African Americans
in the South who moved to cities in the North and West
during the Great Migration from 1916 to 1970—relocated
to Chicago. There he began playing clubs and bars on the
city's South and West sides while earning a living working
in a paper mill and later driving a truck. In 1944 he bought
his first electric guitar, which cut more easily through the
noise of crowded bars. He soon broke with country blues
by playing electric guitar in a shimmering slide style. In 1946
pianist Sunnyland Slim, another Delta native, helped Waters
land a contract with Aristocrat Records, for which he made

several unremarkable recordings. By 1948 Aristocrat had become Chess Records (taking its name from Leonard and Phil Chess, the Polish immigrant brothers who owned and operated it), and Waters was recording a string of hits for it that began with "I Feel Like Going Home" and "I Can't Be Satisfied." His early, aggressive, electrically amplified band—including pianist Otis Spann, guitarist Jimmie Rodgers, and harmonica virtuoso Little Walter—created closely integrated support for his passionate singing, which featured dramatic shouts, swoops, and falsetto moans. His repertoire, much of which he composed, included lyrics that were mournful ("Blow Wind Blow," "Trouble No More"), boastful ("Got My Mojo Working," "I'm Your Hoochie Coochie Man"), and frankly sensual (the unusual 15-bar blues "Rock Me"). In the process Waters became the foremost exponent of modern Chicago blues.

Tours of clubs in the South and Midwest in the 1940s and '50s gave way after 1958 to concert tours of the United States and Europe, including frequent dates at jazz, folk, and blues festivals. Over the years, some of Chicago's premier blues musicians did stints in Waters's band, including harmonica players James Cotton and Junior Wells, as well as guitarist Buddy Guy. Toward the end of his career, Waters concentrated on singing and played guitar only occasionally. A major influence on a variety of rock musicians—most notably the Rolling Stones (who took their name from his song "Rollin' Stone" and made a pilgrimage to Chess to record)—Waters was inducted into the Rock and Roll Hall of Fame in 1987.

## BILLIE HOLIDAY

(b. April 7, 1915, Philadelphia, Pa., U.S.—d. July 17, 1959, New York, N.Y.),

Billie Holiday, born Elinore Harris, was one of the greatest American jazz singers from the 1930s to the '50s.

*Billie Holiday, 1958.* Reprinted with permission of *Down Beat* magazine

Eleanora (her preferred spelling for Elinore) Harris was the daughter of Clarence Holiday, a professional musician who for a time played guitar with the Fletcher Henderson band. She and her mother used her maternal grandfather's surname, Fagan, for a time; then in 1920 her mother married a man surnamed Gough, and both she and Eleanora adopted his name. It is probable that in neither case did her mother have Eleanora's name legally changed. The singer later adopted her natural father's last name and took the name Billie from a favourite movie actress, Billie Dove. In 1928 she moved with her mother from Baltimore, Md. (where she had spent her childhood), to New York City, and after three years of subsisting by various means, she found a job singing in a Harlem nightclub. She had had no formal musical training, but, with an instinctive sense of musical structure and with a wealth of experience gathered at the root level of jazz and blues, she developed a singing style that was deeply moving and individual.

In 1933 Holiday made her first recordings, with Benny Goodman and others. Two years later a series of recordings with Teddy Wilson and members of Count Basie's band brought her wider recognition and launched her career as the leading jazz singer of her time. She toured with Basie and with Artie Shaw in 1937 and 1938 and in the latter year opened at the plush Café Society in New York City. About 1940 she began to perform exclusively in cabarets and in concert. Her recordings between 1936 and 1942 marked her peak years. During that period she was often associated with saxophonist Lester Young, who gave her the nickname "Lady Day."

In 1947 Holiday was arrested for a narcotics violation and spent a year in a rehabilitation centre. No longer able to obtain a cabaret license to work in New York City, Holiday nonetheless packed New York's Carnegie Hall 10 days after her release. She continued to perform in concert and in clubs outside of New York City, and she made several tours during her later years. Her constant struggle with heroin addiction ravaged her voice, although not her technique.

Holiday's dramatic intensity rendered any lyric profound. Among the songs identified with her were "Fine and Mellow," "The Man I Love," "Billie's Blues," "God Bless the Child," and "I Wished on the Moon," and "Strange Fruit," the musical rendition of an anti-lynching poem written by a New York schoolteacher. The vintage years of Holiday's professional and private liaison with Young were marked by some of the best recordings of the interplay between a vocal line and an instrumental obbligato. In 1956 she wrote an autobiography, *Lady Sings the Blues* (with William Dufty), that was made into a motion picture in 1972.

## FRANK SINATRA

(b. Dec. 12, 1915, Hoboken, N.J., U.S.—d. May 14, 1998, Los Angeles, Calif.)

F rancis Albert Sinatra, or Frank Sinatra, was an American singer and motion-picture actor who, through a long career and a very public personal life, became one of the most sought-after performers in the entertainment industry; he is often hailed as the greatest American singer of 20th-century popular music.

Sinatra's father, Martin, was a tavern owner and part-time prizefighter, and his mother, Natalie—known to all as "Dolly"—was a domineering influence in both local politics and in her son's life and career. Upon hearing the recordings of Bing Crosby, Sinatra was inspired as a teenager to choose popular singing as a vocation. He joined a local singing group, which toured the country that year, but Sinatra was the only member with serious musical ambitions, and they soon disbanded. For the next few years, Sinatra sang with local dance bands and for remote radio broadcasts. In 1939, while singing and waiting tables in Englewood Cliffs, New Jersey, he was discovered and hired by trumpeter Harry James.

### THE BAND SINGER

Sinatra's six-month tenure with the James band resulted in 10 commercial recordings featuring the young singer. On songs such as "From the Bottom of My Heart," "My Buddy," and "Ciribiribin," Sinatra's warm baritone and sensitivity to lyrics are well showcased. The best-known of the James-

Sinatra recordings is "All or Nothing at All"—unsuccessful in 1939 but a million-seller when rereleased in 1943, after both men had become stars. Sinatra's reputation among industry musicians grew swiftly, and James graciously freed Sinatra from his contract when the singer received a more lucrative offer from bandleader Tommy Dorsey in December 1939.

During the Dorsey period Sinatra proved his mastery of both ballads and up-tempo numbers, and Dorsey arrangers soon tailored their arrangements to highlight Sinatra's skills. Sinatra was featured on memorable recordings such as "I'll Never Smile Again," "I'll Be Seeing You," "Without a Song," and "Oh! Look at Me Now." The 83 commercial recordings that Sinatra made with the Dorsey band from 1940 to 1942 represent his first major body of work.

By 1942 Sinatra's fame had eclipsed that of Dorsey, and the singer yearned for a solo career. After months of bitter negotiations, Sinatra left the Dorsey organization in late 1942; within weeks, he was a cultural phenomenon. As such, he was soon dubbed "Frankieboy," "The Sultan of Swoon," and, most popularly, "The Voice."

## THE COLUMBIA YEARS

A strike by the American Federation of Musicians against the major record companies curtailed Sinatra's recording output during most of 1943–44. His solo recording career for Columbia Records began in earnest in November 1944, when he made dozens of recordings within a three-month period. Songs such as "If You Are but a Dream," "I Fall in Love Too Easily," and his theme song at that time, "Put Your Dreams Away," are some of the first recordings in what would come to be known to fans as the "Columbia era" (1943–52).

Sinatra's success continued unabated until the late 1940s, when he garnered much negative press; it was about this time that the public first read reports of his friendships with organized-crime figures. There was also the widely reported incident, and resulting lawsuit, in which Sinatra punched a gossip columnist, an action for which Sinatra received some vindication in later years when it was revealed that the columnist had collaborated with the FBI to discredit Sinatra. Sinatra began a five-year period of professional decline and personal depression. His divorce from first wife, Nancy, in 1951 and his subsequent stormy marriage to actress Ava Gardner further harmed his reputation. In 1952 his Columbia recording contract was not renewed, his talent agency discontinued its sponsorship, and his network television show was canceled; Sinatra was considered a has-been. Ironically, several of Sinatra's recordings from this period are now considered among his best, especially his 1951 recording of "I'm a Fool to Want You."

## THE ACTOR

Sinatra appeared in several films throughout the 1940s, the best among them being the musicals in which he costarred with dancer Gene Kelly. Of these, *Anchors Aweigh* (1945) and *Take Me Out to the Ballgame* (1949) are pleasant diversions, whereas *On the Town* (1949) ranks among the greatest of film musicals. It was acting, rather than music, that precipitated Sinatra's comeback in 1953. He played the role of the scrappy, tragic soldier, Maggio, in *From Here to Eternity* (1953), and his performance earned him an Oscar for best supporting actor. Sinatra went on to become one of the top film stars of the 1950s and '60s. The political thriller *The Manchurian Candidate* (1962) is perhaps Sinatra's greatest film and features his best performance. In later years, he was memorable in *The Detective* (1968) and in his final starring role in *The First Deadly Sin* (1980).

*Frank Sinatra, sometimes called "Ol' Blue Eyes," is photographed here in 1945 in front of a CBS radio microphone.* Hulton Archive/Getty Images

## The Capitol Years

In 1953 Sinatra's musical style took a dramatic turn. He signed with Capitol Records and, throughout the next nine years, issued a series of recordings widely regarded as his finest body of work. He is often credited with inventing the "concept album"—a collection of songs built around a single theme or mood. His new approach also demanded new arrangements. The in-house arrangers at Capitol were among the best, and with them he produced outstanding up-tempo albums such as *Come Fly with Me* (1958) and *Come Dance with Me!* (1959), as well as more-melancholy works such as *Where Are You?* (1957) and *No One Cares* (1959).

Although Sinatra worked with many extraordinary arrangers, it was Nelson Riddle who, in Sinatra's words, was "the greatest arranger in the world," and critics agreed. Riddle employed everything from quartets to 50-piece orchestras for ballad arrangements that were often characterized by a dominant solo instrument (particularly a mournful trombone). For swing tunes, Riddle developed his trademark "heartbeat rhythm," a steady, driving beat, meant to emulate "the pulse rate of the human heart after a brisk walk," in Riddle's words. Virtually all of the albums the Sinatra-Riddle team made for Capitol—including *In the Wee Small Hours* (1955), *Songs for Swingin' Lovers!* (1956), and *Only the Lonely* (1958)—are masterpieces.

Despite the importance of the Capitol arrangers in determining Sinatra's new sound, the resulting albums were still very much dominated by the singer himself. Sinatra's voice had deepened and grown in power, and his failed marriage to Gardner had infused his ballad singing with a heretofore unseen emotional urgency. He attacked swing numbers with abandon and displayed his jazz influences with an uncanny sense of syncopation and an innate knowledge of "blue notes." Two of his most heralded recordings—*I've Got You Under My Skin* (1956) and *One for My Baby* (1958)—illustrate well his varied approach to moods and tempi.

## THE RAT PACK AND THE MOB

During the late 1950s and early '60s, Sinatra frequently appeared on stage and in films with his close-knit band of friends known variously as "The Clan," "The Summit," or, most popularly, "The Rat Pack." The group performed a largely ad-libbed act of boozy, racial, and misogynist humour that seems dated to the contemporary listener, but was seen as the height of swinging sophistication in the 1960s.

It was also about this time that Sinatra generated more controversy for his connections with organized crime, although most critics now acknowledge that Sinatra's association with underworld figures was largely one of involuntary servitude. There is no question, however, that his fraternizing with notorious criminals such as Sam Giancana eroded his fan base and jeopardized his political friendships.

## THE REPRISE YEARS

Sinatra founded Reprise Records in 1960 and was allowed to record there simultaneously with his Capitol contract, which expired in 1962. During the early 1960s, Sinatra recorded at a furious pace, releasing some 14 albums of new material during the years 1961–63. Sinatra's prodigiousness during these years resulted in some quickly recorded albums of uneven quality, but there were also several classics on par with the best of his Capitol work. His two 1960s masterpieces, *September of My Years* (1965) and the partnership with Brazilian songwriter Antonio Carlos Jobim, *Francis Albert Sinatra and Antonio Carlos Jobim* (1967), rank among Sinatra's greatest albums. He also had success with the hit singles "Strangers in the Night" (1966), "That's Life" (1967), and "My Way" (1969).

## THE MATURE YEARS

Sinatra announced his retirement in 1971, but by 1973 he was recording once again. In his last two decades as a recording artist, he released only seven albums of new material. His well-regarded albums of later years include volume one of the ambitious three-disc *Trilogy* (1980), the ballad collection *She Shot Me Down* (1981), and *L.A. Is My Lady* (1984), which featured an all-star orchestra. He returned to the recording studio after nearly a decade's absence to record *Duets* (1993) and *Duets II* (1994), which paired Sinatra with several contemporary popular singers. The *Duets* albums sold millions of copies and were Sinatra's final recordings.

In addition to his curtailed recording activity, Sinatra virtually retired from films during his later years. He concentrated instead on live performance and gave hundreds of international concerts from the late 1970s, with his final public performance in 1995. Although he suffered from failing memory and various physical infirmities during his last few years, he remained a compelling showman to the end.

## EDITH PIAF

(b. Dec. 19, 1915, Paris, France—d. Oct. 11, 1963, Paris)

Edith Giovanna Gassion—known professionally as Edith Piaf—was a French singer and actress whose interpretation of the *chanson*, or French ballad, made her internationally famous. Among her trademark songs were "Non, je ne regrette rien" ("No, I Don't Regret Anything") and "La Vie en rose" (literally "Life in Pink" [i.e., through "rose-coloured glasses," from an optimistic point of view]).

Piaf's songs and singing style seemed to reflect the tragedies of her own difficult life. Her mother, a café singer, abandoned her at birth, and she was taken in by her grandmother, who reared the girl in a house of prostitution. Piaf became blind at the age of three as a complication of meningitis but recovered her sight four years later. A few years after that she joined her father, a circus acrobat, and accompanied him while he performed. She sang in the streets of Paris until discovered by Louis Leplée, a cabaret owner, who gave her her first nightclub job. It was Leplée who began calling her "la môme piaf," Parisian slang for "little sparrow," in apparent reference to her diminutive size—under 5 feet (142 cm) tall and about 90 pounds (40 kg) in weight. She later adopted the name professionally. Her debut was acclaimed by the actor Maurice Chevalier, who was in the audience that night.

In 1935 Piaf made her theatrical debut, and within a few years she was singing in the large music halls of Paris. Initially her material was standard music hall fare, but eventually she had songwriters such as Marguerite Monnot and Michel Emer writing songs specifically for her. In the mid-1940s she became a mentor to the young Yves Montand, and she worked with him in the film *Étoile sans lumière* (1946; "Star Without Light"). She had an affair with the middleweight boxer Marcel Cerdan, who died in a plane crash on his way to meet her. Her unhappy personal life and unadorned though dramatic style underlined her expressive mezzo-soprano voice, and she was able to move audiences wherever she or her recordings traveled.

In addition to singing, she recorded her thoughts about her life in two books, *Au bal de la chance* (1958; "At the Ball of Fortune"; Eng. trans. *The Wheel of Fortune*) and the posthumously published *Ma vie* (1964; "My Life"; Eng. trans. 1990). Piaf's recordings remain available in the 21st century, and she has been the subject of several biographies as well as plays and movies.

## NAT KING COLE

(b. March 17, 1917, Montgomery, Ala., U.S.—d. Feb. 15, 1965, Santa Monica, Calif.)

American musician Nat King Cole (the byname of Nathaniel Adams Cole) was hailed as one of the best and most influential pianists and small-group leaders of the swing era. Cole attained his greatest commercial success, however, as a vocalist specializing in warm ballads and light swing.

Cole grew up in Chicago where, by age 12, he sang and played organ in the church where his father was pastor. He formed his first jazz group, the Royal Dukes, five years later. In 1937, after touring with a black musical revue, he began playing in jazz clubs in Los Angeles. There he formed the King Cole Trio (originally King Cole and His Swingsters), with guitarist Oscar Moore and bassist Wesley Prince (later replaced by Johnny Miller). The trio specialized in swing music with a delicate touch in that they did not employ a drummer; also unique were the voicings of piano and guitar, often juxtaposed to sound like a single instrument. An influence on jazz pianists such as Oscar Peterson, Cole was known for a compact, syncopated piano style with clean, spare, melodic phrases.

During the late 1930s and early '40s the trio made several instrumental recordings, as well as others that featured their harmonizing vocals. They found their greatest success, however, when Cole began doubling as a solo singer. Their first chart success, "Straighten Up and Fly Right" (1943), was followed by hits such as "Sweet Lorraine," "It's Only a Paper Moon," "(I Love You) For Sentimental Reasons," and "Route 66." Eventually, Cole's piano playing took a backseat to his singing career. Noted for his warm tone and flawless phrasing, Cole was regarded among the top male vocalists, although jazz critics tended to regret his near-abandonment of the piano. He first recorded with a full orchestra (the trio serving as rhythm section) in 1946 for "The Christmas Song," a holiday standard and one of Cole's biggest-selling recordings. By the 1950s, he worked almost exclusively as a singer, with such notable arrangers as Nelson Riddle and Billy May providing lush orchestral accompaniment. "Nature Boy," "Mona Lisa," "Too Young," "A Blossom Fell," and "Unforgettable" were among his major hits of the period. He occasionally revisited his jazz roots, as on the outstanding album *After Midnight* (1956), which proved that Cole's piano skills had not diminished.

Cole's popularity allowed him to become the first African American to host a network variety program, *The Nat King Cole Show*, which debuted on NBC television in 1956. The show fell victim to the bigotry of the times, however, and was canceled after one season; few sponsors were willing to be associated with a black entertainer. Cole had greater success with concert performances during the late 1950s and early '60s and twice toured with his own vaudeville-style reviews, *The Merry World of Nat King Cole* (1961) and *Sights and Sounds* (1963). His hits of the early '60s—"Ramblin' Rose," "Those Lazy, Hazy, Crazy Days of Summer," and "L-O-V-E"—indicate that he was moving even farther away from his jazz roots and concentrating almost exclusively on mainstream pop. Adapting his style, however, was one factor that kept Cole popular up to his early death from lung cancer in 1965.

The prejudices of the era in which Cole lived hindered his potential for even greater stardom. His talents extended beyond singing and piano playing: he excelled as a relaxed and humorous stage personality, and he was also a capable actor, evidenced by his performances in the films *Istanbul* (1957), *China Gate* (1957), *Night of the Quarter Moon* (1959), and *Cat Ballou* (1965); he also played himself in *The Nat "King" Cole Musical Story* (1955) and portrayed blues legend W.C. Handy in *St. Louis Blues* (1958). His daughter Natalie is also a popular singer who achieved her greatest chart success in 1991 with "Unforgettable," an electronically created duet with her father.

## ELLA FITZGERALD

(b. April 25, 1917, Newport News, Va., U.S.—d. June 15, 1996, Beverly Hills, Calif.)

American singer Ella Fitzgerald became world famous for the wide range and rare sweetness of her voice and was an international legend during a career that spanned some six decades.

Singing in a style influenced by the jazz vocalist Connee Boswell, Fitzgerald won amateur talent contests in New York City before she joined the Chick Webb orchestra in 1935; Webb became the teenaged Fitzgerald's guardian when her mother died. She made her first recording, "Love and Kisses," in 1935, and her first hit, "A-Tisket, A-Tasket," followed in 1938. After Webb's death in 1939, she led his band until it broke up in 1942. She then soloed in cabarets and theatres, toured internationally with such pop and jazz stars as Benny Goodman, Louis Armstrong, Duke Ellington, the Mills Brothers, the Ink Spots, and Dizzy Gillespie, and recorded prolifically.

During much of her early career she had been noted for singing and recording novelty songs. Her status rose dramatically in the 1950s when jazz impresario Norman Granz became her manager. From 1956 to 1964 she recorded a 19-volume series of "songbooks," in which she interpreted nearly 250 outstanding songs by Richard Rodgers, Cole Porter, George Gershwin, Duke Ellington, Jerome Kern, Irving Berlin, and Johnny Mercer. This material, combined with the best jazz instrumental support, clearly demonstrated Fitzgerald's remarkable interpretative skills. Although her diction was excellent, her rendition of lyrics was intuitive rather than studied. For many years the star attraction of Granz's Jazz at the Philharmonic concert tours, she was also one of the best-selling jazz vocal recording artists in history. She appeared in films (notably *Pete Kelly's Blues* in 1955), on television, and in concert halls throughout the world. She also recorded a number of live concert albums and produced a notable duet version of *Porgy and Bess* (1957) with Armstrong. During the 1970s she began to experience serious health problems, but she continued to perform periodically, even after heart surgery in 1986, until about 1993.

Fitzgerald's clear tone and wide vocal range were complemented by her mastery of rhythm, harmony, intonation, and articulation. She was an excellent ballad singer, conveying a winsome, ingenuous quality. Her infectious scat singing brought excitement to such concert recordings as *Mack the Knife: Ella in Berlin* and was widely imitated by others. She won 12 Grammy Awards and several other honours.

## LEONARD BERNSTEIN

(b. Aug. 25, 1918, Lawrence, Mass., U.S.—d. Oct. 14, 1990, New York, N.Y.)

American conductor, composer, and pianist Leonard Bernstein was noted for his accomplishments in both classical and popular music, for his flamboyant conducting style, and for his pedagogic flair, especially in concerts for young people.

Bernstein played piano from age 10. He attended Boston Latin School; Harvard University (A.B., 1939), where he took courses in music theory with Arthur Tillman Merritt and counterpoint with Walter Piston; the Curtis Institute of Music, Philadelphia (1939–41), where he studied conducting with Fritz Reiner and orchestration with Randall Thompson; and the Berkshire Music Center at Tanglewood, Mass., where he studied conducting with Serge Koussevitzky. In 1943 Bernstein was appointed assistant conductor of the New York Philharmonic; the first signal of his forthcoming success came on Nov. 14, 1943, when he was summoned unexpectedly to substitute for the conductor Bruno Walter. His technical self-assurance under difficult circumstances and his interpretive excellence made an immediate impression and marked the beginning of a brilliant career. He subsequently conducted the New York City Center orchestra (1945–47) and appeared as guest conductor in the United States, Europe, and Israel. In 1953 he became the first American to conduct at La Scala in Milan. From 1958 to 1969 Bernstein was conductor and musical director of the New York Philharmonic, becoming the first American-born holder of those posts. With this orchestra he made several international tours in Latin America, Europe, the Soviet Union, and Japan. His popularity increased through his appearances not only as conductor and pianist but also as a commentator and entertainer. Bernstein explained classical music to young listeners on such television shows as "Omnibus" and "Young People's Concerts." After 1969 he continued to write music and to perform as a guest conductor with several symphonies throughout the world.

As a composer Bernstein made skillful use of diverse elements ranging from biblical themes, as in the *Symphony No. 1* (1942; also called *Jeremiah*) and the *Chichester Psalms* (1965); to jazz rhythms, as in the *Symphony No. 2* (1949; *The Age of Anxiety*), after a poem by W.H. Auden; to Jewish liturgical themes, as in the *Symphony No. 3* (1963; *Kaddish*). His best-known works are the musicals *On the Town* (1944; filmed 1949), *Wonderful Town* (1953; filmed 1958), *Candide* (1956), and the very popular *West Side Story* (1957; filmed 1961), written in collaboration with Stephen Sondheim and Jerome Robbins. He also wrote the scores for the ballets *Fancy Free* (1944), *Facsimile* (1946), and *Dybbuk* (1974), and he composed the music for the film *On the Waterfront* (1954), for which he received an Academy Award nomination. His *Mass*, written especially for the occasion, was performed at the opening of the John F. Kennedy Center for the Performing Arts in Washington, D.C., in September 1971. In 1989 he conducted two historic performances of Ludwig van Beethoven's *Symphony No. 9 in D Minor* (1824; *Choral*), which were held in East and West Berlin to celebrate the fall of the Berlin Wall.

Bernstein published a collection of lectures, *The Joy of Music* (1959); *Young People's Concerts, for Reading and Listening* (1962, rev. ed. 1970); *The Infinite Variety of Music* (1966); and *The Unanswered Question* (1976), taken from his Charles Eliot Norton lectures at Harvard University (1973).

## PETE SEEGER

(b. May 3, 1919, New York, N.Y., U.S.)

American singer Pete Seeger sustained the folk music tradition and was one of the principal inspirations for younger performers in the folk revival of the 1960s.

Seeger was born to a musically gifted family. His father was the influential musicologist Charles Seeger, and his mother, Constance, was a violin instructor at Juilliard. But it was perhaps the introspective poems of his uncle, Alan Seeger, that most inspired Pete's songwriting. Leaving Harvard after two years in 1938, Seeger hitchhiked and rode freight trains around the country, gathering country ballads, work songs, and hymns and developing a remarkable virtuosity on the five-string banjo. In 1940 he organized the Almanac Singers, a quartet that also featured the folk-singer and composer Woody Guthrie, and appeared at union halls, farm meetings, and wherever his populist political sentiments were welcome. The group disbanded soon after World War II.

In 1948 he formed another group, the Weavers—with Lee Hays, Ronnie Gilbert, and Fred Hellerman—which achieved considerable success on college campuses, in concert, and on several records. Shortly after the group achieved national fame, however, a great deal of controversy was stirred up concerning Seeger's previous activities in left-wing and labour politics, and the Weavers suddenly found themselves blacklisted by much of the entertainment industry. Finding it increasingly difficult to make concert bookings or to sell records, the group broke up in 1952 but reunited three years later when a Christmas concert at Carnegie Hall sparked new interest in their music and message. Seeger left the group in 1958, and it disbanded in 1963. (The Weavers gave two reunion concerts in 1980, and a motion picture documentary about the group, *Wasn't That a Time!*, was released in 1982.)

After the 1950s Seeger usually worked alone or with his family (brother Mike was a member of New Lost City Ramblers; sister Peggy, a singer and multi-instrumentalist, became one of the driving forces behind the British folk music revival with Ewan McColl, her partner in life and in music making). As a solo performer, Seeger was still a victim of blacklisting, especially after his 1961 conviction for contempt of Congress stemming from his refusal in 1955 to answer questions posed to him by the House Committee on Un-American Activities concerning his political activities. Although Seeger's conviction was overturned the following year in an appeal, for several years afterward the major networks refused to allow him to make television appearances. In later years the controversy surrounding the performer gradually subsided.

A beloved fixture at folk festivals, Seeger was given major credit for fostering the growth of the hootenanny (a gathering of performers playing and singing for each other, often with audience participation) as a characteristically informal and personal style of entertainment. Among the many songs that he wrote himself or in collaboration with others were "Where Have All the Flowers Gone," "If I Had a Hammer," "Kisses Sweeter Than Wine," and "Turn, Turn, Turn." His *The Incompleat Folksinger* (1972) is a collection of his writings on the history of folk songs, civil rights, and performers in his lifetime.

In the 1970s and '80s he was active in a program to remove pollution from the Hudson River, building the Hudson River sloop *Clearwater*, promoting festivals for its maintenance, and engaging in environmental demonstrations, particularly antinuclear ones. During this period Seeger also performed regularly with singer-songwriter Arlo Guthrie, Woody Guthrie's son. By the 1990s Seeger had transcended the accusations of the McCarthy era, and he was regarded as a cherished American institution. The motto inscribed on his banjo—"This machine surrounds hate and forces it to surrender"—seemed to have been proven correct. In 1994 he was awarded a National Medal of Arts, the first of many honours that he received as the century approached its turn. Seeger was inducted into the Rock and Roll Hall of Fame in 1996, and the following year he received his first Grammy Award, for *Pete* (1996). In 2009 he won a second Grammy, for a collection that found the artist approaching his 90th birthday with undiminished spirit and hope. Seeger's "musical autobiography" *Where Have All the Flowers Gone* was published in 1996.

## RAVI SHANKAR

(b. April 7, 1920, Benares [now Varanasi], India)

Indian musician, player of the sitar, composer, and founder of the National Orchestra of India, Ravi Shankar was influential in stimulating Western appreciation of Indian music.

Born into a Bengali Brahman (highest caste in Hindu tradition) family, Shankar spent most of his youth studying music and dance and touring extensively in India and Europe with his brother Uday's dance troupe. At age 18 Shankar gave up dancing, and for the next seven years he studied the sitar (a long-necked stringed instrument of the lute family) under the noted musician Ustad Allauddin Khan. After serving as music director of All-India Radio from 1948 until 1956, he began a series of European and American tours.

In the course of his long career, Shankar became the world's best-known exponent of Hindustani (North Indian) classical music, performing with India's most distinguished percussionists and making dozens of successful recordings. He composed the film scores for the Indian director Satyajit Ray's famous *Apu* trilogy (1955–59). In 1962 Shankar founded the Kinnara School of Music in Bombay (now Mumbai) and then established a second Kinnara School in Los Angeles in 1967; he closed both schools some years later, however, having become disenchanted with institutional teaching.

*Indian musician Ravi Shankar plays a sitar in 2004 at a function paying tribute to the former Beatle George Harrison.* Raveendran/AFP/Getty Images

Beginning in the 1960s, his concert performances with the American violinist Yehudi Menuhin and his association with George Harrison, lead guitarist of the then wildly popular British musical group the Beatles, helped bring Indian music to the attention of the West. Shankar won Grammy Awards in 1967 for his album *East Meets West*, with Menuhin; in 1972 for *The Concert for Bangladesh*, with Harrison; and in 2002 for *Full Circle*, a live recording of a performance at Carnegie Hall with his daughter Anoushka Shankar (born 1981).

Especially remarkable among Shankar's accomplishments is his equally expert participation in traditional Indian music and in Indian-influenced Western music. Most characteristic of the latter activity are his concerti for sitar and orchestra, particularly *Raga Mala* ("Garland of Ragas"), first performed in 1981. In addition to his strictly musical undertakings, Shankar wrote two autobiographies, published 30 years apart: *My Life, My Music* (1969) and *Raga Mala* (1999). Shankar continued giving concerts into his 80s, frequently accompanied by Anoushka, who, like her father, specialized in blending Indian and Western traditions. Also a daughter of Shankar is multiple-Grammy-winning singer-songwriter Norah Jones (born 1979), who found her niche in an eclectic blend of jazz, pop, and country music.

## CHARLIE PARKER

(b. Aug. 29, 1920, Kansas City, Kan., U.S.—d. March 12, 1955, New York, N.Y.)

American alto saxophonist, composer, and bandleader, Charlie Parker was the principal stimulus of the modern jazz idiom known as bebop, and—together with Louis Armstrong and Ornette Coleman—was one of the great revolutionary geniuses in jazz.

Parker grew up in Kansas City, Missouri, during the great years of Kansas City jazz and began playing alto saxophone when he was 13. At 14 he quit school and began performing with youth bands, and at 16 he was married—the first of his four marriages. The most significant of his early stylistic influences were tenor saxophone innovator Lester Young and the advanced swing-era alto saxophonist Buster Smith, in whose band Parker played in 1937.

Parker recorded his first solos as a member of Jay McShann's band, with whom he toured the eastern United States in 1940–42. It was at this time that his childhood nickname "Yardbird" was shortened to "Bird." His growing friendship with trumpeter Dizzy Gillespie led Parker to develop his new music in avant-garde jam sessions in New York's Harlem. Bebop grew out of these experiments by Parker, Gillespie, and their adventurous colleagues; the music featured chromatic harmonies and, influenced especially by Parker, small note values and seemingly impulsive rhythms. Parker and Gillespie played in Earl Hines's swing-oriented band and Billy Eckstine's more modern band. In 1944 they formed their own small ensemble, the first working bebop group. The next year Parker made a series of classic recordings with Red Norvo, with Gillespie's quintet ("Salt Peanuts" and "Shaw Nuff"), and for his own first solo recording session ("Billie's Bounce," "Now's the Time," and "Koko"). The new music he was espousing aroused controversy but also attracted a devoted audience. By this time Parker had been addicted to drugs for several years. While working in Los Angeles with Gillespie's group and others, Parker collapsed in the summer of 1946, suffering from heroin and alcohol addiction, and was confined to a state mental hospital.

Following his release after six months, Parker formed his own quintet, which included trumpeter Miles Davis and drummer Max Roach. He performed regularly in New

York City and on tours to major U.S. cities and abroad, played in a Gillespie concert at Carnegie Hall (1947), recorded with Machito's Afro-Cuban band (1949–50), and toured with the popular Jazz at the Philharmonic troupe (1949). A Broadway nightclub, Birdland, was named after him, and he performed there on opening night in late 1949; Birdland became the most famous of 1950s jazz clubs.

The recordings Parker made for the Savoy and Dial labels in 1945–48 (including the "Koko" session, "Relaxin' at Camarillo," "Night in Tunisia," "Embraceable You," "Donna Lee," "Ornithology," and "Parker's Mood") document his greatest period. He had become the model for a generation of young saxophonists. His alto tone was hard and ideally expressive, with a crying edge to his highest tones and little vibrato. One of his most influential innovations was the establishment of eighth notes as the basic units of his phrases. The phrases themselves he broke into irregular lengths and shapes and applied asymmetrical accenting.

Parker's most popular records, recorded in 1949–50, featured popular song themes and brief improvisations accompanied by a string orchestra. These recordings came at the end of a period of years when his narcotics and alcohol addictions had a less disruptive effect on his creative life. By the early 1950s, however, he had again begun to suffer from the cumulative effects of his excesses; while hospitalized for treatment of an ulcer, he was informed that he would die if he resumed drinking. He was banned from playing in New York City nightclubs for 15 months. He missed engagements and failed to pay his accompanying musicians, and his unreliability led his booking agency to stop scheduling performances for him. Even Birdland, where he had played regularly, eventually fired him. His two-year-old daughter died of pneumonia; his fourth marriage fell apart. He twice attempted suicide and again spent time in a mental hospital.

If Parker's life was chaotic in the 1950s, he nonetheless retained his creative edge. From roughly 1950 he abandoned his quintet to perform with a succession of usually small, ad hoc jazz groups; on occasion he performed with Latin American bands, big jazz bands (including Stan Kenton's and Woody Herman's), or string ensembles. Recording sessions with several quartets and quintets produced such pieces as "Confirmation," "Chi-Chi," and "Bloomdido," easily the equals of his best 1940s sessions. Outstanding performances that were recorded at concerts and in nightclubs also attest to his vigorous creativity during this difficult period. He wanted to study with classical composer Edgard Varèse, but, before the two could collaborate, Parker's battle with ulcers and cirrhosis of the liver got the better of him. While visiting his friend Baroness Nica de Koenigswarter, he was persuaded to remain at her home because of his illness; there, a week after his last engagement, he died of a heart attack.

The impact of Parker's tone and technique has already been discussed; his concepts of harmony and melody were equally influential. Rejecting the diatonic scales common to earlier jazz, Parker improvised melodies and composed themes using chromatic scales. Often he played phrases that implied added harmonies or created passages that were only distantly related to his songs' harmonic foundations (chord changes). Yet for all the tumultuous feelings in his solos, he created flowing melodic lines. At slow tempos as well as fast, his were intense improvisations that communicated complex, often subtle emotions. The harmonies and inflections of the blues, which he played with passion and imagination, reverberated throughout his improvisations. Altogether, Parker's lyric art was a virtuoso music resulting from a coordination of nerve, muscle, and intellect that pressed human agility and creativity to their limits.

## TITO PUENTE

(b. April 20, 1923, New York, N.Y., U.S.—d. May 31, 2000, New York, N.Y.)

American bandleader, composer, and musician Tito Puente (born Ernesto Antonio Puente, Jr.) was one of the leading figures in Latin jazz. His bravura showmanship and string of mambo dance hits in the 1950s earned him the nickname "King of Mambo."

The son of Puerto Rican immigrants, Puente grew up in New York City's Spanish Harlem and became a professional musician at age 13. He later studied at the Juilliard School and eventually learned to play a number of instruments, including the piano, saxophone, vibraphone, and timbales (paired high-pitched drums). After an apprenticeship in the historic Machito Orchestra (a New York-based Latin jazz group established in 1939), he served in the navy during World War II.

In 1947 Puente formed his own 10-piece band, which he expanded two years later to include four trumpets, three trombones, and four saxophones, as well as a number of percussionists and vocalists. With other Latin musicians such as Tito Rodríguez and Pérez Prado, he helped give rise in the 1950s to the golden

*Legendary drummer Tito Puente performing in Nice, France, July of 1983.* Getty Images/AFP

age of mambo, a dance form of Cuban origin; his infectious energy and dynamic stage presence quickly made him a star. As his reputation grew, so too did his repertoire, through the addition of other Latin and Afro-Cuban dance rhythms such as Dominican merengue, Brazilian bossa nova, and Cuban cha-cha. The term *salsa* first appeared in the 1960s, when it was used to describe the music that had been the mainstay of Puente's repertoire for decades. Although salsa—as a specific genre—is rooted in the Cuban *son* music, the term has often been applied generically to a wide variety of popularized Latin dance forms, such as those performed by Puente. Aside from his activities as a bandleader and instrumentalist, Puente also wrote many songs, among which "Babarabatiri," "Ran Kan Kan," and "Oye Como Va" have been the most popular.

In the course of his career, Puente recorded some 120 albums and maintained a busy performance schedule, appearing with leading jazz musicians such as George Shearing and Woody Herman, as well as with many stars of Latin music and, in later years, with symphony orchestras. He also performed in several films, including *Radio Days* (1987) and *The Mambo Kings* (1992), and was responsible for introducing American audiences to a number of Latin musicians, most notably Cuban singer Celia Cruz. Puente received five Grammy Awards as well as numerous other honours, and he played 200 to 300 engagements a year until shortly before his death in 2000.

# HANK WILLIAMS

(b. Sept. 17, 1923, Georgiana, Ala., U.S.—d. Jan. 1, 1953, Oak Hill, W.Va.)

American singer, songwriter, and guitarist Hank Williams (born Hiram King Williams) in the 1950s arguably became country music's first superstar. An immensely talented songwriter and an impassioned vocalist, the "Hillbilly Shakespeare," as he often was called, also experienced great crossover success in the popular music market. His iconic status was amplified by his death at age 29 and by his reputation for hard living and heart-on-the-sleeve vulnerability.

As a boy, Williams was the musical protégé of Rufus Payne, an African American street performer who went by the name Tee-Tot and busked on the streets of Georgiana and Greenville, Ala. Probably taught his first chords by Payne, Williams began playing the guitar at age eight. He made his radio debut at age 13; formed his first band, Hank Williams and his Drifting Cowboys, at age 14; and early on began wearing the cowboy hats and western clothing that later were so associated with him. During World War II Williams commuted between Mobile, where he worked in a shipyard, and Montgomery, where he pursued a musical career. At this stage Williams began abusing alcohol, a problem that haunted him the rest of his life, but that came about partly as a result of his attempts to self-medicate agonizing back pain caused by a congenital spinal disorder. Later he would dull his physical pain with morphine, but when he sought to relieve the heartache of his tumultuous relationship with Audrey Sheppard, whom he married in 1942 (they divorced in 1952), alcohol remained his painkiller of choice.

In 1946 Williams landed a songwriting contract with Acuff-Rose Publications and began composing material for singer Molly O'Day. Later that year he received his first recording contract, with Sterling Records; however, it was on the start-up label MGM that he had his first hit, "Move It on Over" in 1947. Shortly thereafter he became a regular on the newly created *Louisiana Hayride* radio program based in Shreveport, La. His breakthrough moment came in 1949 with the release of "Lovesick Blues," an old show tune that Williams parlayed into a chart-topping hit, an invitation to join the Grand Ole Opry in Nashville, and international fame. More than half of the 66 recordings he would make under his own name (he also released a string of religious-themed recordings under the name Luke the Drifter) were Top Ten country and western hits, many of them reaching number one, including "Cold, Cold Heart," "Your Cheatin' Heart," "Hey, Good Lookin'," "Jambalaya (On the Bayou)," and "I'll Never Get Out of This World Alive." His extraordinary "Lost Highway" peaked at number 12.

Williams, who wrote most of his songs himself, crafted direct, emotionally honest lyrics with a poetic simplicity that spoke not only to fans of country and western music but to a much broader audience, as evidenced by the pop hit crooner Tony Bennett had with his cover of "Cold, Cold Heart" in 1951. Williams's music itself was not especially groundbreaking, though he was a deft synthesizer of blues, honky-tonk country, western swing, and other genres. However, his plaintive, bluesy phrasing was unique and became a touchstone of country music. Country music historian Bill Malone wrote that Williams "sang with the quality that has characterized every great hillbilly singer: utter sincerity." Despite Williams's many well-known heartbreak songs, it should also be remembered that he was capable of writing and singing with great joy and humour, as on, for example, "Howlin' at the Moon."

The last years of his life were suffused in increasing sadness and substance abuse. He died of a heart attack in a drug- and alcohol-induced stupor in the backseat of a car, probably in West Virginia, while being driven from Knoxville, Tenn., to a concert in Canton, Ohio. Red Foley, Roy Acuff, and Ernest Tubb, among others, sang Williams's gospel-influenced "I Saw the Light" at his funeral, which was attended by thousands. His son, Hank Williams, Jr., a successful country performer in his own right (like Williams's grandson, Hank Williams III), sang Williams's songs in the film biography *Your Cheatin' Heart* (1964).

## MARIA CALLAS

(b. Dec. 2, 1923, New York, N.Y., U.S.—d. Sept. 16, 1977, Paris, France)

American-born Greek operatic soprano Maria Callas, originally named Maria Cecilia Sophia Anna Kalogeropoulos, revived classical coloratura roles in the mid-20th century with her lyrical and dramatic versatility.

Callas was the daughter of Greek immigrants and early developed an interest in singing. Accompanied by her mother, she left the United States in 1937 to study at the Athens Conservatory with soprano Elvira de Hidalgo; in 1966 she became a Greek citizen and relinquished her U.S. citizenship. She sang locally in *Cavalleria rusticana* and *Boccaccio* and returned to the United States in 1945.

Her career began in earnest in August 1947, when she appeared in Verona in *La gioconda*. Soon, under the tutelage of conductor Tullio Serafin, she made debuts in Venice, Turin, and Florence. In 1949 she first appeared in Rome, Buenos Aires, and Naples, and in 1950 in Mexico City. Her powerful soprano voice, capable of sustaining both lyric and coloratura roles, was, although not perfect in control, intensely dramatic; combined with her strong sense of theatre and her scrupulously high artistic standards, it took her quickly to the forefront of contemporary opera stars. Her talents made possible the revival of 19th-century bel canto works, notably those of Bellini and Donizetti, that had long been dropped from standard repertoires.

Callas made her debut at the prestigious La Scala in Milan in 1950, singing in *I Vespri siciliani*. In 1952 she appeared at Covent Garden, London. Her American debut took place in November 1954 at Chicago's Lyric Opera in the title role of *Norma*, a performance she repeated before a record audience at the Metropolitan Opera in New York City. Callas's recordings were enthusiastically received, and she was one of the most popular singers of the period. Her much-publicized volatile temperament resulted in several protracted feuds with rivals and managers.

After a final operatic performance as Tosca at Covent Garden (July 1965), Callas made the film *Medea* (1971) and taught master classes in opera at Juilliard (1972) before a last U.S. and European concert tour (1973–74). By the time of her retirement, she had performed more than 40 different roles and had recorded more than 20 complete operas.

## CLIFTON CHENIER

(b. June 25, 1925, Opelousas, La., U.S. — d. Dec. 12, 1987, Lafayette, La.)

American popular musician Clifton Chenier was a pioneer in the development of zydeco music— a bluesy, southern Louisiana blend of French, African American, Native American, and Afro-Caribbean traditions. He was a master keyboard accordionist, a bold vocalist, and the unofficial (but virtually undisputed) "King of Zydeco."

Chenier was born to a family of sharecroppers (tenant farmers) in south-central Louisiana and spent much of his youth working in the cotton fields. He received his first accordion as a gift from his father, who was an established accordionist in the local house-party (dance) and Saturday-dinner circuit. Chenier immediately recruited a washboard (*frottoir*) player—his brother Cleveland—to provide the lively, syncopated scraping that has remained a rhythmic hallmark of zydeco music. Inspired by recordings of earlier accordion virtuoso Amadie (or Amédé) Ardoin, as well as by the live performances of many local Cajun and Creole musicians, Chenier quickly became a formidable force in the zydeco tradition.

Chenier left his hometown of Opelousas in his early 20s for Lake Charles in southwestern Louisiana, where he worked for several years as a truck driver for the nearby petroleum companies. During his off-hours he played and listened to music, and his musical style increasingly gravitated toward rhythm and blues. The emblematic features of zydeco—such as the French-based Louisiana Creole language and the ever-popular waltz and two-step dance forms—were never fully excised from his performances, however. In the mid-1950s Chenier signed with Specialty Records, for which he produced mostly rhythm-and-blues recordings with a zydeco tint, notably the hit song "Ay-Tete-Fee" (sung in Louisiana Creole). With his band, the Zodico Ramblers—which, aside from the keyboard accordion and washboard, featured drums, guitar, bass, piano, and saxophone—Chenier emerged as a star of rhythm and blues. His brilliance faded over the next decade, however, and his career remained inert for some years before it was revived and redirected by Arhoolie Records, a label specializing in recordings of regional music traditions. With Arhoolie's support and encouragement, Chenier recalibrated his music back toward its zydeco roots and released a number of successful albums, including *Louisiana Blues and Zydeco* (1965), *King of the Bayous* (1970), and *Bogalusa Boogie* (1975).

Throughout the 1970s Chenier toured nationally and internationally as the King of Zydeco, donning a large gold-and-burgundy mock crown in many of his performances to acknowledge and amplify his popular status. By late in the decade, however, both he and his music had lost their lustre; he had developed a severe kidney infection related to diabetes and had to have a portion of his foot amputated. Although Chenier experienced somewhat of a comeback in the early 1980s—when he expanded his band to include a trumpet—his illness continued to take its musical and physical toll, and he ultimately succumbed to it in 1987.

## B.B. KING

(b. Sept. 16, 1925, Itta Bena, near Indianola, Miss., U.S.)

American guitarist and singer B.B. King (born Riley B. King) was a principal figure in the development of blues and from whose style leading popular musicians drew inspiration.

King was reared in the Mississippi Delta, and gospel music in church was the earliest influence on his singing. To his own impassioned vocal calls, King played lyrical single-string guitar responses with a distinctive vibrato; his guitar style was influenced by T-Bone Walker, by delta blues players (including his cousin Bukka White), and by such jazz guitarists as Django Reinhardt and Charlie Christian. He worked for a time as a disk jockey in Memphis, Tennessee (notably at station WDIA), where he acquired the name B.B. (for Blues Boy) King. In 1951 he made a hit record of "Three O'Clock Blues," which led to virtually continuous tours of clubs and theatres throughout the country. He often played 300 or more one-night stands a year with his 13-piece band. A long succession of hits, including "Every Day I Have the Blues," "Sweet Sixteen," and "The Thrill Is Gone," enhanced his popularity. By the late 1960s rock guitarists acknowledged his influence and priority; they introduced King (and his guitar—which was named Lucille) to a broader white public, who until then had heard blues chiefly in derivative versions.

King's relentless touring strengthened his claim to the title of undisputed king of the blues, and he was a regular fixture on the *Billboard* charts through the mid-1980s. His strongest studio albums of this era were those that most closely tried to emulate the live experience, and he found commercial success through a series of all-star collaborations. On *Deuces Wild* (1997), King enlisted such artists as Van Morrison, Bonnie Raitt, and Eric Clapton to create a fusion of blues, pop, and country that dominated the blues charts for almost two years. Clapton and King collaborated on the more straightforward blues album *Riding with the King* (2000), which featured a collection of standards from King's catalog. He recaptured the pop magic of *Deuces Wild* with *80* (2005), a celebration of his 80th birthday that featured Sheryl Crow, John Mayer, and a standout performance by Elton John. King returned to his roots with *One Kind Favor* (2008), a collection of songs from the 1940s and '50s including blues classics by the likes of John Lee Hooker and Lonnie Johnson. Joining King in the simple four-part arrangements on the T-Bone Burnett–produced album were stalwart New Orleans pianist Dr. John, ace session drummer Jim Keltner, and stand-up bassist Nathan East. The album earned King his 15th Grammy Award.

In 2008 the B.B. King Museum and Delta Interpretive Center opened in Indianola, with exhibits dedicated to King's music, his influences, and the history of the delta region. King's autobiography, *Blues All Around Me*, written with David Ritz, was published in 1996.

## MILES DAVIS

(b. May 26, 1926, Alton, Ill., U.S.—d. Sept. 28, 1991, Santa Monica, Calif.)

American jazz musician Miles Dewey Davis III—or simply, Miles Davis—was a great trumpeter who as a bandleader and composer was one of the major influences on the art from the late 1940s.

## STARTING OUT

Davis grew up in East St. Louis, Ill., where his father was a prosperous dental surgeon. He began studying trumpet in his early teens; fortuitously, in light of his later stylistic development, his first teacher advised him to play without vibrato. Davis played with jazz bands in the St. Louis area before moving to New York City in 1944 to study at the Institute of Musical Art (now the Juilliard School)—although he skipped many classes and instead was schooled through jam sessions with masters such as Dizzy Gillespie and Charlie Parker. Davis and Parker recorded together often during the years 1945–48.

Davis's early playing was sometimes tentative and not always fully in tune, but his unique, intimate tone and his fertile musical imagination outweighed his technical shortcomings. By the early 1950s Davis had turned his limitations into considerable assets. Davis explored the trumpet's middle register, experimenting with harmonies and rhythms and varying the phrasing of his improvisations. With the occasional exception of multinote flurries, his melodic style was direct and unornamented.

## COOL JAZZ AND MODAL JAZZ

In the summer of 1948, Davis formed a nonet that included the renowned jazz artists Gerry Mulligan, J.J. Johnson, Kenny Clarke, and Lee Konitz, as well as players on French horn and tuba, instruments rarely heard in a jazz context. Mulligan, Gil Evans, and pianist John Lewis did most of the band's arrangements, which juxtaposed the flexible, improvisatory nature of bebop with a thickly textured orchestral sound. The group was short-lived but during its brief history recorded a dozen tracks that were originally released as singles (1949–50). These recordings changed the course of modern jazz and paved the way for the West Coast styles of the 1950s. The tracks were later collected in the album *Birth of the Cool* (1957).

During the early 1950s Davis recorded albums that rank among his best. In 1954, having overcome drug addiction, Davis embarked on a two-decade period during which he was considered the most innovative musician in jazz. He formed classic small groups in the 1950s that featured saxophone legends John Coltrane and Cannonball Adderley, pianists Red Garland and Bill Evans, bassist Paul Chambers, and drummers "Philly" Joe Jones and Jimmy Cobb. Davis's albums recorded during this era, including *'Round About Midnight* (1956), *Steamin'* (1956), and *Milestones* (1958), among others, affected the work of numerous other artists. He capped this period of his career with *Kind of Blue* (1959), perhaps the most celebrated album in the history of jazz. A mellow, relaxed collection, the album includes the finest recorded examples of modal jazz, a style in which improvisations are based upon sparse chords and nonstandard scales rather than on complex, frequently changing chords.

Released concurrently with the small-group recordings, Davis's albums with pieces arranged and conducted by Gil Evans—*Miles Ahead* (1957), *Porgy and Bess* (1958), and *Sketches of Spain* (1960)—were also monuments of the genre. The Davis-Evans collaborations were marked by complex arrangements, a near-equal emphasis on orchestra and soloist, and some of Davis's most soulful and emotionally powerful playing. Davis and Evans occasionally collaborated in later years, but never again so memorably as on these three masterful albums.

## FREE JAZZ AND FUSION

The early 1960s were transitional, less-innovative years for Davis. He began forming another soon-to-be-classic small group in late 1962 with bassist Ron Carter, pianist Herbie Hancock, and teenage drummer Tony Williams; tenor saxophonist Wayne Shorter joined the lineup in 1964. Davis's new quintet was characterized by a light, free sound and a repertoire that extended from the blues to avant-garde and free jazz. Compared with the innovations of other modern jazz groups of the 1960s, the Davis quintet's experimentations in polyrhythm and polytonality were more subtle but equally daring. *Live at the Plugged Nickel* (1965), *E.S.P.* (1965), *Miles Smiles* (1966), and *Nefertiti* (1967) were among the quintet's timeless, influential recordings. About the time of *Miles in the Sky* and *Filles de Kilimanjaro* (both 1968), Davis began experimenting with electronic instruments. With other musicians, including keyboardists Chick Corea and Joe Zawinul and guitarist John McLaughlin, Davis cut *In a Silent Way* (1969), regarded as the seminal album of the jazz fusion movement. It was considered by purists to be Davis's last true jazz album.

Davis won new fans and alienated old ones with the release of *Bitches Brew* (1969), an album on which he fully embraced the rhythms, electronic instrumentation, and studio effects of rock music. A cacophonous kalcidoscope of layered sounds, rhythms, and textures, the album's influence was heard in such 1970s fusion groups as Weather Report and Chick Corea's Return to Forever. Davis continued in this style for a few years, with the album *Live-Evil* (1970) and the film sound track *A Tribute to Jack Johnson* (1970) being particular highlights.

## LEGACY

Davis was injured in an auto accident in 1972, curtailing his activities, then retired from 1975 through 1980. He returned to public notice with *The Man with the Horn* (1981) and subsequently dabbled in a variety of musical styles, concentrating mostly on jazz-rock dance music, but there were also notable experiments in other styles. Davis won several Grammy Awards during this period for such albums as *We Want Miles* (1982), *Tutu* (1986), and *Aura* (1989). One of the most-memorable events of Davis's later years occurred at the Montreux Jazz Festival in 1991, when he joined with an orchestra conducted by Quincy Jones to perform some of the classic Gil Evans arrangements of the late 1950s. Davis died less than three months later. His final album, *Doo-Bop* (1992), was released posthumously.

## CHUCK BERRY

(b. Oct. 18, 1926, St. Louis, Mo., U.S.)

Singer, songwriter, and guitarist Chuck Berry (born Charles Edward Anderson Berry) was one of the most popular and influential performers in rhythm-and-blues and rock-and-roll music in the 1950s, '60s, and '70s.

Raised in a working-class African American neighbourhood on the north side of the highly segregated city of St. Louis, Berry grew up in a family proud of its African-American and Native American ancestry. He gained early exposure to music through his family's participation in the choir of the Antioch Baptist Church, through the blues and country western music he heard on the radio, and through music classes, especially at Sumner High School. Berry was still attending high school when he was sent to serve three years for armed robbery at a

Missouri prison for young offenders. After his release
and return to St. Louis, he worked at an auto plant,
studied hairdressing, and played music in small nightclubs. Berry traveled to Chicago in search of a recording
contract; he signed with the Chess label, and in 1955 his
first recording session produced "Maybellene", which
stayed on the pop charts for 11 weeks, cresting at number
five. Berry followed this success with extensive tours
and hit after hit, including "Roll Over Beethoven"
(1956), "Rock and Roll Music" (1957), and "Johnny B.
Goode" (1958). His vivid descriptions of consumer culture and teenage life, the distinctive sounds he coaxed
from his guitar, and the rhythmic and melodic virtuosity of his piano player (Johnny Johnson) made Berry's
songs staples in the repertoire of almost every rock-and-
roll band.

At the peak of his popularity, federal authorities
prosecuted Berry for violating the Mann Act, alleging
that he transported an underage female across state lines
"for immoral purposes." After two trials tainted by rac-
ist overtones, Berry was convicted and remanded to
prison. Upon his release he placed new hits on the pop
charts, including "No Particular Place to Go" in 1964,
at the height of the British Invasion, whose prime movers,
the Beatles and the Rolling Stones, were hugely influenced by Berry (as were the Beach Boys). In 1972 Berry
achieved his first number one hit, "My Ding-A-Ling."
Although he recorded more sporadically in the 1970s
and '80s, he continued to appear in concert, most often
performing with backing bands comprising local musicians. Berry's public visibility increased in 1987 with the
publication of his book *Chuck Berry: The Autobiography* and
the release of the documentary film *Hail! Hail! Rock 'n'
Roll*, featuring footage from his 60th birthday concert

and guest appearances by Keith Richards and Bruce Springsteen.

Berry is undeniably one of the most influential figures in the history of rock music. In helping to create rock and roll from the crucible of rhythm and blues, he combined clever lyrics, distinctive guitar sounds, boogie-woogie rhythms, precise diction, an astounding stage show, and musical devices characteristic of country western music and the blues in his many best-selling single records and albums. A distinctive if not technically dazzling guitarist, Berry used electronic effects to replicate the ringing sounds of bottleneck blues guitarists in his recordings. He drew upon a broad range of musical genres in his compositions, displaying an especially strong interest in Caribbean music on "Havana Moon" (1957) and "Man and the Donkey" (1963), among others. Influenced by a wide variety of artists—including guitar players Carl Hogan, Charlie Christian, and T-Bone Walker and vocalists Nat King Cole, Louis Jordan, and Charles Brown—Berry played a major role in broadening the appeal of rhythm-and-blues music during the 1950s. He fashioned his lyrics to appeal to the growing teenage market by presenting vivid and humorous descriptions of high-school life, teen dances, and consumer culture. Many popular-music performers have recorded Berry's songs.

An appropriate tribute to Berry's centrality to rock and roll came when his song "Johnny B. Goode" was among the pieces of music placed on a copper phonograph record attached to the side of the Voyager 1 satellite, hurtling through outer space, in order to give distant or future civilizations a chance to acquaint themselves with the culture of the planet Earth in the 20th century. In 1984 he was presented with a Grammy Award for lifetime achievement. He was inducted into the Rock and Roll Hall of Fame in 1986.

# ANTONIO CARLOS JOBIM

(b. Jan. 25, 1927, Rio de Janeiro, Braz.—d. Dec. 8, 1994, New York, N.Y., U.S.)

**B**razilian songwriter, composer, and arranger Antonio Carlos Jobim transformed the extroverted rhythms of the Brazilian samba into an intimate music, the bossa nova ("new wrinkle" or "new wave"), which became internationally popular in the 1960s.

"Tom" Jobim—as he was popularly known—first began playing piano when he was 14 years old, on an instrument given to his sister by their stepfather. He quickly showed an aptitude for music, and his stepfather sent him to a series of highly accomplished classically trained musicians for lessons. During the course of his studies, Jobim was particularly inspired by the music of Brazilian composer Heitor Villa-Lobos (1887–1959), whose Western classical works regularly employed Brazilian melodic and rhythmic materials. When it came time to choose a career, Jobim initially showed no interest in pursuing music professionally, opting instead to become an architect. He soon became disenchanted with the choice, however, and left the field to devote himself fully to music.

Jobim subsequently performed in the clubs of Rio de Janeiro, transcribed songs for composers who could not write music, and arranged music for various recording artists before becoming music director of Odeon Records, one of the largest record companies in Brazil. In 1958 he began collaborating with singer-guitarist João Gilberto, whose recording of Jobim's song "Chega de Saudade" (1958; "No More Blues") is widely recognized as the first bossa nova single. Although the song itself met a cold reception, the bossa nova album that bears its name—*Chega de Saudade* (1959)—took Brazil by storm the following year. Also in 1959, Jobim and composer Luís Bonfá became

*Brazilian composer Antonio Carlos Jobim, shown here around 1970, is best known for his "bossa nova," which became an international sensation.* Michael Ochs/Archives/Getty Images

noted for their collaboration with lyricist Vinícius de Moraes on the score for *Orfeo negro* (*Black Orpheus*), which won an Academy Award for best foreign film. By the early 1960s, Jobim's music was being played around the world.

Jobim maintained a second home in the United States, where bossa nova's fusion of understated samba pulse (quiet percussion and unamplified guitars playing subtly complex rhythms) and gentle, breathy singing with the melodious and sophisticated harmonic progressions of cool jazz found a long-lasting niche in popular music. In 1962 he appeared at Carnegie Hall with his leading jazz interpreters, tenor saxophonist Stan Getz and guitarist Charlie Byrd. Jobim collaborated on many albums, such as *Getz/Gilberto* (1963) and *Frank Sinatra & Antonio Carlos Jobim* (1967). He also recorded solo albums, most notably *Jobim* (1972) and

*A Certain Mr. Jobim* (1965), and composed classical works and film scores. Of the more than 400 songs Jobim produced in the course of his musical career, "Samba de uma nota só" ("One-Note Samba"), "Desafinado" ("Slightly Out of Tune"), "Meditação" ("Meditation"), "Corcovado" ("Quiet Nights of Quiet Stars"), "Garota de Ipanema" ("The Girl from Ipanema"), "Wave," and "Dindi" have been particularly popular.

## RAY CHARLES

(b. Sept. 23, 1930, Albany, Ga., U.S.—d. June 10, 2004, Beverly Hills, Calif.)

American pianist, singer, composer, and bandleader Ray Charles Robinson was a leading entertainer, often billed as "the Genius." Charles was credited with the early development of soul music, a style based on a melding of gospel, rhythm and blues, and jazz music.

When Charles was an infant his family moved to Greenville, Florida, and he began his musical career at age five on a piano in a neighbourhood café. He began to go blind at six, possibly from glaucoma, completely losing his sight by age seven. He attended the St. Augustine School for the Deaf and Blind, where he concentrated on musical studies, but left school at age 15 to play the piano professionally after his mother died from cancer (his father had died when the boy was 10).

Charles built a remarkable career based on the immediacy of emotion in his performances. After emerging as a blues and jazz pianist indebted to Nat King Cole's style in the late 1940s, Charles recorded the boogie-woogie classic *"Mess Around"* and the novelty song "It Should've Been Me" in 1952–53. His arrangement for Guitar Slim's "The Things That I Used to Do" became a blues million-seller in 1953. By 1954 Charles had created a successful combination of blues and gospel influences and signed on with Atlantic Records. Propelled by Charles's distinctive raspy voice, "I've Got a Woman" and "Hallelujah I Love You So" became hit records. "What'd I Say" led the rhythm-and-blues sales charts in 1959 and was Charles's own first million-seller.

Charles's rhythmic piano playing and band arranging revived the "funky" quality of jazz, but he also recorded in many other musical genres. He entered the pop market with the best-sellers "Georgia on My Mind" (1960) and "Hit the Road, Jack" (1961). His album *Modern Sounds in Country and Western Music* (1962) sold more than one million copies, as did its single, "I Can't Stop Loving You." Thereafter his music emphasized jazz standards and renditions of pop and show tunes.

From 1955 Charles toured extensively in the United States and elsewhere with his own big band and a gospel-style female backup quartet called The Raeletts. He also appeared on television and worked in films such as *Ballad in Blue* (1964) and *The Blues Brothers* (1980) as a featured act and sound track composer. He formed his own custom recording labels, Tangerine in 1962 and Crossover Records in 1973. The recipient of many national and international awards, he received 13 Grammy Awards, including a lifetime achievement award in 1987. In 1986 Charles was inducted into the Rock and Roll Hall of Fame and received a Kennedy Center Honor. He published an autobiography, *Brother Ray, Ray Charles' Own Story* (1978), written with David Ritz.

## PATSY CLINE

(b. Sept. 8, 1932, Winchester, Va., U.S. — d. March 5, 1963, near Camden, Tenn.)

American country and western singer Patsy Cline (born Virginia Patterson Hensley) helped bridge the gap between country music and more mainstream audiences.

Known in her youth as "Ginny," she began to sing with local country bands while a teenager, sometimes accompanying herself on guitar. By the time she had reached her early 20s, Cline was promoting herself as "Patsy" and was on her way toward country music stardom. She first recorded on the Four Star label in 1955, but it was with the advent of television culture in the late 1950s that she gained a wider audience. Cline began appearing on the radio and on *Town and Country Jamboree*, a local television variety show that was broadcast every Saturday night from Capitol Arena in Washington, D.C.

Singing "Walkin' After Midnight" as a contestant on the CBS television show *Arthur Godfrey's Talent Scouts*, Cline took first prize—the opportunity to appear on Godfrey's morning show for two weeks. She thereby gained national exposure both for herself and for her song. Three years later she became a regular performer on the Grand Ole Opry radio broadcasts from Nashville, Tenn., which largely defined the country music genre. Although Cline preferred traditional country music, which typically included vocalizations such as yodeling, the country music industry—coming into increasing competition with rock and roll—was trying to increase its appeal to a more mainstream audience. After her recording of "I Fall to Pieces" remained a popular seller for 39 consecutive weeks, she was marketed as a pop singer and was backed by strings and vocals. Cline never fully donned the pop music mantle, however: she did not eliminate yodeling from her repertoire, she dressed in distinctly western-style clothing, and she favoured country songs—especially heart-wrenching ballads of lost or waning love—over her three popular songs "Walkin' After Midnight," "I Fall to Pieces," and "Crazy" (written by a young Willie Nelson).

Cline's life was cut short in March 1963 by an airplane crash that also killed fellow entertainers Cowboy Copas and Hawkshaw Hawkins. In her short career, however, she helped usher in the modern era for American country singers; she figures prominently, for instance, as singer Loretta Lynn's mentor in Lynn's autobiography, *Coal Miner's Daughter* (1976). Cline was elected to the Country Music Hall of Fame in 1973.

## JAMES BROWN

(b. May 3, 1933, Barnwell, S.C., U.S. — d. Dec. 25, 2006, Atlanta, Ga.)

Known as "the Godfather of Soul," American singer, songwriter, arranger, and dancer James Brown was one of the most important and influential entertainers in 20th-century popular music. His remarkable achievements earned him the sobriquet "the Hardest-Working Man in Show Business."

Brown was raised mainly in Augusta, Ga., by his great-aunt, who took him in at about the age of five when his parents divorced. Growing up in the segregated South during the Great Depression of the 1930s, Brown was so impoverished that he was sent home from grade school for "insufficient clothes," an experience that he never forgot and that perhaps explains his penchant as an adult for wearing ermine coats, velour jumpsuits, elaborate capes, and conspicuous gold jewelry. Neighbours taught him how to play drums, piano, and guitar, and he learned about gospel music in churches and at tent revivals, where preachers would scream, yell, stomp their feet, and fall to their knees during sermons to provoke responses from the congregation.

At age 15 Brown and some companions were arrested while breaking into cars. He was sentenced to 8 to 16 years of incarceration but was released after 3 years for good behaviour. While at the Alto Reform School, he formed a gospel group. Subsequently secularized and renamed the

Flames (later the Famous Flames), it soon attracted the attention of rhythm-and-blues and rock-and-roll shouter Little Richard, whose manager helped promote the group. Intrigued by their demo record, Ralph Bass, the artists-and-repertoire man for the King label, brought the group to Cincinnati, Ohio, to record for King Records' subsidiary Federal. Brown's first recording, "Please, Please, Please" (1956) eventually sold three million copies and launched his extraordinary career. Along with placing nearly 100 singles and almost 50 albums on the best-seller charts, Brown broke new ground with two of the first successful "live and in concert" albums—his landmark *Live at the Apollo* (1963), and his 1964 follow-up, *Pure Dynamite! Live at the Royal*.

During the 1960s Brown was known as "Soul Brother Number One." His hit recordings of that decade have often been associated with the emergence of the black aesthetic and black nationalist movements, especially the songs "Say It Loud—I'm Black and I'm Proud" (1968), "Don't Be a Drop-Out" (1966), and "I Don't Want Nobody to Give Me Nothin' (Open Up the Door, I'll Get It Myself)" (1969). In the 1970s Brown became "the Godfather of Soul," and his hit songs stimulated several dance crazes and were featured on the sound tracks of a number of "blaxploitation" films (sensational, low-budget, action-oriented motion pictures with African American protagonists). When hip-hop emerged as a viable commercial music in the 1980s, Brown's songs again assumed centre stage as hip-hop disc jockeys frequently incorporated samples (audio snippets) from his records. He also appeared in several motion pictures, including *The Blues Brothers* (1980) and *Rocky IV* (1985), and attained global status as a celebrity, especially in Africa, where his tours attracted enormous crowds and generated a broad range of new musical fusions. Yet Brown's life continued to be marked by difficulties, including the tragic death of his third wife, charges of drug use, and a period of imprisonment for a 1988 high-speed highway chase in which he tried to escape pursuing police officers.

Brown's uncanny ability to "scream" on key, to sing soulful slow ballads as well as electrifying up-tempo tunes, to plumb the rhythmic possibilities of the human voice and instrumental accompaniment, and to blend blues, gospel, jazz, and country vocal styles together made him one of the most influential vocalists of the 20th century. His extraordinary dance routines featuring deft deployment of microphones and articles of clothing as props, acrobatic leaps, full-impact knee landings, complex rhythmic patterns, dazzling footwork, dramatic entrances, and melodramatic exits redefined public performance within popular music and inspired generations of imitators (not least Michael Jackson). His careful attention to every aspect of his shows, from arranging songs to supervising sidemen, from negotiating performance fees to selecting costumes, guaranteed his audiences a uniformly high level of professionalism every night and established a precedent in artistic autonomy. In the course of an extremely successful commercial career, Brown's name was associated with an extraordinary number and range of memorable songs, distinctive dance steps, formative fashion trends, and even significant social issues. A skilled dancer and singer with an extraordinary sense of timing, Brown played a major role in bringing rhythm to the foreground of popular music. In addition to providing melody and embellishment, the horn players in his bands functioned as a rhythm section (they had to think like drummers), and musicians associated with him (Jimmy Nolan, Bootsy Collins, Fred Wesley, and Maceo Parker) have played an important role in creating the core vocabulary and grammar of funk music. Brown was inducted into the Rock and Roll Hall of Fame in 1986.

# ELVIS PRESLEY

(b. Jan. 8, 1935, Tupelo, Miss., U.S.—d. Aug. 16, 1977, Memphis, Tenn.)

American popular singer Elvis Aaron Presley, widely known as the "King of Rock and Roll," was one of rock music's dominant performers from the mid-1950s until his death.

Presley grew up dirt-poor in Tupelo, moved to Memphis as a teenager, and, with his family, was off welfare only a few weeks when producer Sam Phillips at Sun Records, a local blues label, responded to his audition tape with a phone call. Several weeks' worth of recording sessions ensued with a band consisting of Presley, guitarist Scotty Moore, and bassist Bill Black. Their repertoire consisted of the kind of material for which Presley would become famous: blues and country songs, Tin Pan Alley ballads, and gospel hymns. Presley knew some of this music from the radio, some of it from his parents' Pentecostal church and the group sings he attended at the Reverend H.W. Brewster's black Memphis church, and some of it from the Beale Street blues clubs he began frequenting as a teenager.

Presley was already a flamboyant personality, with relatively long greased-back hair and wild-coloured clothing combinations, but his full musical personality did not emerge until he and the band began playing with blues singer Arthur ("Big Boy") Crudup's song "That's All Right Mama" in July 1954. They arrived at a startling synthesis, eventually dubbed rockabilly, retaining many of the original's blues inflections but with Presley's high tenor voice adding a lighter touch and with the basic rhythm striking a much more supple groove. This sound was the hallmark of the five singles Presley released on Sun over the next year. Although none of them became a national hit, by August 1955, when he released the fifth, "Mystery Train," arguably his greatest record ever, he had attracted a substantial

Southern following for his recordings, his live appearances in regional roadhouses and clubs, and his radio performances on the nationally aired *Louisiana Hayride*. (A key musical change came when drummer D.J. Fontana was added, first for the *Hayride* shows but also on records beginning with "Mystery Train.")

Presley's management was then turned over to Colonel Tom Parker, a country music hustler who had made stars of Eddy Arnold and Hank Snow. Parker arranged for Presley's song catalog and recording contract to be sold to major New York City-based enterprises, Hill and Range and RCA Victor, respectively. Sun received a total of $35,000; Elvis got $5,000. He began recording at RCA's studios in Nashville, Tennessee, with a somewhat larger group of musicians but still including Moore, Black, and Fontana and began to create a national sensation with a series of hits: "Heartbreak Hotel," "Don't Be Cruel," "Love Me Tender" (all 1956), "All Shook Up" (1957), and more.

From 1956 through 1958 Presley completely dominated the best-seller charts and ushered in the age of rock and roll, opening doors for both white and black rock artists. His television appearances, especially those on Ed Sullivan's Sunday night variety show, set

*Legendary American popular singer Elvis Presley poses for a portrait in the 1950s.* Getty Images

records for the size of the audiences. Even his films, a few slight vehicles, were box office smashes.

Presley became the teen idol of his decade, greeted everywhere by screaming hordes of young women, and, when it was announced in early 1958 that he had been drafted and would enter the U.S. Army, there was that rarest of all pop culture events, a moment of true grief. More important, he served as the great cultural catalyst of his period. Elvis projected a mixed vision of humility and self-confidence, of intense commitment and comic disbelief in his ability to create frenzy. He inspired literally thousands of musicians—initially those more or less like-minded Southerners, from Jerry Lee Lewis and Carl Perkins on down, who were the first generation of rockabillies, and, later, people who had far different combinations of musical and cultural influences and ambitions. From John Lennon to Bruce Springsteen, Bob Dylan to Prince, it was impossible to think of a rock star of any importance who did not owe an explicit debt to Presley.

Beyond even that, Presley inspired his audience. "It was like he whispered his dream in all our ears and then we dreamed it," said Springsteen at the time of Presley's death. You did not have to want to be a rock and roll star or even a musician to want to be like Elvis—which meant, ultimately, to be free and uninhibited and yet still a part of the everyday. Literally millions of people—an entire generation or two—defined their sense of personal style and ambition in terms that Elvis first personified.

As a result, he was anything but universally adored. Those who did not worship him found him despicable (no one found him ignorable). Preachers and pundits declared him an anathema, his Pentecostally derived hip-swinging stage style and breathy vocal asides obscene. Racists denounced him for mingling black music with white (and Presley was always scrupulous in crediting his black sources, one of the things that made him different from the Tin Pan Alley writers and singers who had for decades lifted black styles without credit). He was pronounced responsible for all teenage hooliganism and juvenile delinquency. Yet, in every appearance on television, he appeared affable, polite, and soft-spoken, almost shy. It was only with a band at his back and a beat in his ear that he became "Elvis the Pelvis."

In 1960 Presley returned from the army, where he had served as a soldier in Germany rather than joining the Special Services entertainment division. Those who regarded him as commercial hype without talent expected him to fade away. Instead, he continued to have hits from recordings stockpiled just before he entered the army. Upon his return to the States, he picked up pretty much where he had left off, churning out a series of more than 30 movies (from *Blue Hawaii* to *Change of Habit*) over the next eight years, almost none of which fit any genre other than "Elvis movie," which meant a light comedic romance with musical interludes. Most had accompanying soundtrack albums, and together the movies and the records made him a rich man, although they nearly ruined him as any kind of artist. Presley did his best work in the 1960s on singles either unconnected to the films or only marginally stuck into them, recordings such as "It's Now or Never ('O Sole Mio')" (1960), "Are You Lonesome Tonight?," "Little Sister" (both 1961), "Can't Help Falling in Love," "Return to Sender" (both 1962), and "Viva Las Vegas" (1964). Presley was no longer a controversial figure; he had become one more predictable mass entertainer, a personage of virtually no interest to the rock audience that had expanded so much with the advent of the new sounds of the Beatles, the Rolling Stones, and Dylan.

By 1968 the changes in the music world had overtaken Presley—both movie grosses and record sales had fallen. In

*Ann-Margret and Elvis Presley in* Viva Las Vegas *(1964).* © 1964 Metro-Goldwyn-Mayer Inc.; photograph from a private collection

December his one-man Christmas TV special aired; a tour de force of rock and roll and rhythm and blues, it restored much of his dissipated credibility. In 1969 he released a single having nothing to do with a film, "Suspicious Minds"; it went to number one. He also began doing concerts again and quickly won back a sizable following, although it was not nearly as universal as his audience in the 1950s. For much of the next decade, he was again one of the top live attractions in the United States. Presley was now a mainstream American entertainer, an icon but not so much an idol. He had married in 1967 without much furor, became a parent with the birth of his daughter, Lisa Marie, in 1968, and got divorced in 1973. He made no more movies, and his recordings were of uneven quality. Hits were harder to come by—"Suspicious Minds" was his last number one and "Burning Love" (1972) his final Top Ten entry. But, thanks to the concerts, spectaculars best described by critic Jon Landau as an apotheosis of American musical comedy, he remained a big money earner.

However, Presley had also developed a lethal lifestyle. Spending almost all his time when not on the road in Graceland, his Memphis estate, he lived nocturnally, surrounded by sycophants and stuffed with greasy foods and a variety of prescription drugs. His shows deteriorated in the final two years of his life, and his recording career came to a virtual standstill. Finally, in the summer of 1977, the night before he was to begin yet another concert tour, he died of a heart attack brought on largely by drug abuse. He was 42 years old.

## LUCIANO PAVAROTTI

(b. Oct. 12, 1935, Modena, Italy—d. Sept. 6, 2007, Modena)

Italian operatic lyric tenor Luciano Pavarotti was considered one of the finest bel canto opera singers of the 20th century. Even in the highest register, his voice was noted for its purity of tone, and his concerts, recordings, and television appearances—which provided him ample opportunity to display his ebullient personality—gained him a wide popular following.

Pavarotti graduated from a teaching institute in Modena (1955) and then taught elementary school for two years. He studied opera privately, mostly in Mantua. After winning the Concorso Internazionale, a singing competition, he made his professional operatic debut in 1961 as Rodolfo in *La Bohème* (1896) in Reggio nell'Emilia, Italy. He then played in opera houses throughout Europe and Australia and performed the role of Idamante in Mozart's *Idomeneo* (1781) at the Glyndebourne Festival in 1964. He made his first appearance in the United States in Miami in 1965, singing opposite Joan Sutherland as Edgardo in *Lucia di Lammermoor* (1835). In 1968 he made his debut at the Metropolitan Opera House in New York City, and from 1971 he was a regular performer there. Pavarotti toured the world, performing to as many as 500,000 fans at a time in outdoor venues, as a solo performer or as one of the "Three Tenors" (with Plácido Domingo and José Carreras). Among his many prizes and awards were five Grammy Awards and a Kennedy Center Honor in 2001.

His most notable operatic roles included the Duke in Giuseppe Verdi's *Rigoletto* (1851), Tonio in Gaetano Donizetti's *La Fille du régiment* (1840; a part remarkable for its demanding sequence of high Cs), Arturo in Vincenzo Bellini's *I puritani* (1835), and Radamès in Verdi's *Aida* (1871), all of which are available as sound recordings. He performed in a number of televised opera broadcasts. In addition to his opera work, Pavarotti also recorded a collection of Italian love songs (*Amore* [1992; "Love"]) and a pop album (*Ti adoro* [2003; "I Adore You"]).

With William Wright he wrote *Pavarotti: My Own Story* (1981) and *Pavarotti: My World* (1995). In 2004

Pavarotti gave his final performance on the operatic stage, although he continued to sing publicly until 2006. His last public appearance was in the opening ceremony of the 2006 Winter Olympics in Turin, Italy, where he sang his signature aria, *Nessun dorma*, from Giacomo Puccini's *Turandot* (first performed 1926).

## BUDDY HOLLY

(b. Sept. 7, 1936, Lubbock, Texas, U.S.—d. Feb. 3, 1959, near Clear Lake, Iowa)

American singer and songwriter Charles Hardin Holley, professionally known as Buddy Holly, produced some of the most distinctive and influential work in rock music.

Holly (the *e* was dropped from his last name—probably accidentally—on his first record contract) was the youngest of four children in a family of devout Baptists in the West Texas town of Lubbock, and gospel music was an important part of his life from an early age. A good student possessed of infectious personal charm, Holly was declared "King of the Sixth Grade" by his classmates. He became seriously interested in music at about age 12 and pursued it with remarkable natural ability.

The African American rhythm and blues that Holly heard on the radio had a tremendous impact on him, as it did on countless other white teenagers in the racially seg-regated United States of the 1950s. Already well versed in country music, bluegrass, and gospel and a seasoned per-former by age 16, he became a rhythm-and-blues devotee. By 1955, after hearing Elvis Presley, Holly was a full-time rock and roller. Late that year he bought a Fender Stratocaster electric guitar and developed a style of play-ing featuring ringing major chords that became his trademark. In 1956 he signed with Decca Records'

Nashville, Tennessee, division, but the records he made for them were uneven in quality, and most sold poorly.

In 1957 Holly and his new group, the Crickets (Niki Sullivan on second guitar and background vocals, Joe B. Mauldin on bass, and the great Jerry Allison on drums), began their association with independent producer Norman Petty at his studio in Clovis, New Mexico. Together they created a series of recordings that display an emotional intimacy and sense of detail that set them apart from other 1950s rock and roll. As a team, they threw away the rule book and let their imaginations loose. Unlike most independent rock-and-roll producers of the time, Petty did not own any cheap equipment. He wanted his recordings to sound classy and expensive, but he also loved to experiment and had a deep bag of sonic tricks. The Crickets' records feature unusual microphone placement techniques, imaginative echo chamber effects, and over-dubbing, a process that in the 1950s meant superimposing one recording on another. While crafting tracks such as "Not Fade Away," "Peggy Sue," "Listen to Me," and "Everyday," Holly and the Crickets camped out at Petty's studio for days at a time, using it as a combination laboratory and playground. They were the first rock and rollers to approach the recording process in this manner.

When the Crickets' first single, "That'll Be the Day," was released in 1957, their label, Brunswick, did nothing to promote it. Nevertheless, the record had an irrepressible spirit, and by year's end it became an international multi-million-seller. Soon after, Holly became a star and an icon. Holly and the Crickets' association with Petty (who, serving as their manager, songwriting partner, and publisher, owned their recordings) was far from all beneficial, however. According to virtually all accounts, Petty collected the Crickets' royalty checks and kept the money. By 1959 the hit records tapered off, and Holly was living in New York with his new bride. Estranged from the Crickets and broke, he was also contemplating legal action against Petty. This left him little choice but to participate in the doomed "Winter Dance Party of 1959" tour through the frozen Midwest, during which he and coheadliners Ritchie Valens and the Big Bopper (J.P. Richardson) were killed in a plane crash.

The music of Holly and the Crickets, their innovative use of the studio, and the fact that they wrote most of their songs themselves made them the single most important influence on the Beatles, who knew every Holly record backward and forward. In 1986 Holly was inducted into the Rock and Roll Hall of Fame, and in 1996 he was honoured by the National Academy of Recording Arts and Sciences with a lifetime achievement award.

## THE ROLLING STONES

The original members were Mick Jagger (b. July 26, 1943, Dartford, Kent, Eng.), Keith Richards (b. Dec. 18, 1943, Dartford, Kent, Eng.), Brian Jones (b. Feb. 28, 1942, Cheltenham, Gloucestershire, Eng.—d. July 3, 1969, Hartfield, Sussex), Bill Wyman (b. Oct. 24, 1936, London, Eng.), and Charlie Watts (b. June 2, 1941, London, Eng.). Later members were Mick Taylor (b. Jan. 17, 1948, Hereford, East Hereford and Worcester, Eng.), Ron Wood (b. June 1, 1947, London, Eng.), and Darryl Jones (b. Dec. 11, 1961, Chicago, Ill., U.S.).

Formed in 1962, the Rolling Stones are a British rock group that has drawn on Chicago blues stylings to create a unique vision of the dark side of post-1960s counterculture.

No rock band has sustained consistent activity and global popularity for so long a period as the Rolling Stones, still capable, more than 45 years after their formation, of filling the largest stadia in the world. Though several of their mid-1960s contemporaries—notably Bob Dylan, Paul McCartney, Eric Clapton, and Van Morrison—have maintained individual positions in rock's front line, the Rolling Stones' nucleus of singer Jagger, guitarist Richards, and drummer Watts remains rock's most durable ongoing partnership.

In the process, the Stones have become rock's definitive, emblematic band: a seamless blend of sound, look, and public image. That they are the mold from which various generations of challengers have been struck—from the Who, Led Zeppelin, and Aerosmith (via the New York Dolls), the Clash, the Sex Pistols all the way to Guns N' Roses and Oasis—is virtually inarguable. In their onstage personae, Jagger and Richards established the classic rock band archetypes: the preening, narcissistic singer and the haggard, obsessive guitarist.

Formed in London as an alliance between Jagger, Richards, and multi-instrumentalist Brian Jones along with Watts and bassist Wyman, the Stones began as a grubby conclave of students and bohemians playing a then-esoteric music based on Chicago ghetto blues in pubs and clubs in and around West London. Their potential for mass-market success seemed negligible at first, but by 1965 they were second only to the Beatles in the collective affection of teenage Britain. However, whereas the Beatles of the mid-1960s had longish hair, wore matching suits, and appeared utterly charming, the Stones had considerably longer hair, all dressed differently, and seemed thoroughly intimidating. As the Beatles grew ever more respectable and reassuring, the Stones became correspondingly more rebellious and threatening. The Stones—specifically Jagger, Richards, and Jones—were subjected to intense police and press harassment for drug use and all-purpose degeneracy, whereas the Beatles, who were in private life no less fond of marijuana, sex, and alcohol, were welcomed at Buckingham Palace and made Members of the Order of the British Empire (M.B.E.) by the queen.

The Stones' early repertoire consisted primarily of recycled gems from the catalogs of the blues and rock-and-roll titans of the 1950s: their first five singles and the bulk of their first two albums were composed by others. The turning point was reached when, spurred on by the example of the Beatles' John Lennon and Paul McCartney, Jagger and Richards began composing their own songs, which not only ensured the long-term viability of the band but

*The British rock group the Rolling Stones in 1967. From left to right: Brian Jones, Keith Richards, Bill Wyman, Charlie Watts, and Mick Jagger.* Getty Images/Keystone

also served to place the Jagger-Richards team firmly in creative control of the group. Jones had been their prime motivating force in their early days, and he was the band's most gifted instrumentalist as well as its prettiest face, but he had little talent for composition and became increasingly marginalized. His textural wizardry dominated their first all-original album, *Aftermath* (1966), which featured him on marimba, dulcimer, sitar, and assorted keyboards as well as on his customary guitar and harmonica. Thereafter, however, he declined in both creativity and influence, becoming a depressive, drug-sodden liability eventually fired by the band mere weeks before his death.

The Jagger-Richards songwriting team created its first bona fide classic, "(I Can't Get No) Satisfaction," in 1965 and enjoyed a string of innovative hit singles well into 1966, including "Paint It Black," "19th Nervous Breakdown," "Get off My Cloud," "Have You Seen Your Mother, Baby," and "Lady Jane," but the era of art-pop and psychedelia, which coincided with the Beatles' creative peak, represented a corresponding trough for the Stones. The fashions of the era of whimsy and flower power did not suit their essentially dark and disruptive energies, and their psychedelic album *Their Satanic Majesties Request* (1967) contributed little beyond its title to their legend. Furthermore, they were hampered by seemingly spending as much time in court and jail as they did in the studio or on tour. However, as the mood of the time darkened, the Stones hit a new stride in 1968 with the epochal single "Jumpin' Jack Flash," which reconnected them to their blues-rock roots, and the album *Beggars Banquet*. Replacing Jones with the virtuosic but self-effacing guitarist Mick Taylor, they returned to the road in 1969, almost instantly becoming rock's premier touring attraction.

By the end of 1970 the Beatles had broken up, Jimi Hendrix was dead, and Led Zeppelin had barely appeared on the horizon. Though Led Zeppelin eventually outsold the Stones by five albums to one, no group could challenge their central position in the rock pantheon. Moreover, the death of Brian Jones combined with Taylor's lack of onstage presence elevated public perception of Richards's status from that of Jagger's right-hand man to effective coleader of the band.

The period between "Jumpin' Jack Flash" and the double album *Exile on Main Street* (1972) remains their creative and iconic peak. Including the studio albums *Let It Bleed* (1969) and *Sticky Fingers* (1971) plus the in-concert *Get Yer Ya-Yas Out!* (1970), it gave them the repertoire and image that still defines them and on which they have continued to trade ever since: an incendiary blend of sex, drugs, satanism, and radical politics delivered with their patented fusion of Jagger's ironic distance and Richards's tatterdemalion intensity. Their records and concerts at this time both explored and provided the soundtrack for the contradictions of a collapsing counterculture at a time when almost everybody else still seemed to be in a state of psychedelic euphoria.

Their recordings of this period found them adding country music to their list of influences and—most notably on *Beggars Banquet*—adding more and more acoustic guitar textures to their already impressive command of musical light and shade. Yet their blues-powered foray into the era's heart of darkness bore bitter fruit indeed: when a young black man was murdered by Hell's Angels at a disastrous free concert at the Altamont Speedway in Livermore, Calif., during their 1969 American tour, it seemed to many observers that the Stones' own aura of decadence and danger was somehow to blame for the tragedy.

The quality of their music began to decline after *Exile on Main Street*. Jagger and Richards began to act out the group's fascination with the juxtaposition of high society and lowlife: the singer became a jet-set figure; the guitarist, a full-time junkie who finally "cleaned up" in 1977 and thereby saved both his own life and the band's future. Taylor left in 1975 to be replaced by Wood, formerly of the Faces, and, despite the occasional bright spot like *Some Girls* (1978), *Emotional Rescue* (1980), or "Start Me Up" (1981), the Stones' albums and singles became increasingly predictable, though their tours continued to sell out. Both Jagger and Richards recorded solo albums that performed relatively poorly in the marketplace, though Richards's work was significantly more favourably reviewed than Jagger's.

The Stones embarked on their *Steel Wheels* album and tour in 1989. Wyman retired in 1992 and was replaced on tour by Daryl Jones, formerly a bassist for Miles Davis and Sting, and in the studio by a variety of guest musicians. Jagger, Richards, Watts, and Wood continue to trade as the Rolling Stones, and, whenever they tour, audiences flock in the thousands to discover if the old lions can still roar.

Several prominent directors have sought to translate the electricity of the Stones as live performers to the screen, including Jean-Luc Godard, with the impressionistic *Sympathy for the Devil* (1968); Hal Ashby, with *Let's Spend the Night Together* (1982); and, perhaps most notably, David Maysles, Albert Maysles, and Charlotte Zwerin, with *Gimme Shelter* (1970), which covered the group's 1969 tour and Altamont Speedway concert. More recently, in the wake of the group's well-received album *A Bigger Bang* (2005), director Martin Scorsese, long a fan of the group, focused less on the spectacle of a Stones' concert and more on the band as performers. The result, *Shine a Light* (2008), met with critical acclaim and confirmed that the Rolling Stones remained a major presence in the rock scene of the 21st century.

## PHILIP GLASS

(b. Jan. 31, 1937, Baltimore, Md., U.S.)

Philip Glass is an American composer of innovative instrumental, vocal, and operatic music, who variously has employed minimalist, atonal, and non-Western elements in his work.

Glass studied flute as a boy and enrolled at age 15 at the University of Chicago, where he studied mathematics and philosophy and graduated in 1956. His interest in atonal music drew him on to study composition at the Juilliard School of Music (M.S., 1962) in New York City and then to Paris to study under Nadia Boulanger. His acquaintance there with the Indian sitarist Ravi Shankar decisively affected Glass's compositional style, and he temporarily jettisoned such traditional formal qualities as harmony, tempo, and melody in his music. Instead he began creating ensemble pieces in a monotonous and repetitive style; these works consisted of a series of syncopated rhythms ingeniously contracted or extended within a stable diatonic structure. Such minimalist music, played by a small ensemble using electronically amplified keyboard and wind instruments, earned Glass a small but enthusiastic following in New York City by the late 1960s.

Glass's opera *Einstein on the Beach* (1976), composed in collaboration with Robert Wilson, earned him broader acclaim; this work showed a renewed interest in classical Western harmonic elements, though his interest in startling rhythmic and melodic changes remained the work's most dramatic feature. Glass's opera *Satyagraha* (1980) was a more authentically "operatic" portrayal of incidents from the early life of Mohandas K. Gandhi. In this work, the dronelike repetition of symmetrical sequences of chords attained a haunting and hypnotic power well attuned to the religio-spiritual themes of the libretto, adapted from the Hindu scripture the *Bhagavadgītā*. The opera *The Voyage* (1992) had mixed reviews, but the fact that it had been commissioned by the New York Metropolitan Opera (to commemorate the 500th anniversary of Christopher Columbus's arrival in the Americas) confirmed Glass's growing acceptance by the classical music establishment.

## SMOKEY ROBINSON AND THE MIRACLES

In addition to Smokey Robinson (b. Feb. 19, 1940, Detroit, Mich., U.S.), the principal members of the group were Warren Moore (b. Nov. 19, 1939, Detroit, Mich., U.S.), Bobby Rogers (b. Feb. 19, 1940, Detroit, Mich., U.S.), Ronnie White (b. April 5, 1939, Detroit, Mich., U.S.), and Claudette Rogers (b. 1942)

Smokey Robinson and the Miracles were an American vocal group that helped define the Motown sound of the 1960s; the group was led by one of the most gifted, influential singer-songwriters in 20th-century popular music.

Whether writing for fellow artists Mary Wells, the Temptations, or Marvin Gaye or performing with the Miracles, singer-lyricist-arranger-producer Robinson created songs that were supremely balanced between the joy and pain of love. At once playful and passionate, Robinson's graceful lyrics led Bob Dylan to call him "America's greatest living poet."

Coming of age in the doo-wop era and deeply influenced by jazz vocalist Sarah Vaughan, Robinson formed the Five Chimes with school friends in the mid-1950s. After some personnel changes, the group, as the Matadors, auditioned unsuccessfully for Jackie Wilson's manager; however, they greatly impressed Wilson's songwriter Berry Gordy, who soon became their manager and producer. Most important, Gordy became Robinson's mentor, harnessing his prodigious but unformed composing talents, and Robinson, assisted by the Miracles, became Gordy's inspiration for the creation of Motown Records.

With the arrival of Claudette Rogers, the group changed its name to the Miracles and released "Got a Job" on End Records in 1958. The Miracles struggled onstage in their first performance at the Apollo Theatre that year, but good fortune came their way in the form of Marv Tarplin, guitarist for the Primettes, who were led by Robinson's friend Diana Ross. Tarplin became an honorary (but essential) Miracle, while Robinson introduced Gordy to the Primettes, who soon became the Supremes. In 1959 Robinson and Claudette Rogers were married, and "Bad Girl," licensed to Chess Records, peaked nationally at number 93. The fiery "Way Over There" and the shimmering "(You Can) Depend on Me" were followed in 1960 by "Shop Around," the second version of which became an enormous hit, reaching number one on the rhythm-and-blues charts and number two on the pop charts.

While Robinson was writing such vital songs as "My Guy" for Mary Wells, "I'll Be Doggone" for Marvin Gaye, and "My Girl" for the Temptations, he and the Miracles proceeded to record stunning compositions, including "You've Really Got a Hold on Me" (1962), "I'll Try Something New" (1962), "Ooo Baby Baby" (1965), "Choosey Beggar" (1965), "The Tracks of My Tears" (1965), and "More Love" (1967, written following the premature birth and death of Robinson's twin daughters). The Miracles complemented their songs of aching romance and mature love with buoyant numbers such as "Mickey's Monkey" (1963), "Going to a Go-Go" (1965), "I Second That Emotion" (1967), and "The Tears of a Clown" (1970).

In 1972 Robinson left the Miracles to pursue a solo career. Without him, the Miracles enjoyed moderate success in subsequent years (the disco-era "Love Machine [Part 1]" hit number one on the pop charts in 1975), while Robinson produced such solo hits as "Cruisin'" (1979) and "Being with You" (1981). He also unintentionally inspired the new soul radio format that took its name from the title track of his 1975 conceptual album *A Quiet Storm*. Robinson was inducted into the Rock and Roll Hall of Fame in 1987.

## PARLIAMENT-FUNKADELIC

The original members were George Clinton (b. July 22, 1941, Kannapolis, N.C., U.S.), Raymond Davis (b. March 29, 1940, Sumter, S.C., U.S.), Calvin Simon (b. May 22, 1942, Beckley, W.Va., U.S.), Fuzzy Haskins (b. June 8, 1941, Elkhorn, W.Va., U.S.), and Grady Thomas (b. Jan. 5, 1941, Newark, N.J., U.S.). Later members included Michael Hampton (b. Nov. 15, 1956, Cleveland, Ohio, U.S.), Bernie Worrell (b. April 19, 1944, Long Beach, N.J., U.S.), Billy Bass Nelson (b. Jan. 28, 1951, Plainfield, N.J., U.S.), Eddie Hazel (b. April 10, 1950, Brooklyn, N.Y., U.S.—d. Dec. 23, 1992), Tiki Fulwood (b. May 23, 1944, Philadelphia, Pa., U.S.—d. Oct. 29, 1979), Bootsy Collins (b. Oct. 26, 1951, Cincinnati, Ohio, U.S.), Fred Wesley (b. July 4, 1943, Columbus, Ga., U.S.), Maceo Parker (b. Feb. 14, 1943, Kinston, N.C., U.S.), Jerome Brailey (b. Aug. 20, 1950, Richmond, Va., U.S.), Garry Shider (b. July 24, 1953, Plainfield, N.J., U.S.), Glen Goins (b. Jan. 2, 1954, Plainfield, N.J., U.S.—d. July 29, 1978, Plainfield), and Gary ("Mudbone") Cooper (b. Nov. 24, 1953, Washington, D.C., U.S.)

Parliament-Funkadelic, also known as P-Funk, was a massive group of performers that greatly influenced black music in the 1970s.

The group scored 13 Top Ten rhythm-and-blues and pop hits from 1967 to 1983 (including six number one rhythm-and-blues hits) under a variety of names, including the Parliaments, Funkadelic, Bootsy's Rubber Band, and the Brides of Funkenstein, as well as under the name of its founding father, Clinton.

The band combined the hard rock of Jimi Hendrix, the funky rhythms of James Brown, and the showstopping style of Sly and the Family Stone to fashion an outrageous tribal funk experience. P-Funk emphasized the aesthetics of funk as a means of self-fulfillment; to "give up the funk" meant to achieve transcendence.

Organized and produced by Clinton, the original Parliaments began as a doo-wop quintet based in Plainfield. The group's first charting single, "(I Wanna) Testify," in 1967 led to their first tour, but legal problems that arose with the demise of their record company resulted in the loss of the group's name. Performing throughout the northeastern United States and recording in Detroit, the group began to emphasize its backing band, Funkadelic. Led by bassist Nelson, guitarist Hazel, drummer Fulwood, and classically trained keyboardist Worrell, Funkadelic incorporated the influence of amplified, psychedelic rock into its distinctive sound.

By 1970 Clinton was producing albums for both the renamed Parliament and Funkadelic—essentially the same entity recording for different labels. In the process he recruited key new performers: Collins on bass, Wesley on trombone, and Parker on saxophone (all from James Brown's band the JBs), along with drummer Brailey, vocalist Cooper, lead guitarist Hampton, and vocalist-guitarists Shider and Goins. Success came in 1976 with the release of Parliament's album *Mothership Connection* and the single "Give Up the Funk (Tear the Roof Off the Sucker)," which earned a gold record. Other hit singles followed, including "Flash Light" (1977) by Parliament, "One Nation Under a Groove" (1978) by Funkadelic, and "Atomic Dog" (1982) by Clinton.

P-Funk reached its peak in the late 1970s, sporting a massive stage act (with more than 40 performers) that showcased Clinton's visionary album concepts, Collins's spectacular bass effects, and Worrell's synthesizer innovations. However, by the early 1980s the large overhead and multifaceted legal identity of the group led to a collapse of the enterprise.

P-Funk defined the dance music of its time and influenced a range of styles from hard rock to house music. The P-Funk catalog is among the most sampled by rap music producers. Parliament-Funkadelic was inducted into the Rock and Roll Hall of Fame in 1997.

## THE BEATLES

The principal members were Paul McCartney (b. June 18, 1942, Liverpool, Merseyside, Eng.), John Lennon (b. Oct. 9, 1940, Liverpool, Merseyside, Eng.—d. Dec. 8, 1980, New York, N.Y., U.S.), George Harrison (b. Feb. 25, 1943, Liverpool, Merseyside, Eng.—d. Nov. 29, 2001, Los Angeles, Calif., U.S.), and Ringo Starr (b. July 7, 1940, Liverpool, Merseyside, Eng.). Other early members included Stuart Sutcliffe (b. June 23, 1940, Edinburgh, Scot.—d. April 10, 1962, Hamburg, W. Ger.) and Pete Best (b. Nov. 24, 1941, Madras [now Chennai], India).

The Beatles were a British musical quartet and a global cynosure for the hopes and dreams of a generation that came of age in the 1960s.

Formed around the nucleus of Lennon and McCartney, who first performed together in Liverpool in 1957, the group grew out of a shared enthusiasm for American rock and roll. Lennon, a guitarist and singer, and McCartney, a bassist and singer, were largely self-taught as musicians. Precocious composers, they gathered around themselves a changing cast of accompanists, adding by the end of 1957 Harrison, a lead guitarist, and then, in 1960 for several formative months, Sutcliffe, who brought into the band a brooding sense of bohemian style. After dabbling in skiffle, a jaunty sort of folk music popular in Britain in the late 1950s, and assuming several different names (the Quarrymen, the Silver Beetles, and, finally, the Beatles), the band added a drummer, Best, and joined a small but booming "beat music" scene.

In autumn 1961 Brian Epstein, a local Liverpool record store manager, saw the band, fell in love, became their manager, and proceeded to bombard the major British music companies with letters and tape recordings of the band. The group finally won a contract with Parlophone, a subsidiary of the giant EMI group of music labels. The man in charge of their career at Parlophone was George Martin, a classically trained musician who from the start put his stamp on the Beatles, first by suggesting the band hire a more polished drummer (they chose Starr) and then by rearranging their second recorded song (and first big British hit), "Please Please Me."

Throughout the winter and into the spring of 1963, the Beatles continued their rise to fame in England by producing spirited recordings of original tunes and also by playing classic American rock and roll on a variety of radio programs. In these months, fascination with the Beatles breached the normal barriers of taste, class, and age, transforming their recordings and live performances into matters of widespread public comment. In the fall of that year, when they made a couple of appearances on British television, the evidence of popular frenzy prompted British newspapermen to coin a new word for the phenomenon: *Beatlemania*. In early 1964, after equally tumultuous appearances on American television, the same phenomenon erupted in the United States and provoked a so-called British Invasion of Beatles imitators from the United Kingdom.

Beatlemania was something new. Musicians performing in the 19th century certainly excited a frenzy, but that was before the mass media created the possibility of collective frenzy. Later pop music idols sold similarly large numbers of records, but without provoking anything approaching the hysteria caused by the Beatles. By the summer of 1964, when the Beatles appeared in *A Hard Day's Night*, a movie that dramatized the phenomenon of Beatlemania, the band's effect was evident around the world.

The popular hubbub convinced Lennon and McCartney of their songwriting abilities and sparked an outpouring of creative experimentation all but unprecedented in the history of rock music. Between 1965 and 1967 the music of the Beatles rapidly changed and evolved, becoming ever more subtle, sophisticated, and varied. Their repertoire in these years ranged from the chamber pop ballad "Yesterday" and the enigmatic folk tune "Norwegian Wood" (both in 1965) to the hallucinatory hard rock song "Tomorrow Never Knows" (1966), with a lyric inspired by Timothy Leary's handbook *The Psychedelic Experience* (1964). It also included the carnivalesque soundscape of "Being for the Benefit of Mr. Kite!" (1967), which featured stream-of-consciousness lyrics by Lennon and a typically imaginative arrangement (by George Martin) built around randomly spliced-together snippets of recorded steam organs.

In 1966 the Beatles announced their retirement from public performing to concentrate on exploiting the full resources of the recording studio. A year later, in June 1967, this period of widely watched creative renewal was climaxed by the release of *Sgt. Pepper's Lonely Hearts Club Band*, an album avidly greeted by young people around the world as indisputable evidence not only of the band's genius but also of the era's utopian promise. More than a band of musicians, the Beatles had come to personify, certainly in the minds of millions of young listeners, the

*The Beatles celebrate the completion of their album* Sgt. Pepper's Lonely Hearts Club Band *in May of 1967.* Getty Images/John Pratt

joys of a new counterculture of hedonism and uninhibited experimentation.

In those years the Beatles effectively reinvented the meaning of rock and roll as a cultural form. The American artists they chose to emulate—including Chuck Berry, Little Richard, Elvis Presley, the Everly Brothers, Buddy Holly, the rock composers Jerry Leiber and Mike Stoller, and, after 1964, folksinger Bob Dylan, among others— became widely regarded as canonic sources of inspiration, offering "classical" models for aspiring younger rock musicians. At the same time, the original songs the Beatles wrote and recorded dramatically expanded the musical range and expressive scope of the genre they had inherited.

After 1968 and the eruption of student protest movements in countries as different as Mexico and France, the Beatles insensibly surrendered their role as de facto leaders of an inchoate global youth culture. They nevertheless continued for several more years to record and release new music and maintained a level of popularity rarely rivaled before or since. The band continued to enjoy widespread popularity. The following year *Abbey Road* went on to become one of the band's best-loved and biggest-selling albums.

Meanwhile, personal disagreements magnified by the stress of symbolizing the dreams of a generation had begun to tear the band apart. Lennon and McCartney fell into bickering and mutual accusations of ill will, and in the spring of 1970 the Beatles formally disbanded. In the years that followed, all four members went on to produce solo albums of variable quality and popularity. Lennon released a corrosive set of songs with his new wife, Yoko Ono, and McCartney went on to form a band, Wings, that turned out a fair number of commercially successful recordings in the 1970s. Starr and Harrison, too, initially had some success as solo artists.

In 1980 Lennon was murdered by a demented fan outside the Dakota, an apartment building in New York City known for its celebrity tenants. The event provoked a global outpouring of grief. Lennon is memorialized in Strawberry Fields, a section of Central Park across from the Dakota that Yoko Ono landscaped in her husband's honour.

In the years that followed, the surviving former Beatles continued to record and perform as solo artists. McCartney in particular remained musically active, both in the pop field, producing new albums every few years, and in the field of classical music—in 1991 he completed

*Liverpool Oratorio*; and in 1999 he released a new classical album, *Working Classical*. McCartney was knighted by the queen of England in 1997. Starr was also very visible in the 1990s, touring annually with his All-Star Band, a rotating group of rock veterans playing their hits on the summertime concert circuit. Beginning in 1988, Harrison recorded with Bob Dylan, Tom Petty, Jeff Lynne, and Roy Orbison in a loose amalgam known as the Traveling Wilburys, but, for most of the 1980s and '90s, he had a low profile as a musician while acting as the producer of several successful films. After surviving a knife attack at his home in 1999, Harrison succumbed to a protracted battle with cancer in 2001.

Early in the 1990s McCartney, Harrison, and Starr had joined to add harmonies to two previously unreleased vocal recordings by Lennon. These new songs by "the Beatles" served as a pretext for yet another publicity blitz, aimed at creating a market for a lavishly produced quasi-historical series of archival recordings assembled under the supervision of the band and released in 1995 and 1996 as *The Beatles Anthology*, a collection of six compact discs that supplemented a 10-hour-long authorized video documentary of the same name. A compilation of the band's number one singles, *1*, appeared in 2000 and enjoyed worldwide success, topping the charts in such countries as England and the United States.

The Beatles were inducted into the Rock and Roll Hall of Fame in 1988, and Lennon (1994), McCartney (1999), and Harrison (2004) were also inducted as solo performers. In April 2009 it was announced that on September 9 there would be a simultaneous release of specially packaged, digitally remastered versions of the Beatles' entire catalog and a Beatles version of the popular electronic music game *Rock Band*.

## JOAN BAEZ

(b. Jan. 9, 1941, Staten Island, N.Y., U.S.)

American folksinger and political activist Joan Chandos Baez interested young audiences in folk music during the 1960s. Despite the inevitable fading of the folk music revival, Baez continued to be a popular performer into the 21st century. By touring with younger performers throughout the world and staying politically engaged, she reached a new audience both in the United States and abroad.

The daughter of a physicist of Mexican descent whose teaching and research took him to various communities in New York, California, and elsewhere, Baez moved often

*This photo, taken at a Washington D.C. civil rights rally in 1963, shows folk singers Joan Baez and Bob Dylan performing.* Getty Images/National Archive

and acquired little formal musical training. Her first instrument was the ukulele, but she soon learned to accompany her clear soprano voice on the guitar. Her first album, *Joan Baez*, was released in 1960. Although some considered her voice too pretty, her youthful attractiveness and activist energy put her in the forefront of the 1960s folk-song revival, popularizing traditional songs through her performances in coffeehouses, at music festivals, and on television and through her record albums, which were best sellers from 1960 through 1964 and remained popular. She was instrumental in the early career of Bob Dylan, with whom she was romantically involved for several years. Two of the songs with which she is most identified are her 1971 cover of the Band's song "The Night They Drove Old Dixie Down" and her own song "Diamonds and Rust," which she recorded on her acclaimed album of the same name, issued in 1975.

An active participant in the 1960s protest movement, Baez made free concert appearances for UNESCO, civil rights organizations, and anti-Vietnam War rallies. In 1964 she refused to pay federal taxes that went toward war expenses, and she was jailed twice in 1967. Throughout the years, she remained deeply committed to social and political causes, lending her voice in many concerts for a variety of causes. Among Baez's noteworthy recordings are *Diamonds and Rust*, *Very Early Joan* (1983), *Speaking of Dreams* (1989), *Play Me Backwards* (1992), *Gone from Danger* (1997), and *Bowery Songs* (2004). She wrote *Daybreak* (1968), an autobiography, and a memoir titled *And a Voice to Sing With* (1987).

## PLÁCIDO DOMINGO

(b. Jan. 21, 1941, Madrid, Spain)

Spanish-born singer, conductor, and opera administrator Plácido Domingo, with his resonant, powerful voice, imposing physical stature, good looks, and remarkable dramatic ability, was one of the most popular tenors of his time.

Domingo's parents were noted performers in zarzuela, a form of Spanish light opera. The family moved to Mexico when he was eight. He studied piano and conducting at the National Conservatory of Music, but he changed his emphasis when his rich vocal ability was revealed. In 1961 he made his operatic debut in Mexico City and then went to Dallas to perform in its opera company. From 1962 to 1965 he was a resident performer at Tel Aviv's Hebrew National Opera. He made his debut at the New York City Opera in 1965, at the Metropolitan Opera House in New York City in 1968 (subsequently becoming a regular performer there), and at La Scala in Milan in 1969. Over the course of an opera career that lasted more than 45 years, Domingo sang an unprecedented number of different roles—more than 120—and he continued to learn new parts into his 60s.

A prolific and versatile performer, Domingo made numerous recordings and several film versions of operas, and he ventured into popular music as well. With Luciano Pavarotti and José Carreras, he performed around the world as one of the "Three Tenors," exposing millions of people to the operatic repertoire. He received 11 Grammy Awards in several categories, as well as a Kennedy Center Honor (2000), the U.S. Medal of Freedom (2002), and an honorary British knighthood (2002), among many other honours. In 2009 he was awarded the first Birgit Nilsson Prize for outstanding achievement in classical music.

From 1996 he was artistic director, then from 2001 general director, of the Washington (D.C.) Opera, and from 2000 he was general director of the Los Angeles Opera. Domingo also conducted major symphony and opera orchestras in the United States and Europe. His motto, he claimed, was "If I rest, I rust." His autobiography, *My First Forty Years*, was published in 1983.

## THE BEACH BOYS

The original members were Brian Wilson (b. June 20, 1942, Inglewood, Calif., U.S.), Dennis Wilson (b. Dec. 4, 1944, Inglewood, Calif., U.S.—d. Dec. 28, 1983, Marina del Rey, Calif.), Carl Wilson (b. Dec. 21, 1946, Los Angeles, Calif., U.S.—d. Feb. 6, 1998, Los Angeles), Michael Love (b. March 15, 1941, Los Angeles, Calif., U.S.), and Alan Jardine (b. Sept. 3, 1942, Lima, Ohio, U.S.). Significant later members included David Marks (b. Aug. 22, 1948, Newcastle, Pa., U.S.) and Bruce Johnston (original name William Baldwin; b. June 24, 1944, Chicago, Ill., U.S.)

The dulcet melodies and distinctive vocal mesh of the American rock group the Beach Boys defined the 1960s youthful idyll of sun-drenched southern California.

Initially perceived as a potent pop act—celebrants of the surfing and hot rod culture of the Los Angeles Basin during the 1960s—the Beach Boys and lead singer-bassist-producer Brian Wilson later gained greater respect as muses of post-World War II American suburban angst. Notwithstanding sales of 70 million albums, their greatest achievement was their ability to express the bittersweet middle-class aspirations of those who had participated in America's great internal westward movement in the 1920s. The Beach Boys extolled the promise of a fragile California dream that their parents had had to struggle to sustain.

Growing up in suburban Los Angeles (Hawthorne), the Wilson brothers were encouraged by their parents to explore music. Their father, Murry, who operated a small machinery shop, was also a songwriter. While still teenagers, Brian, drummer Dennis, and guitarist Carl joined with cousin Love and friends Jardine and Marks to write and perform pop music in the alloyed spirit of Chuck Berry and the harmonies-driven Four Freshmen and Four Preps.

Dennis, a novice surfer and adolescent habitué of the Manhattan Beach surfing scene, goaded Brian and the rest of the group (then called the Pendletons) into writing songs that glorified the emerging sport. The regional success in 1961 of the Beach Boys' first single, "Surfin'," led in 1962 to their signing as Capitol Records' first rock act. Brian's latent ambitions as a pop composer were unleashed; for years he would write almost all the group's songs, often with collaborators (most frequently Love). The Beach Boys soon appeared on *Billboard*'s U.S. singles charts with such odes to cars and surfing as "409" and "Surfin' Safari," while their debut album reached number 14. After the commercial triumph of the follow-up album and single, "Surfin' U.S.A.," in 1963, Brian assumed complete artistic control. Their next album, *Surfer Girl*, was a landmark for the unheard-of studio autonomy he secured from Capitol as writer, arranger, and producer. Redolent of the Four Freshmen but actually inspired by "When You Wish Upon a Star" from Walt Disney's film *Pinocchio* (1940), the title track combined a childlike yearning with sophisticated pop poignance. Like his hero, pioneering producer Phil Spector, the eccentric Brian proved gifted at crafting eclectic arrangements with crisply evocative rock power (e.g., "Little Deuce Coupe," "Fun, Fun, Fun," "I Get Around," and "Don't Worry Baby").

After the first of a series of stress- and drug-related breakdowns in 1964, Brian withdrew from touring and was replaced first by singer-guitarist Glen Campbell, then by veteran surf singer-musician Johnston. Brian focused thereafter on the Beach Boys' studio output, surpassing all his role models with his band's masterwork, *Pet Sounds*

(1966). A bittersweet pastiche of songs recalling the pangs of unrequited love and other coming-of-age trials, *Pet Sounds* was acknowledged by Paul McCartney as the catalyst for the Beatles' *Sgt. Pepper's Lonely Hearts Club Band* (1967). Brian soon eclipsed himself again with "Good Vibrations," a startlingly prismatic "pocket symphony" that reached number one in the autumn of 1966. His self-confidence stalled, however, when an even more ambitious project called *Dumb Angel*, then *Smile*, failed to meet its appointed completion date in December 1966. Exhausted and depressed, Brian went into seclusion as the rest of the band cobbled remains of the abortive album into a tuneful but tentative release titled *Smiley Smile* (1967).

For the remainder of the decade, the Beach Boys issued records of increasing commercial and musical inconsistency. They departed Capitol amid a legal battle over back royalties and signed with Warner Brothers in 1970. When the splendid *Sunflower* sold poorly, Brian became a recluse, experimenting with hallucinogens and toiling fitfully while the rest of the group produced several strong but modest-selling albums in the early 1970s. Meanwhile, *Endless Summer*, a greatest hits compilation, reached number one in the charts in 1974. In 1976 an uneven but commercially successful album, *15 Big Ones*, signaled the reemergence of the still drug-plagued Brian. In 1977 Dennis released a critically acclaimed solo album, *Pacific Ocean Blue*. Despite personal turmoil, the reunited Beach Boys seemed destined for a new artistic peak when Dennis drowned in 1983. The excellent *The Beach Boys* was released in 1985. In 1988 Brian released a critically acclaimed self-titled solo album, the other Beach Boys had a number one hit with "Kokomo," and the group was inducted into the Rock and Roll Hall of Fame. In the 1990s the Beach Boys continued to tour and record, with Love continuing his longtime role as the band's business mind. Brian released another solo album (*Imagination*) and collaborated on albums with Van Dyke Parks (*Orange Crate Art*) and with his daughters Carnie and Wendy (*The Wilsons*), who were successful performers in their own right. Carl, who was considered the group's artistic anchor during the turbulent 1970s and '80s, died of cancer in 1998.

In 2004 Brian released *Gettin' In over My Head*, with contributions from Paul McCartney, Eric Clapton, and Elton John. The landmark work of this period in Brian's career, however, was his solo album, *Smile*. He was presented with a Kennedy Center Honor in 2007, and in 2008 he released *That Lucky Old Sun*, a nostalgic celebration of southern California made in collaboration with Scott Bennett and Parks.

# BOB DYLAN

(b. May 24, 1941, Duluth, Minn., U.S.)

American folksinger Bob Dylan (born Robert Allen Zimmerman) moved from folk to rock music in the 1960s and infused the lyrics of rock and roll, theretofore concerned mostly with boy-girl romantic innuendo, with the intellectualism of classic literature and poetry. Dylan has sold more than 58 million albums, written more than 500 songs recorded by more than 2,000 artists, and performed all over the world.

He grew up in the northeastern Minnesota mining town of Hibbing, where his father co-owned Zimmerman Furniture and Appliance Co. He acquired his first guitar at age 14 and as a high school student played in a series of rock and roll bands. In 1959, just before enrolling at the University of Minnesota in Minneapolis, he served a brief stint playing piano for rising pop star Bobby Vee. Fascinated by folksinger Woody Guthrie, he began performing folk music in coffeehouses, adopting the last name Dylan (after the Welsh poet Dylan Thomas). Restless and determined to meet Guthrie—who was confined to a hospital in New Jersey—he relocated to the East Coast.

Arriving in late January 1961, Dylan relied on the generosity of various benefactors who, charmed by his performances in Greenwich Village, provided meals and shelter. He quickly built a following and within four months was hired to play harmonica for a Harry Belafonte recording session. In September 1961 talent scout–producer John Hammond, Sr., signed him to Columbia Records.

Dylan's eponymous first album was released in March 1962 to mixed reviews. His singing voice—a cowboy lament laced with Midwestern patois, with an obvious nod to Guthrie—confounded many critics. By comparison, Dylan's second album, *The Freewheelin' Bob Dylan* (released in May 1963), sounded a clarion call. Young ears everywhere quickly assimilated his quirky voice, which established him as part of the burgeoning counterculture. Moreover, his first major composition, "Blowin' in the Wind," served notice that this was no cookie-cutter recording artist. About this time Dylan signed a seven-year management contract with Albert Grossman, who soon replaced Hammond with another Columbia producer, Tom Wilson.

In April 1963 Dylan played his first major New York City concert at Town Hall. That summer, Dylan made his first appearance at the Newport (Rhode Island) Folk Festival and was virtually crowned the king of folk music. The prophetic title song of his next album, *The Times They Are A-Changin'* (1964), provided an instant anthem.

Dylan was perceived as a singer of protest songs, a politically charged artist with a whole other agenda. He spawned imitators at coffeehouses and record labels everywhere. At the 1964 Newport Folk Festival, while previewing songs from *Another Side of Bob Dylan*, he confounded his core audience by performing songs of a personal nature, rather than his signature protest repertoire. A backlash from purist folk fans began and continued for three years as Dylan defied convention at every turn.

On his next album, *Bringing It All Back Home* (1965), electric instruments were openly brandished—a violation of folk dogma—and only two protest songs were included. The folk rock group the Byrds covered "Mr. Tambourine Man" from that album, adding electric 12-string guitar and three-part harmony vocals, and took it to number one on the singles chart. Dylan's mainstream audience skyrocketed. His purist folk fans, however, fell off in droves.

In June 1965 Dylan recorded his most ascendant song yet, "Like a Rolling Stone." Devoid of obvious protest references, set against a rough-hewn, twangy rock underpinning, and fronted by a snarling vocal that lashed out at all those who questioned his legitimacy, "Like a Rolling Stone" spoke to yet a new set of listeners and reached number two on the popular music charts. And the album containing the hit single, *Highway 61 Revisited*, further vindicated his abdication of the protest throne.

At the 1965 Newport Folk Festival, Dylan bravely showcased his electric sound. After an inappropriately short 15-minute set, Dylan left the stage to a hail of booing—mostly a response to the headliner's unexpectedly abbreviated performance rather than to his electrification. Nonetheless, reams were written about his electric betrayal and banishment from the folk circle. By the time of his next public appearance, at the Forest Hills (New York) Tennis Stadium a month later, the audience had been "instructed" by the press how to react. After a well-received acoustic opening set, Dylan was joined by his new backing band (Al Kooper on keyboards, Harvey Brooks on bass, and, from the Hawks, Canadian guitarist Robbie Robertson and drummer Levon Helm). Dylan and the band were booed throughout the performance.

Backed by Robertson, Helm, and the rest of the Hawks (Rick Danko on bass, Richard Manuel on piano, and Garth Hudson on organ and saxophone), Dylan toured incessantly in 1965 and 1966, always playing to sold-out audiences. On Nov. 22, 1965, Dylan married Sara Lowndes. They split their time between a townhouse in Greenwich Village and a country estate in Woodstock, New York.

In February 1966, at the suggestion of his new producer, Bob Johnston, Dylan recorded at Columbia's Nashville, Tennessee, studios, along with Kooper, Robertson, and the cream of Nashville's studio musicians. A week's worth of marathon sessions produced *Blonde on Blonde*. The critically acclaimed album pushed Dylan to the zenith of his popularity. He toured Europe with the Hawks (soon to reemerge as the Band) until the summer of 1966, when a motorcycle accident in Woodstock brought Dylan's amazing seven-year momentum to an abrupt halt. He retreated to his home in Woodstock and virtually disappeared for two years.

In 1967 the Band moved to Woodstock to be closer to Dylan. Occasionally they coaxed him into the basement studio of their communal home to play music together, and recordings from these sessions ultimately became the double album *The Basement Tapes* (1975). In early 1968 Columbia released a stripped-down album of new Dylan songs titled *John Wesley Harding*. It reached number two on the pop album charts.

In January 1968 Dylan made his first postaccident appearance at a memorial concert for Woody Guthrie in New York City—with shorter hair, spectacles, and a neglected beard. At this point Dylan adopted the stance he held for the rest of his career: sidestepping the desires of the critics, he went in any direction but those called for in print. When his audience and critics were convinced that his muse had left him, Dylan would deliver an album at full strength, only to withdraw again.

Dylan returned to Tennessee to record *Nashville Skyline* (1969), which helped launch an entirely new genre, country rock. It charted at number three, but, owing to the comparative simplicity of its lyrics, people questioned whether Dylan remained a cutting-edge artist. Meanwhile, rock's first bootleg album, *The Great White Wonder*—containing unreleased, "liberated" Dylan recordings—appeared in independent record stores.

Over the next quarter century Dylan continued to record, toured sporadically, and was widely honoured, though his impact was never as great or as immediate as it had been in the 1960s. In 1970 Princeton University awarded him an honorary doctorate of music. In August 1971 Dylan made a rare appearance at a benefit concert that former Beatle George Harrison had organized for the newly independent country of Bangladesh. At the end of the year, Dylan purchased a house in Malibu, California; he had already left Woodstock for New York City in 1969.

In 1973 he appeared in director Sam Peckinpah's film *Pat Garrett and Billy the Kid* and contributed to the soundtrack, including "Knockin' on Heaven's Door." *Writings and Drawings*, an anthology of his lyrics and poetry, was published the next year. In 1974 he toured for the first time in eight years, reconvening with the Band.

Released in January 1975, Dylan's next studio album, *Blood on the Tracks*, was a return to lyrical form. It topped the charts, as did *Desire*, released one year later. In 1975 and 1976 Dylan toured North America, announcing shows only hours before appearing. Filmed and recorded, the *Rolling Thunder Revue*—including Joan Baez, Allen

Ginsberg, Ramblin' Jack Elliott, and Roger McGuinn—came to motion-picture screens in 1978 as part of the Dylan-edited *Renaldo and Clara*.

Lowndes and Dylan divorced in 1977. They had four children, including son Jakob, whose band, the Wallflowers, experienced pop success in the 1990s. Dylan was also stepfather to a child from Lowndes's previous marriage. In 1978 Dylan mounted a yearlong world tour and released *Street-Legal* and *Bob Dylan at Budokan*. In a dramatic turn-about, he converted to Christianity in 1979 and for three years recorded and performed only religious material. He received a Grammy Award in 1980 for best male rock vocal performance with his "gospel" song "Gotta Serve Somebody."

By 1982, when Dylan was inducted into the Songwriters Hall of Fame, his open zeal for Christianity was waning. In 1985 he participated in the all-star charity recording "We Are the World," organized by Quincy Jones, and published his third book, *Lyrics: 1962–1985*. Dylan toured again in 1986–87, backed by Tom Petty and the Heartbreakers. A year later he was inducted into the Rock and Roll Hall of Fame, and the Traveling Wilburys (Dylan, Petty, Harrison, Jeff Lynne, and Roy Orbison) formed at his house in Malibu and released their first album. In 1989 Dylan once again returned to form with *Oh Mercy*.

When *Life* magazine published a list of the 100 most influential Americans of the 20th century in 1990, Dylan was included, and in 1991 he received a Grammy Award for lifetime achievement. As the 1990s drew to a close, Dylan, who was called the greatest poet of the second half of the 20th century by Allen Ginsberg, was the recipient of several national and international honours. In 1998, in a comeback of sorts, he won three Grammy Awards—including album of the year—for *Time Out of Mind*. Another

Grammy (for best contemporary folk album) came Dylan's way in 2001, for *Love and Theft*.

In 2003 he cowrote and starred in the film *Masked & Anonymous* and, because of the effects of carpal tunnel syndrome, began playing electric piano exclusively in live appearances. The next year he released what portended to be the first in a series of autobiographies, *Chronicles: Volume 1*. In 2005 *No Direction Home*, a documentary directed by Martin Scorsese, appeared on television. In 2006 Dylan turned his attention to satellite radio as the host of the weekly *Theme Time Radio Hour* and released his 44th album, *Modern Times*, which won the 2007 Grammy Award for best contemporary folk album.

In presenting to Dylan Spain's Prince of Asturias Prize for the Arts in 2007, the jury called him a "living myth in the history of popular music and a light for a generation that dreamed of changing the world." In 2008 the Pulitzer Prize Board awarded him a special citation for his "profound impact on popular music and American culture." Dylan was still actively performing in his 60s.

## ARETHA FRANKLIN

(b. March 25, 1942, Memphis, Tenn., U.S.)

American singer Aretha Louise Franklin defined the golden age of soul music of the 1960s.

Franklin's mother, Barbara, was a gospel singer and pianist. Her father, C.L. Franklin, presided over the New Bethel Baptist Church of Detroit, Michigan, and was a minister of national influence. A singer himself, he was noted for his brilliant sermons, many of which were recorded by Chess Records.

Franklin's parents separated when she was six, and she remained with her father in Detroit. Her mother died when Aretha was 10. As a young teen, Franklin performed with her father on his gospel programs in major cities throughout the country and was recognized as a vocal prodigy. Her central influence, Clara Ward of the renowned Ward Singers, was a family friend. Other gospel greats of the day—Albertina Walker and Jackie Verdell—helped shape young Franklin's style. Her album *The Gospel Sound of Aretha Franklin* (1956) captures the electricity of her performances as a 14-year-old.

At age 18, with her father's blessing, Franklin switched from sacred to secular music. She moved to New York City, where Columbia Records executive John Hammond, who had signed Count Basie and Billie Holiday, arranged her recording contract and supervised sessions highlighting her in a blues-jazz vein. From that first session, "Today I Sing the Blues" (1960) remains a classic. But, as her Detroit friends on the Motown label enjoyed hit after hit, Franklin struggled to achieve crossover success. Columbia placed her with a variety of producers who marketed her to both adults ("If Ever You Should Leave Me," 1963) and teens ("Soulville," 1964). Without targeting any particular genre, she sang everything from Broadway ballads to youth-oriented rhythm and blues. Critics recognized her talent, but the public remained lukewarm until 1966, when she switched to Atlantic Records, where producer Jerry Wexler allowed her to sculpt her own musical identity.

At Atlantic, Franklin returned to her gospel-blues roots, and the results were sensational. "I Never Loved a Man (the Way I Love You)" (1967), recorded at Fame Studios in Florence, Alabama, was her first million-seller. Surrounded by sympathetic musicians playing spontaneous arrangements and devising the background vocals herself, Franklin refined a style associated with Ray Charles—a rousing mixture of gospel and rhythm and blues—and raised it to new heights. As a civil rights–minded nation lent greater support to black urban music, Franklin was crowned the "Queen of Soul." "Respect," her 1967 cover of Otis Redding's spirited composition, became an anthem operating on personal, sexual, and racial levels. "Think" (1968), which Franklin wrote herself, also had more than one meaning. For the next half-dozen years, she became a hit maker of unprecedented proportions; she was "Lady Soul."

In the early 1970s she triumphed at the Fillmore West in San Francisco before an audience of flower children and on whirlwind tours of Europe and Latin America. Her return to church, *Amazing Grace* (1972), is considered one of the great gospel albums of any era. By the late 1970s disco cramped Franklin's style and eroded her popularity. But in 1982, with help from singer-songwriter-producer Luther Vandross, she was back on top with a new label, Arista, and a new dance hit, "Jump to It," followed by "Freeway of Love" (1985). A reluctant interviewee, Franklin kept her private life private, claiming that the popular perception associating her with the unhappiness of singers Bessie Smith and Billie Holiday was misinformed.

In 1987 Franklin became the first woman inducted into the Rock and Roll Hall of Fame. While her album sales in the 1990s and 2000s failed to approach the numbers of previous decades, Franklin remained the Queen of Soul, and in 2009 she electrified a crowd of more than one million with her performance of "My Country 'Tis of Thee" at the presidential inauguration of Barack Obama.

## JIMI HENDRIX

(b. Nov. 27, 1942, Seattle, Wash., U.S.—d. Sept. 18, 1970, London, Eng.)

American rock guitarist, singer, and composer Jimi Hendrix fused American traditions of blues, jazz, rock, and soul with techniques of British avant-garde rock to redefine the electric guitar in his own image.

Though his active career as a featured artist lasted a mere four years, Hendrix altered the course of popular music and became one of the most successful and influential musicians of his era. An instrumentalist who radically redefined the expressive potential and sonic palette of the electric guitar, he was the composer of a classic repertoire of songs ranging from ferocious rockers to delicate, complex ballads. He also was the most charismatic in-concert performer of his generation. Moreover, he was a visionary who collapsed the genre boundaries of rock, soul, blues, and jazz and an iconic figure whose appeal linked the

*Rock guitar legend Jimi Hendrix is seen here in the middle of his performance at the Isle of Wight Festival in August of 1970.* Getty Images/Evening Standard

concerns of white hippies and black revolutionaries by clothing black anger in the colourful costumes of London's Carnaby Street.

A former paratrooper whose honourable medical discharge exempted him from service in the Vietnam War, Hendrix spent the early 1960s working as a freelance accompanist for a variety of musicians, both famous and obscure. His unorthodox style and penchant for playing at high volume, however, limited him to subsistence-level work until he was discovered in a small New York City club and brought to England in August 1966. Performing alongside two British musicians, he stunned London's clubland with his instrumental virtuosity and extroverted showmanship. Members of the Beatles, the Rolling Stones, and the Who were among his admirers, but it proved a lot easier for Hendrix to learn their tricks than it was for them to learn his.

Hendrix had an encyclopaedic knowledge of the musical roots on which the cutting-edge rock of his time was based, but, thanks to his years on the road with the likes of Little Richard and the Isley Brothers, he also had hands-on experience of the cultural and social worlds in which those roots had developed and a great admiration for the work of Bob Dylan, the Beatles, and the Yardbirds. Speedily adapting the current musical and sartorial fashions of late 1966 London to his own needs, he was soon able not only to match the likes of the Who at their own high-volume, guitar-smashing game but also to top them with what rapidly became the hottest-ticket show in town.

By November his band, the Jimi Hendrix Experience, had their first Top Ten single, "Hey Joe." Two more hits, "Purple Haze" and "The Wind Cries Mary," followed before their first album, *Are You Experienced?*, was released in the summer of 1967, when it was second in impact only to the Beatles' *Sgt. Pepper's Lonely Hearts Club Band*. Its immediate successor, *Axis: Bold as Love*, followed that December. Hendrix was flown to California for a scene-stealing appearance at the Monterey Pop Festival, which rendered him a sensation in his homeland less than a year after his departure.

Relocating back to the United States in 1968, he enjoyed further acclaim with the sprawling, panoramic double album *Electric Ladyland*, but the second half of his career proved frustrating. Legal complications from an old contract predating his British sojourn froze his recording royalties, necessitating constant touring to pay his bills; and his audiences were reluctant to allow him to progress beyond the musical blueprint of his earliest successes. He was on the verge of solving both these problems when he died of an overdose of barbiturates. In his all-too brief career, Hendrix managed to combine and extend the soaring improvisational transcendence of John Coltrane, the rhythmic virtuosity of James Brown, the bluesy intimacy of John Lee Hooker, the lyrical aesthetic of Bob Dylan, the bare-knuckle onstage aggression of the Who, and the hallucinatory studio fantasias of the Beatles. His work provides a continuing source of inspiration to successive generations of musicians to whom he remains a touchstone for emotional honesty, technological innovation, and an all-inclusive vision of cultural and social brotherhood.

## JONI MITCHELL

(b. Nov. 7, 1943, Fort McLeod, Alta., Can.)

Canadian experimental singer-songwriter Joni Mitchell (born Roberta Joan Anderson) enjoyed her greatest popularity in the 1970s. Like her contemporary of the 1960s, Bob Dylan, she helped turn pop music into an art form.

Mitchell studied commercial art in her native Alberta before moving to Toronto in 1964 and performing at local folk clubs and coffeehouses. After a brief marriage to folksinger Chuck Mitchell, she relocated to New York City, where in 1967 she made her eponymous debut album (also known as *Songs to a Seagull*). This concept album was acclaimed for the maturity of its lyrics.

With each successive release, Mitchell gained a larger following, from *Clouds* (which in 1969 won a Grammy Award for best folk performance) to the mischievous euphoria of *Ladies of the Canyon* (1970) to *Blue* (1971), which was her first million-selling album. By the early 1970s Mitchell had branched out from her acoustic base to experiment with rock and jazz, with *The Hissing of Summer Lawns* (1975) marking her transition to a more complex, layered sound. Whereas earlier albums were more confessional in their subject matter, *The Hissing of Summer Lawns*, on which she satirized the role of the 1970s housewife, showed Mitchell's movement toward social observation. Although she had a number of pop hits, especially in 1970 with "Big Yellow Taxi" and "Woodstock," Mitchell's impact was as a long-term "album artist." With its carefully precise yet improvisational feel, her music is at times difficult to listen to. She does not opt for straight melody or satisfying conclusions. "My music is not designed to grab instantly. It's designed to wear for a lifetime, to hold up like a fine cloth," she once said.

With *Hejira* (1976) and *Don Juan's Reckless Daughter* (1977), she continued to disregard commercial considerations, while *Mingus* (1979) was considered by many as beyond the pale. An album that began as a collaboration with the jazz bassist Charles Mingus ended up as a treatment of his themes after his death. Mitchell delved not only deeper into jazz but also into black history; the album was as much a voice for the dispossessed as it was a biography of Mingus.

Having proved that she could make commercially successful albums and win critical acclaim, Mitchell became a prestige artist. Moreover, because her songs had become hits for others, she was a source of considerable publishing revenue for her record companies. As a result, they went along with her musical experiments. After *Mingus*, however, Mitchell stood back a little from the pop world. From the beginning of her career she had illustrated her own album covers, so it was not surprising that in the 1980s she began to develop her visual art, undecided about whether to concentrate more on painting or music.

Although not as prolific as in the 1960s and '70s, Mitchell continued to create penetrating, imaginative music, from *Dog Eat Dog* (1985) to the more reflective *Night Ride Home* (1991) and the Grammy Award-winning *Turbulent Indigo* (1994). Having dealt with international political and social issues such as Ethiopian famine on *Dog Eat Dog*, she returned, by the early 1990s, to more personal subject matter—singing about true love, for instance, on *Turbulent Indigo*. One of the first women in modern rock to achieve enviable longevity and critical recognition, Mitchell has been a major inspiration to everyone from Dylan and Prince to a later generation of female artists such as Suzanne Vega and Alanis Morissette. Although she regularly collaborated with producers and arrangers,— Mitchell always had control over her material. Her songs have been covered by a range of stars, including Dylan, Fairport Convention, Judy Collins, Johnny Cash, and Crosby, Stills and Nash. Though unworried about pop chart trends, in 1997 she enjoyed major success with a new, young audience when Janet Jackson sampled from Mitchell's *Big Yellow Taxi* for the massive hit *Got 'Til It's*

*Gone.* In 1997 she published a new collection of her work, entitled *Joni Mitchell: The Complete Poems and Lyrics.* That year she was also inducted into the Rock and Roll Hall of Fame.

## LED ZEPPELIN

The members were Jimmy Page (b. Jan. 9, 1944, Heston, Middlesex, Eng.), Robert Plant (b. Aug. 20, 1948, West Bromwich, West Midlands, Eng.), John Paul Jones (original name John Baldwin; b. Jan. 3, 1946, Sidcup, Kent, Eng.), and John Bonham (b. May 31, 1948, Redditch, Hereford and Worcester, Eng. — d. Sept. 25, 1980, Windsor, Berkshire).

The British rock band Led Zeppelin was extremely popular in the 1970s, and although their musical style was diverse, they came to be well known for their influence on the development of heavy metal.

Initially called the New Yardbirds, Led Zeppelin was formed in 1968 by Jimmy Page, the final lead guitarist for the legendary British blues band the Yardbirds. Bassist and keyboard player Jones, like Page, was a veteran studio musician; vocalist Plant and drummer Bonham came from little-known provincial bands. The group was influenced by various kinds of music, including early rock and roll, psychedelic rock, blues, folk, Celtic, Indian, and Arabic music. Although acoustic and folk-based music was part of the band's repertoire from its inception, it was the bottom-heavy, loud, raw, and powerful electric style that gained them their following and notoriety early on; their first two albums included many of the songs that prompted Led Zeppelin's categorization as a precursor of heavy metal. The heaviness of songs such as "Dazed and Confused" and "Whole Lotta Love" was created by Bonham's enormous drum sound and through Page's production techniques, in which he emphasized drums and bass, resulting in a sonic spaciousness that has kept the records sounding fresh years after they were made. Page and Jones also wrote most of the band's music, while Plant contributed lyrics and some musical ideas. Although Page was responsible for the majority of their signature riffs (the short, repeated musical ideas that often structure a song), Jones wrote the riff for the celebrated "Black Dog" and several other songs. Jones also contributed much to the arrangement of songs. Page's guitar solos were based primarily on melodic ideas derived from the blues scale ("Heartbreaker" is a good example), and he is especially known for creating multiple, simultaneous guitar parts—a kind of guitar orchestra—in such songs as "Achilles Last Stand" and "The Song Remains the Same." Page is considered one of rock's guitar heroes, but, because he was more interested in creating a distinctive mood and sound on a recording than in displaying his virtuosity, he frequently chose not to include a guitar solo in Zeppelin songs.

Plant's voice rounded out Led Zeppelin's sound. Exaggerating the vocal style and expressive palette of blues singers such as Howlin' Wolf and Muddy Waters, Plant created the sound that has defined much hard rock and heavy metal singing: a high range, an abundance of distortion, loud volume, and emotional excess ("Whole Lotta Love" is a classic example). Plant was, however, capable of a broader stylistic range, including tender ballads ("The Rain Song") and songs showing the influence of Indian and Arabic vocal styles ("Kashmir").

Led Zeppelin's best-known song is "Stairway to Heaven"; its gentle acoustic beginning eventually builds to an exhilarating climax featuring a lengthy electric guitar solo. This combination of acoustic and electric sections was typical for Page, who from the band's beginning was interested in juxtaposing what he called "light and shade."

The song appeared on the band's fourth and most famous album, released untitled, which showed only four runic symbols (intended to represent the band members) on the cover and had the mystical, mythological lyrics to "Stairway" printed on the inner sleeve. The sense of mystery and ritual that this created became an important part of the band's image.

Thanks in part to their manager, Peter Grant, the band enjoyed phenomenal commercial success throughout the 1970s. While Led Zeppelin never received the kind of critical acclaim or mainstream acceptance accorded the Beatles or the Rolling Stones, their influence on rock music has been prodigious. They are regularly cited as the progenitors of both hard rock and heavy metal. Their sound has been imitated by bands from Black Sabbath to Nirvana. They also inspired hard rock bands to include acoustic elements in their music and were among the first to experiment with Indian and North African music. Page's style has served as an important model for most rock guitarists, and Bonham is often cited as the model for metal or hard rock drumming.

Led Zeppelin disbanded in 1980 after Bonham's accidental death. The group re-formed for short, one-off performances in 1985 (the Live Aid benefit), 1988 (Atlantic Records' 40th anniversary concert), and 1995 (the band's induction into the Rock and Roll Hall of Fame). Much more momentous was the group's full-blown concert in London in December 2007 to honour Atlantic's legendary cofounder Ahmet Ertegun, at which Bonham's son, Jason, played the drums.

## THE WHO

The principal members were Pete Townshend (b. May 19, 1945, London, Eng.), Roger Daltrey (b. March 1, 1944, London, Eng.),

John Entwistle (b. Oct. 9, 1944, London, Eng.—d. June 27, 2002, Las Vegas, Nev., U.S.), and Keith Moon (b. Aug. 23, 1946, London. Eng.—d. Sept. 7, 1978, London). Moon was replaced by Kenny Jones (b. Sept. 16, 1948, London, Eng.).

The Who was a British rock group that was among the most popular and influential bands of the 1960s and '70s and that originated the rock opera.

Though primarily inspired by American rhythm and blues, the Who took a bold step toward defining a uniquely British rock vernacular in the 1960s. Eschewing the Beatles' idealized romance and the Rolling Stones' cocky swagger, the Who shunned pretension and straight-forwardly dealt with teenage travails. At a time when rock music was uniting young people all over the world, the Who were friendless, bitter outsiders.

Townshend and Entwistle joined Daltrey in his group, the Detours, in 1962; with drummer Doug Sandom they became, in turn, the Who and the High Numbers. Moon replaced Sandom in early 1964, after which the group released a self-consciously mod single ("I'm the Face") to little notice and became the Who again in late 1964. The West London quartet cultivated a Pop art image to suit the fashion-obsessed British "mod" subculture and matched that look with the rhythm-and-blues sound that mod youth favoured. Townshend ultimately acknowledged that clothing made from the Union Jack, sharp suits, pointy boots, and short haircuts were a contrivance, but it did the trick, locking in a fanatically devoted core following. Fashion, however, was strictly a starting point for the Who; by the late 1960s the mods were history, and the Who were long past needing to identify themselves with the uniform of any movement.

The band's early records dealt with alienation, uncertainty, and frustration, lashing out with tough lyrics, savage power chords and squalling feedback by guitarist-songwriter Townshend, the kinetic assault of drummer Moon and bassist Entwistle, and the macho brawn of singer Daltrey. The four singles that introduced the Who between January 1965 and March 1966 — "I Can't Explain," "Anyway, Anyhow, Anywhere," "My Generation," and "Substitute" — declared themselves in an unprecedented fury of compressed sonic aggression, an artistic statement intensified onstage by Townshend's habit of smashing his guitar to climax concerts. While other groups were moving toward peace-and-love idealism, the Who sang of unrequited lust ("Pictures of Lily"), peer pressure ("Happy Jack"), creepy insects (Entwistle's "Boris the Spider"), and gender confusion ("I'm a Boy"). As one instrument after another ended in splinters, the Who firmly declared themselves proponents of making violent rage a form of rock catharsis.

Until the 1967 release of *The Who Sell Out*, a sardonic concept album presented as a pirate radio broadcast, the Who were primarily a singles group. They were, however, more successful in this regard in Britain than in the United States ("I Can See for Miles," released in 1967, was the group's only *Billboard* Top Ten single). It was the 1969 rock opera *Tommy* — and a memorable performance at Woodstock that summer — that made the Who a world-class album-rock act. In the process, Townshend was recognized as one of rock's most intelligent, articulate, and self-conscious composers.

The Who cemented their standing with *Who's Next* (1971), an album of would-be teen anthems ("Won't Get Fooled Again," "Baba O'Riley") and sensitive romances ("Behind Blue Eyes," "Love Ain't for Keeping"), all reflecting Townshend's dedication to his "avatar," the Indian mystic Meher Baba. That same year, Entwistle released a solo album, the darkly amusing *Smash Your Head Against the Wall*; Townshend issued his first solo album, *Who Came*

*First*, in 1972; and Daltrey offered his, *Daltrey*, in 1973. Still, the Who continued apace, releasing Townshend's second magnum rock opera, *Quadrophenia*, in 1973, *The Who by Numbers* in 1975, and *Who Are You* in 1978.

Moon ("the Loon"), whose excessive lifestyle was legendary, died of an accidental drug overdose in 1978 and was replaced by Jones. So constituted, the Who released *Face Dances* (1981) and *It's Hard* (1982) before disbanding in 1982. Daltrey pursued acting while letting his solo career taper off. Entwistle released occasional records to little effect. Townshend busied himself briefly as a book editor while undertaking a variety of solo ventures—from well-received Who-like rock records such as *Empty Glass* (1980) to *The Iron Man* (1989), a less-successful experiment in musical theatre that nevertheless paved the way for the triumphant delivery of *Tommy* to Broadway in 1993. Townshend, Daltrey, and Entwistle reunited for tours in 1989 and 1996–97. The Who was about to embark on a U.S. tour in 2002 when Entwistle died.

*Tommy* remains the Who's most enduring creation. On its way to the theatre, *Tommy* became an all-star orchestral album in 1972 and a garish film with Daltrey in the title role in 1975. *Quadrophenia* also was made into a film, in 1979, and was revived by the touring Who as a stagy rock spectacle in the 1990s.

In 2005 and 2006 Townshend serialized a novella, *The Boy Who Heard Music*, online, and a set of related songs constituted *Wire & Glass*, the mini-opera that made up part of *Endless Wire* (2006), which was the first album of new Who material since 1982. A full-blown musical based on this material and also titled *The Boy Who Heard Music* premiered in July 2007 at Vassar College in Poughkeepsie, N.Y. A year later the Who were celebrated (and performed) at a VH1 Rock Honors concert.

# BOB MARLEY

(b. Feb. 6, 1945, Nine Miles, St. Ann, Jam.—d. May 11, 1981, Miami, Fla., U.S.)

The thoughtful, ongoing distillation of early ska, rock steady, and reggae forms by Jamaican singer-songwriter Bob Marley blossomed in the 1970s into an electrifying rock-influenced hybrid that made the musician an international superstar.

The son of a white rural overseer, Norval Sinclair Marley, and the black daughter of a local *custos* (respected backwoods squire), the former Cedella Malcolm, Bob Marley would forever remain the unique product of parallel worlds—his poetic worldview was shaped by the countryside, his music by the tough West Kingston ghetto streets. Marley's maternal grandfather was not just a prosperous farmer but also a bush doctor adept at the mysticism-steeped herbal healing that guaranteed respect in Jamaica's remote hill country. As a child Marley was known for his shy aloofness, his startling stare, and his penchant for palm reading. Virtually kidnapped by his absentee father (who had been disinherited by his own prominent family for marrying a black woman), the preadolescent Marley was taken to live with an elderly woman in Kingston until a family friend rediscovered the boy by chance and returned him to Nine Miles.

By his early teens Marley was back in West Kingston, living in a government-subsidized tenement in Trench Town, a desperately poor slum. In the early 1960s, while a schoolboy serving an apprenticeship as a welder, Marley was exposed to the languid, jazz-infected shuffle-beat rhythms of ska, a Jamaican amalgam of American rhythm and blues and native mento (folk-calypso) strains then catching on commercially. Marley was a fan of Fats

Domino, the Moonglows, and pop singer Ricky Nelson, but, when his big chance came in 1961 to record with producer Leslie Kong, he cut "Judge Not," a peppy ballad he had written based on rural maxims learned from his grandfather. Among his other early tracks was "One Cup of Coffee," issued in 1963 in England on the Island Records label.

Marley also formed a vocal group in Trench Town with friends who would later be known as Peter Tosh (original name Winston Hubert MacIntosh) and Bunny Wailer (original name Neville O'Reilly Livingston). The trio, which named itself the Wailers (because, as Marley stated, "We started out crying"), received vocal coaching by noted singer Joe Higgs. Later they were joined by vocalist Junior Braithwaite and backup singers Beverly Kelso and Cherry Green.

In December 1963 the Wailers entered Coxsone Dodd's Studio One facilities to cut "Simmer Down," a song by Marley that he had used to win a talent contest in Kingston. "Simmer Down" was an urgent anthem from the shantytown precincts of the Kingston underclass. A huge overnight smash, it played an important role in recasting the agenda for stardom in Jamaican music circles. No longer did one have to parrot the stylings of overseas entertainers; it was possible to write raw, uncompromising songs for and about the disenfranchised people of the West Indian slums.

This bold stance transformed both Marley and his island nation, engendering the urban poor with a pride that would become a pronounced source of identity in Jamaican culture—as would the Wailers' Rastafarian faith, a creed popular among the impoverished people of the Caribbean, who worshiped the late Ethiopian emperor Haile Selassie I as the African redeemer foretold in popular

*Jamaican singer-songwriter Bob Marley performing live on stage.* Echoes/
Redferns/Getty Images

quasi-biblical prophecy. The Wailers did well in Jamaica
during the mid-1960s with their ska records, even during
Marley's sojourn to Delaware in 1966 to visit his relocated
mother and find temporary work. Reggae material created
in 1969–71 increased the contemporary stature of the
Wailers; and, once they signed in 1972 with the (by that
time) international label Island and released *Catch a Fire*,
their uniquely rock-contoured reggae gained a global audience. It also earned the charismatic Marley superstar
status, which gradually led to the dissolution of the original
triumvirate about early 1974. Although Peter Tosh would
enjoy a distinguished solo career before his murder in 1987,
many of his best solo albums (such as *Equal Rights* [1977])

were underappreciated, as was Bunny Wailer's excellent solo album *Blackheart Man* (1976).

Eric Clapton's version of the Wailers' "I Shot the Sheriff" in 1974 spread Marley's fame. Meanwhile, Marley continued to guide the skilled Wailers band through a series of potent, topical albums. By this point Marley also was backed by a trio of female vocalists that included his wife, Rita; she, like many of Marley's children, later experienced her own recording success. Featuring eloquent songs like "No Woman No Cry," "Exodus," "Could You Be Loved," "Coming in from the Cold," "Jamming," and "Redemption Song," Marley's landmark albums included *Natty Dread* (1974), *Live!* (1975), *Rastaman Vibration* (1976), *Exodus* (1977), *Kaya* (1978), *Uprising* (1980), and the posthumous *Confrontation* (1983). Exploding in Marley's reedy tenor, his songs were public expressions of personal truths—eloquent in their uncommon mesh of rhythm and blues, rock, and venturesome reggae forms and electrifying in their narrative might.

He also loomed large as a political figure and in 1976 survived what was believed to have been a politically motivated assassination attempt. Marley's attempt to broker a truce between Jamaica's warring political factions led in April 1978 to his headlining the "One Love" peace concert. His sociopolitical clout also earned him an invitation to perform in 1980 at the ceremonies celebrating majority rule and internationally recognized independence for Zimbabwe. In April 1981, the Jamaican government awarded Marley the Order of Merit. A month later he died of cancer.

Although his songs were some of the best-liked and most critically acclaimed music in the popular canon, Marley was far more renowned in death than he had been in life. *Legend* (1984), a retrospective of his work, became the best-selling reggae album ever, with international sales of more than 12 million copies.

## ERIC CLAPTON

(b. March 30, 1945, Ripley, Surrey, Eng.)

**B**ritish rock musician Eric Clapton (born Eric Patrick Clapp) was a highly influential guitarist in the late 1960s and early 1970s and later became a major singer-songwriter.

Clapton was raised by his grandparents after his mother abandoned him at an early age. He began playing the guitar in his teens and briefly studied at the Kingston College of Art. After playing lead guitar with two minor bands, in 1963 he joined the Yardbirds, a rhythm-and-blues group in which his blues-influenced playing and commanding technique began to attract attention. Clapton left the Yardbirds in 1965 when they pursued commercial success with a pop-oriented style. That same year he joined John Mayall's Bluesbreakers, and his guitar playing soon became the group's principal drawing card as it attracted a fanatic following on the London club scene.

In 1966 Clapton left the Bluesbreakers to form a new band with two other virtuoso rock musicians, bassist Jack Bruce and drummer Ginger Baker. This group, Cream, achieved international popularity with its sophisticated, high-volume fusion of rock and blues that featured improvisatory solos. Clapton's mastery of blues form and phrasing, his rapid runs, and his plaintive vibrato were widely imitated by other rock guitarists. The high energy and emotional intensity of his playing on such songs as "Crossroads" and "White Room" set the standard for the rock guitar solo. Cream disbanded in late 1968, however, after having recorded such albums as *Disraeli Gears* (1967), *Wheels of Fire* (1968), and *Goodbye* (1969).

In 1969 Clapton and Baker formed the group Blind Faith with keyboardist-vocalist Steve Winwood and bassist Rick Grech, but the group broke up after recording only one album. Clapton emerged as a capable vocalist on his first solo album, which was released in 1970. He soon assembled a trio of strong session musicians (bassist Carl Radle, drummer Jim Gordon, and keyboardist Bobby Whitlock) into a new band called Derek and the Dominos, with Clapton as lead guitarist, vocalist, and songwriter. The guitarist Duane Allman joined the group in making the classic double album *Layla and Other Assorted Love Songs* (1970), which is regarded as Clapton's masterpiece and a landmark among rock recordings. Disappointed by *Layla*'s lacklustre sales and addicted to heroin, Clapton went into seclusion for two years. Overcoming his addiction, he made a successful comeback with the album *461 Ocean Boulevard* (1974), which included his hit remake of Bob Marley's "I Shot the Sheriff." On the album Clapton adopted a more relaxed approach that emphasized his songwriting and vocal abilities rather than his guitar playing. Over the next 20 years Clapton produced a string of albums, including *Slowhand* (1977), *Backless* (1978), *Money and Cigarettes* (1983), *August* (1986), *Unplugged* (1992)—which featured the Top Five hit "Tears in Heaven," written after the death of his son—and *From the Cradle* (1994). He explored his musical influences with a pair of Grammy-winning collaborations: *Riding with the King* (2000) with blues legend B.B. King and *The Road to Escondido* (2006) with roots guitarist J.J. Cale. The critical and commercial success of these albums solidified his stature as one of the world's greatest rock musicians. *Clapton*, an autobiography, was published in 2007. In 2000 Clapton was inducted into the Rock and Roll Hall of Fame.

# KING SUNNY ADE

(b. Sept. 1, 1946, Oshogbo, Nigeria)

Nigerian popular musician Sunday Adeniyi, popularly known as King Sunny Ade, was in the vanguard of the development and international popularization of juju music—a fusion of traditional Yoruba vocal forms and percussion with Western rock and roll.

"King" Sunny Ade enjoyed noble status not only through birth into the Yoruba royalty of southwestern Nigeria but also through popular acclaim as the "King of Juju" since the late 1970s. In his youth Ade played highlife, a type of urban dance music that emerged in Ghana in the late 19th century and blended elements of church music, military brass-band music, sea shanties, and various local African traditions. In the mid-1960s Ade abandoned highlife for juju, a related musical genre that arose in Nigeria in the 1920s as an expression of the urban Yoruba working class. He assembled his own juju band, the Green Spots, which he later renamed the African Beats, reflecting the re-Africanization of the genre that had been occurring since the early 1950s in conjunction with a growing sense of nationalism.

Prior to Ade's formation of the African Beats, one of his most notable predecessors, I.K. Dairo, had already modified juju through incorporation of Yoruba "talking" drums—which replicate the tones of Yoruba language—and through extensive use of the call-and-response vocal structure that is typical of the traditional music of many sub-Saharan African peoples, including the Yoruba. Upon this musical foundation, Ade laid a tapestry of guitar voices infused with the rhythmic and melodic colours of rock and roll. Ade's early albums with the African Beats, most notably *Sound Vibration* (1977) and *The Royal Sound* (1979), were tremendously successful, and, when the press

This photo from around 1960 shows Nigerian popular musician King Sunny Ade performing with a band onstage. Jon Sievert/Michael Ochs Archives/ Getty Images

declared Ade the King of Juju in 1977, the title became integral to his professional persona.

In the early 1980s Ade signed with Island Records, and the release of *Juju Music* (1982) propelled him, his band, and juju into the international limelight. Ade's next album with Island, the synthesizer-enriched *Synchro System* (1983), drew an even more thunderous response and prompted a surge in international bookings. By the mid-1980s Ade had exposed much of the non-African world to Nigerian juju. After his separation from Island in 1985, Ade focused his musical activity at home, at which time he also began to shift the topics of his lyrics from the ills of Nigerian society to more-intimate matters of personal struggle. Although he maintained a tight schedule of recording and performances in Nigeria, he continued to make inter-mittent appearances abroad on the rapidly expanding world music concert and festival circuit, where both he and juju music continued to enjoy a strong following.

## DAVID BOWIE

(b. Jan. 8, 1947, London, Eng.)

British singer, songwriter, and actor David Bowie (born David Robert Jones) was most prominent in the 1970s and best known for his distinctive voice, shifting personae, and prescient sense of musical trends.

To call Bowie a transitional figure in rock history is less a judgment than a job description. Every niche he ever found was on a cusp, and he was at home nowhere else — certainly not in the unmoneyed London suburb where his childhood was as reserved as his adult life would be glamorous.

Gifted as a musician, actor, writer, and artist (Bowie attended art school from the age of 12), he would ulti-mately find his place as a performer utilizing all these skills. Nothing if not an eclectic musician in his own right,

*Here David Bowie performs onstage during the final day of the Isle of Wight rock festival in England, 2004.* Getty Images/Dave Hogan

Bowie had similarly diverse tastes regarding the work of others, being an admirer of the showmanship of British actor and musician Anthony Newley as well as the romantic lyricism of Belgian musician Jacques Brel.

During the mod era of the 1960s Bowie fronted various bands from whose shadow he—having renamed himself to avoid confusion with the singer of the Monkees—emerged as a solo singer-songwriter. "Space Oddity," the science-fiction single that marks the real beginning of his career, reached the Top Ten in Britain in 1969, the song's well-timed release coming just after the Apollo 11 Moon mission. Bowie's third album, *The Man Who Sold the World* (1970), displayed an unprecedented hybrid of folk, art rock, and heavy metal sounds. But it wasn't until *Hunky Dory* (1971) that Bowie became truly popular, the hit single "Changes" being the prime vector of that fame.

The singer's ever-changing appearance, too, created a record-selling buzz. At once lighthearted and portentous, Bowie's dramatic chameleonlike approach was tailor-made for the 1970s, his signature decade. Bowie created a series of inspired, daringly grandiose pastiches that insisted on utopia by depicting its alternative as inferno, beginning with the emblematic rock-star martyr fantasy *The Rise and Fall of Ziggy Stardust and the Spiders from Mars* (1972). In the process he stayed so hard on the heels of the zeitgeist that the doom-saying of *Diamond Dogs* (1974) and the disco romanticism of *Young Americans* (1975) were released less than a year apart.

Bowie's public disclosure of his bisexuality, rather than derailing his growing popularity, boosted his enigmatic allure. Similarly, his later recantation of such sexual proclivities had no negative affect on his career. Yet all this public display of personal matters took a private toll. By 1977 Bowie had decamped, ditching his idiosyncratic version of the main-stream for the avant-garde austerities of the minimalist album *Low*, a collaboration in Berlin with Brian Eno, the influential musician and producer who is perhaps best known for his ambient albums. As music, *Low* and its sequels, *Heroes* (1977) and *Lodger* (1979), would prove to be Bowie's most influential and lasting, serving as a blueprint for a later generation of techno-rock. In the short run, the albums marked the end of his significant mass audience impact, though not his sales. In addition to Eno, Bowie also collaborated with guitarists Mick Ronson and Carlos Alomar as well as ace nouveau-funk producer Nile Rodgers for "Let's Dance" (1983).

In the 1980s, despite the impressive artistic resolve of *Scary Monsters* (1980) and the equally impressive commercial success of *Let's Dance* (1983), which produced three American Top 20 hits, Bowie's once-innovative work seemed to have lost the musical, intellectual, and boundary-pushing edge of his previous efforts. In tandem with an acting career that, since his arresting debut in Nicolas Roeg's *The Man Who Fell to Earth* (1976), largely failed to jell, his vague later albums oscillated between would-be commercial moves for which he did not seem to have the heart (*Never Let Me Down* [1987]) and would-be artistic statements for which he had lost his shrewdness (*Outside* [1995]). Yet his 1970s work including, in addition to his own output, service as a producer on landmark albums from Mott the Hoople, Lou Reed, and Iggy and the Stooges remains a vital and compelling index to a time it did its part to shape. Bowie was inducted into the Rock and Roll Hall of Fame in 1996. Ten years later, he was awarded the Grammy Lifetime Achievement Award.

## NUSRAT FATEH ALI KHAN
(b. Oct. 13, 1948, Lyallpur [now Faisalabad] Pak.—d. Aug. 16, 1997, London, Eng.)

Pakistani singer Nusrat Fateh Ali Khan is considered one of the greatest performers of *qawwali*, a Sufi Muslim devotional music characterized by simple melodies, forceful rhythms, and energetic improvisations that encourage a state of euphoria in the listener.

Nusrat's father, Ustad Fateh Ali Khan, and two of his uncles, Ustad Mubarik Ali Khan and Ustad Salamat Ali Khan, were famous *qawwal*s (practitioners of *qawwali*) who sang in the classical form. Although Nusrat began to display a penchant for music and a particular aptitude for singing before he had reached age 10, he did not begin to devote himself to the *qawwali* tradition until he sang at his father's funeral in 1964. Two years later he gave his first public performance as a *qawwal*, singing with his uncles, with whom he continued to perform until 1971, when Ustad Mubarik died.

*Qawwali* originated in 12th-century Persia. The lyrics are based on medieval Sufi poems that often use images of romantic love to express deep religious faith. The traditionally male *qawwal*, who knows these poems by heart, unites phrases and passages from different poems to create a new expression. *Qawwali* performances are typically held in shrines and are marked by passionate shouting and dancing. *Qawwali* is similar in spirit to American gospel music.

Following his father's death, Nusrat continued to study the recordings of his father and uncles, using them as a springboard from which to develop his own style. Within just a few years he had established himself throughout Pakistan as the outstanding *qawwal* of his generation, singing powerfully and expressively in a very high register (a family trademark), with remarkable stamina and melodic creativity. In concert he was usually accompanied by tabla (a pair of single-headed drums played with the hands), harmoniums (or reed organs; small keyboard instruments with a foot-operated bellows), and backing vocals.

As he matured as a performer, Nusrat made various adjustments to his style, such as increasing the tempo, as a means to elevate *qawwali* to a new level of aesthetic and spiritual resonance with contemporary—and international—audiences. In 1985 he gave a concert in the United Kingdom, and word of his talent began to spread. He was soon performing regularly throughout Europe. He first toured the United States in 1989, and in the 1990s he contributed to the sound tracks of several popular films. Nusrat also worked with a number of internationally recognized figures in popular and art music. Popular musician Peter Gabriel promoted Nusrat on the world music circuit through his WOMAD (World of Music, Arts and Dance) festivals and through recordings on his Real World Records label. Meanwhile, composer Michael Brook helped increase the accessibility of Nusrat's vocalizations by recasting them within Western rhythmic frameworks. Nusrat believed in the universality of the musical message and strove throughout his career to make his music transcend religious and cultural boundaries. When he died suddenly in 1997, Nusrat was mourned by fans across the globe.

## BRUCE SPRINGSTEEN
(b. Sept. 23, 1949, Freehold, N.J., U.S.)

American singer, songwriter, and bandleader Bruce Springsteen became the archetypal rock performer of the 1970s and '80s.

Springsteen grew up in Freehold, a mill town where his father worked as a labourer. His rebellious and artistic side led him to the nearby Jersey shore, where his imagination was sparked by the rock band scene and the boardwalk life, high and low. After an apprenticeship in bar bands on the mid-Atlantic coast, Springsteen turned himself into a solo singer-songwriter in 1972 and auditioned for talent scout John Hammond, Sr., who immediately signed him to Columbia Records. His first two albums, released in 1973, reflect folk rock, soul, and rhythm-and-blues influences, especially those of Van Morrison, Bob Dylan, and Stax/ Volt Records. Springsteen's voice, a rough baritone that he used to shout on up-tempo numbers and to more sensual effect on slower songs, was shown to good effect here, but his sometimes spectacular guitar playing, which ranged from dense power chord effects to straight 1950s rock and roll, had to be downplayed to fit the singer-songwriter format.

With his third album, *Born to Run* (1975), Springsteen transformed into a full-fledged rock and roller, heavily indebted to Phil Spector and Roy Orbison. The album, a diurnal song cycle, was a sensation even before it hit the shelves; indeed, the week of the album's release, Columbia's public relations campaign landed Springsteen on the covers of both *Time* and *Newsweek*. Three years passed before the follow-up, the darker, tougher *Darkness on the Edge of Town* (1978), appeared. With "Hungry Heart," from *The River* (1980), Springsteen finally scored an international hit single.

By then, however, he was best known for his stage shows, three- and four-hour extravaganzas with his E Street Band that blended rock, folk, and soul with dramatic intensity and exuberant humour. The band, a crew of mixed stereotypes—from rock-and-roll bandit to cool music professional—was more like a gang than a musical unit, apparently held together by little other than faith in its leader. Springsteen's refusal, after *Born to Run*, to cooperate with much of the record company's public relations and marketing machinery, coupled with his painstaking recording process and the draining live shows, helped earn his reputation as a performer of principle as well as of power and popularity.

*Nebraska* (1982), a stark set of acoustic songs, most in some way concerned with death, was an unusual interlude.

It was *Born in the U.S.A.* (1984) and his subsequent 18-month world tour that cinched Springsteen's reputation as the preeminent writer-performer of his rock-and-roll period. Springsteen's social perspective has been distinctly working-class throughout his career, a point emphasized both by his 1995 album, *The Ghost of Tom Joad*, which concerned itself with the economically and spiritually destitute in America and by his 1994 hit single (his first in eight years), the AIDS-related "Streets of Philadelphia," from the film *Philadelphia*, for which he won both an Academy Award and a Grammy Award.

The other side of Springsteen's work is reflected in the albums that he produced in the period beginning with *Tunnel of Love* (1987) and including *Human Touch* and *Lucky Town* (released simultaneously in 1992). The songs on these albums are intensely personal reflections on intimate relationships. In general, they have not been as popular.

Bridging all this is the five-record set *Bruce Springsteen and the E Street Band Live 1975–1985* (1986), which captures as much of his highly visual stage show of that period as can be rendered in a solely audio form. The breakup of the E Street Band in 1989 and general trends in pop music fashion curbed Springsteen's popularity. In 1998 he put together a box set, *Tracks*, consisting for the most part of leftover material that had failed to make the cut on his albums with the band. This grandiose gesture established him as prolix beyond all but a couple of peers. Sales of *Tracks* were trivial compared with those for *Live*.

In 1999 Springsteen reunited the E Street Band. They appeared with him when he alone was inducted into the Rock and Roll Hall of Fame in early 1999, then spent a year touring with him, resulting in a live album (*Live in New York City* [2001]) but only a handful of new songs. On Sept. 21, 2001, Springsteen performed the national debut of his song "My City of Ruins" on a television special. It

*Bruce Springsteen (left) and Steven Van Zandt (right) performing with the E Street Band at the Super Bowl halftime show in 2009.* Getty Images/ Streeter Lecka

was written about Asbury Park but took on a different tone in the wake of the September 11 attacks. That tone continued on *The Rising*, his 2002 album with the E Street Band, which weighed the consequences of the attacks and their aftermath. Beginning on the Rising tour, Springsteen became an adamant critic of the U.S. government, especially regarding the Iraq War. Springsteen's 2005 solo tour, following the release of the *Devils and Dust* album, explored the full depth of his song catalog and continued his opposition to the administration's policies.

*We Shall Overcome: The Seeger Sessions* (2006) took a turn unanticipated by even the closest Springsteen observers. He made the recording over a period of 10 years with a folk-roots band and a horn section. It featured traditional American folk songs ("Oh, Mary, Don't You Weep," "Froggie Went A-Courtin'," and "John Henry") as well as songs associated with its inspiration, Pete Seeger ("My Oklahoma Home," "How Can I Keep from Singing," and "Bring 'Em Home"). Springsteen's tour of the United States and Europe in 2006 featured a 20-piece band.

*Magic* (2007), another E Street Band album, spoke sometimes metaphorically and sometimes explicitly in opposition to the war and government intrusions on civil liberties. Springsteen continued his commentary through a worldwide tour with the E Street Band in 2007 and 2008. After the April 2008 death of the E Street Band organist and accordionist Danny Federici from melanoma, the band's playing acquired a darker urgency of tone. The later stages of the *Magic* tour featured arguably the most assertive, inspired playing Springsteen and the group had ever done.

*Working on a Dream*, released in early 2009, concerned itself lyrically with thoughts of love and life, how fleeting both are and what it takes to stay the course. The music on the album was a much more sophisticated version of what

Springsteen had done on his first two albums, with a greater emphasis on harmony, especially vocal harmonies characteristic of the later work of the Beach Boys. In the lyrics, Springsteen's knack for particular detail served him well.

On Feb. 1, 2009, Springsteen and the band were the featured entertainment at halftime of Super Bowl XLIII; with an average viewership of 98.7 million, the game was the most-watched televised sports event in American history. Many fans and much of the press criticized Springsteen for commercializing himself this way. But in the aftermath, it was generally agreed that he had managed to condense the structure, message, humour, and athleticism of his live show into the 12 minutes allotted. On the largest popular culture platform available, Springsteen established that some rock artists remained determined to sustain their vitality and creative ambitions all the way to the end.

## STEVIE WONDER

(b. May 13, 1950, Saginaw, Mich., U.S.)

American singer, songwriter, and multi-instrumentalist, Stevie Wonder was a child prodigy who developed into one of the most creative musical figures of the late 20th century.

Blind from birth and raised in inner-city Detroit, he was a skilled musician by age eight. Renamed Little Stevie Wonder by Berry Gordy, Jr., the president of Motown Records—to whom he was introduced by Ronnie White, a member of the Miracles—Wonder made his recording debut at age 12. The soulful quality of his high-pitched singing and the frantic harmonica playing that characterized his early recordings were evident in his first hit single, "Fingertips (Part 2)," recorded during a show at Chicago's

Regal Theatre in 1963. But Wonder was much more than a freakish prepubescent imitation of Ray Charles, as audiences discovered when he demonstrated his prowess with piano, organ, harmonica, and drums. By 1964 he was no longer described as "Little," and two years later his fervent delivery of the pounding soul of "Uptight (Everything's Alright)," which he also had written, suggested the emergence of both an unusually compelling performer and a composer to rival Motown's stable of skilled songwriters. (He had already cowritten, with Smokey Robinson, "The Tears of a Clown.")

Over the next five years Wonder had hits with "I Was Made to Love Her," "My Cherie Amour" (both cowritten with producer Henry Cosby), and "For Once in My Life," songs that suited dancers as well as lovers. *Where I'm Coming From*, an album released in 1971, hinted not merely at an expanded musical range but, in its lyrics and its mood, at a new introspection. *Music of My Mind* (1972) made his concerns even more plain. In the interim he had been strongly influenced by Marvin Gaye's *What's Going On*, the album in which his Motown stablemate moved away from the label's "hit factory" approach to confront the divisive social issues of the day. Any anxieties Gordy may have felt about his protégé's declaration of independence were amply calmed by the run of recordings with which Wonder obliterated the competition in the mid-1970s. Those albums produced a steady stream of classic hit songs, among them "Superstition," "You Are the Sunshine of My Life," "Higher Ground," "Living for the City," "Don't You Worry 'Bout a Thing," "Boogie on Reggae Woman," "I Wish," and "Sir Duke."

Although still only in his mid-20s, Wonder appeared to have mastered virtually every idiom of African-American popular music and to have synthesized them all into a language of his own. His command of the new generation of electronic keyboard instruments made him a pioneer and an inspiration to rock musicians, the inventiveness of his vocal phrasing was reminiscent of the greatest jazz singers, and the depth and honesty of his emotional projection came straight from the black church music of his childhood. Such a fertile period was unlikely to last forever, and it came to an end in 1979 with a fey and overambitious extended work called *Stevie Wonder's Journey Through the Secret Life of Plants*. Thereafter his recordings became sporadic and often lacked focus, although his concerts were never less than rousing. The best of his work formed a vital link between the classic rhythm-and-blues and soul performers of the 1950s and '60s and their less commercially constrained successors. Yet, however sophisticated his music became, he was never too proud to write something as apparently slight as the romantic gem "I Just Called to Say I Love You" (1984). He was inducted into the Rock and Roll Hall of Fame in 1989 and received a Grammy Award for lifetime achievement in 2005. In 2008 the Library of Congress announced that Wonder was the recipient of its Gershwin Prize for Popular Song.

## THE SEX PISTOLS

The original members were Johnny Rotten (byname of John Lydon; b. Jan. 31, 1956, London, Eng.), Steve Jones (b. May 3, 1955, London, Eng.), Paul Cook (b. July 20, 1956, London, Eng.), and Glen Matlock (b. Aug. 27, 1956, London, Eng.). A later member was Sid Vicious (byname of John Simon Ritchie; b. May 10, 1957, London, Eng.—d. Feb. 2, 1979, New York, N.Y., U.S.).

The Sex Pistols created the British punk movement of the late 1970s and, with the song "God Save the Queen," became a symbol of the United Kingdom's social and political turmoil.

Thrown together in September 1975 by manager Malcolm McLaren to promote Sex, his London clothing store, the Sex Pistols began mixing 1960s English pop music influences (the Small Faces, the Who) with those of 1970s rock renegades (Iggy and the Stooges, the New York Dolls) in an attempt to strip rock's complexities to the bone. By the summer of 1976 the Sex Pistols had attracted an avid fan base and successfully updated the energies of the 1960s mods for the malignant teenage mood of the '70s. Heavily stylized in their image and music, media-savvy, and ambitious in their use of lyrics, the Sex Pistols became the leaders of a new teenage movement—called punk by the British press—in the autumn of 1976. Their first single, "Anarchy in the U.K.," was both a call to arms and a state-of-the-nation address. When they used profanity on live television in December 1976, the group became a national sensation. Scandalized in the tabloid press, the Sex Pistols were dropped by their first record company, EMI, in January 1977; their next contract, with A&M Records, was severed after only a few days in March.

Signing quickly with Virgin Records, the Sex Pistols released their second single, "God Save the Queen," in June 1977 to coincide with Queen Elizabeth II's Silver Jubilee (the 25th anniversary of her accession to the throne). Although banned by the British media, the single rose rapidly to number two on the charts. As "public enemies number one," the Sex Pistols were subjected to physical violence and harassment.

Despite a second Top Ten record, "Pretty Vacant," the Sex Pistols stalled. Barely able to play in the United Kingdom because of local government bans, they became mired in preparations for a film and the worsening drug use of Rotten's friend Vicious, who had replaced Matlock in February 1977. Their bunker mentality is evident on their third Top Ten hit, "Holidays in the Sun." By the time their album *Never Mind the Bollocks, Here's the Sex Pistols* reached number one in early November, Rotten, Vicious, Jones, and Cook had recorded together for the last time.

A short, disastrous U.S. tour precipitated the group's split in January 1978 following their biggest show to date, in San Francisco. Attempting to keep the Sex Pistols going with the film project that became *The Great Rock 'n' Roll Swindle* (1980), McLaren issued records with an increasingly uncontrollable Vicious as the vocalist. A cover version of Eddie Cochran's "C'mon Everybody" became the group's best-selling single following Vicious's fatal heroin overdose in New York City in February 1979 while out on bail (charged with the murder of his girlfriend, Nancy Spungen). That same month McLaren was sued by Rotten, and the Sex Pistols disappeared into receivership, only to be revived some years after the 1986 court case that restored control of their affairs to the group. A reunion tour in 1996 finally allowed the original quartet to play their hit songs in front of supportive audiences. This anticlimactic postscript, however, did not lessen the impact of their first four singles and debut album, which shook the foundations of rock music and sent tremors through British society. In 2006 the Sex Pistols were inducted into the Rock and Roll Hall of Fame.

# PRINCE

(b. June 7, 1958, Minneapolis, Minn., U.S.)

Prince (born Prince Rogers Nelson) is a singer, guitarist, songwriter, producer, dancer, and performer on keyboards, drums, and bass who was among the most talented American musicians of his generation. A considerable number of his recordings feature him in all the performing roles.

Prince's recording career began with funk and soul marketed to a black audience; his early music also reflected the contemporary musical impact of disco. Later records incorporated a vast array of influences, including jazz, punk, heavy metal, the Beatles, and hip-hop, usually within an overall approach most informed by funky up-tempo styles and soulful ballads; the latter often featured his expressive falsetto singing.

Taking an early interest in music, Prince began playing the piano at age 7 and mastered the guitar and drums by the time he joined his first band at age 14. With very few African American residents, his hometown, Minneapolis, Minnesota, was an unlikely site for the development of a major black star, but Prince even managed to lead other local musicians, most notably Jimmy Jam and Terry Lewis, to major success.

Mirrored by correspondingly intense music, Prince's lyrics often address sexuality and desire with frankness and imagination. Much of his work, in its lyrics and imagery, struggles with the constriction of social conventions and categories. As one of his biographers put it, "The whole thrust of Prince's art can be understood in terms of a desire to escape the social identities thrust upon him by simple virtue of his being small, black, and male."

Prince explored typographical oddities in his song titles and lyrics as another way of evading convention. In 1993 he announced that he had changed his name to a combination of the male and female gender signs. There is also a strong religious impulse in some of his music, sometimes fused into a kind of sacred erotic experience that has roots in African American churches.

"Little Red Corvette" (1983) was Prince's first big cross-over hit, gaining airplay on MTV at a time when virtually no black artists appeared on the influential new medium. *Purple Rain* (1984) made him one of the major stars of the

1980s and remains his biggest-selling album. Three of its singles were hits: the frenetic "Let's Go Crazy," the androgynous but vulnerable "When Doves Cry," and the anthemic title cut. Thereafter he continued to produce inventive music of broad appeal; outside the United States he was particularly popular in Britain and the rest of Europe.

Throughout most of his career, Prince's prolific inventiveness as a songwriter clashed with his record company's policy of releasing only a single album each year. As a backlog of his completed but unreleased recordings piled up, he gave songs to other performers—some of whom recorded at and for Paisley Park, the studio and label he established in suburban Minneapolis—and even organized ostensibly independent groups, such as the Time, to record his material. His 1996 album *Emancipation* celebrated the forthcoming end of his Warner Brothers contract, which enabled him to release as much music as he liked on his NPG label. Later he explored marketing his work on the Internet and through private arrangements with retail chains as a means of circumventing the control of large record companies. In 1999, however, he released *Rave Un2 the Joy Fantastic* under the Arista label; a collaboration with Sheryl Crow, Chuck D, Ani DiFranco, and others, the album received mixed reviews and failed to find a large audience. Prince (who, following the formal termination of his contract with Warner Brothers in 1999, stopped using the symbol as his name) was inducted into the Rock and Roll Hall of Fame in 2004. That year he also released *Musicology*, an album that both sold well and was much praised by critics.

## MADONNA

(b. Aug. 16, 1958, Bay City, Mich., U.S.)

The immense popularity in the 1980s and '90s of American singer, songwriter, actress, and entrepreneur

Madonna (born Madonna Louise Ciccone) allowed her to achieve levels of power and control unprecedented for a woman in the entertainment industry.

Born into a large Italian-American family, Madonna studied dance at the University of Michigan and with the Alvin Ailey American Dance Theater in New York City in the late 1970s before relocating briefly to Paris as a member of Patrick Hernandez's disco revue. Returning to New York City, she performed with a number of rock groups before signing with Sire Records. Her first hit, "Holiday," in 1983, provided the blueprint for her later material—an upbeat dance-club sound with sharp production and an immediate appeal. Madonna's melodic pop incorporated catchy choruses and her lyrics concerned love, sex, and relation-ships—ranging from the breezy innocence of "True Blue" (1986) to the erotic fantasies of "Justify My Love" (1990) to the spirituality of later songs such as "Ray of Light" (1998). Criticized by some as being limited in range, her sweet, girlish voice nonetheless was well-suited to pop music.

Madonna was the first female artist to exploit fully the potential of the music video. She collaborated with top designers (Jean-Paul Gaultier), photographers (Steven Meisel and Herb Ritts), and directors (Mary Lambert and David Fincher), drawing inspiration from underground club culture or the avant-garde to create distinctive sexual and satirical images—from the knowing ingenue of "Like a Virgin" (1984) to the controversial red-dressed "sinner" who kisses a black saint in "Like a Prayer" (1989). By 1991 she had scored 21 Top Ten hits in the United States and sold some 70 million albums internationally, generating $1.2 billion in sales. Committed to controlling her image and career herself, Madonna became the head of Maverick, a subsidiary of Time-Warner created by the entertainment giant as part of a $60 million deal with the performer. Her success signaled a clear message of financial control to other women in the industry, but in terms of image she was a more ambivalent role model.

In 1992 Madonna took her role as a sexual siren to its full extent when she published *Sex*, a soft-core pornographic coffee-table book featuring her in a variety of "erotic" poses. She was criticized for being exploitative and overcalculating, and writer Norman Mailer said she had become "secretary to herself." Soon afterward Madonna temporarily withdrew from pop music to concentrate on a film career that had begun with a strong performance in *Desperately Seeking Susan* (1985), faltered with the flimsy *Shanghai Surprise* (1986) and *Dick Tracy* (1990), and recovered with *Truth or Dare* (1991, also known as *In Bed with Madonna*), a documentary of one of her tours. She scored massive success in 1996 with the starring role in the film musical *Evita*. That year she also gave birth to a daughter.

In 1998 Madonna released her first album of new material in four years, *Ray of Light*. A fusion of techno music and self-conscious lyrics, it was a commercial and critical success, earning the singer her first musical Grammy Awards (her previous win had been for a video). Her experimentation in electronica continued with *Music* (2000). In 2005 she returned to her roots with *Confessions on a Dance Floor*. Despite a marriage in the 1980s to actor Sean Penn and another to English director Guy Ritchie (married 2000; divorced 2008), with whom she had two sons, Madonna remained resolutely independent. That independent streak, however, did not prevent her from enlisting the biggest names in music to assist on specific projects. This fact was clear on *Hard Candy* (2008), a hip-hop infused effort with writing and vocal and production work by Justin Timberlake, Timbaland, and Pharrell

Williams of the hit-making duo The Neptunes. In 2008 she was inducted into the Rock and Roll Hall of Fame.

## MICHAEL JACKSON

(b. Aug. 29, 1958, Gary, Ind., U.S.—d. June 25, 2009, Los Angeles, Calif., U.S.)

American singer, songwriter, and dancer Michael Joseph Jackson was the most popular entertainer in the world in the early and mid-1980s. Reared in Gary, Ind., in one of the most acclaimed musical families of the rock era, Michael Jackson was the youngest and most talented of five brothers whom his father, Joseph, shaped into a dazzling group of child stars known as the Jackson 5. In addition to Michael, the members of the Jackson 5 (all also born in Gary) were Jackie Jackson (b. May 4, 1951), Tito Jackson (b. Oct. 15, 1953), Jermaine Jackson (b. Dec. 11, 1954), and Marlon Jackson (b. March 12, 1957).

Motown Records president Berry Gordy, Jr., was impressed with the group and signed them in 1969. Sporting the loudest fashions, the largest Afros, the snappiest choreography, and a youthful, soulful exuberance, the Jackson 5 became an immediate success. They scored four consecutive number one pop hits with "I Want You Back," "ABC," "The Love You Save," and "I'll Be There" in 1970. With Michael topping the pop charts as a solo performer with "Ben" and reaching number two with "Rockin' Robin," and with the Jackson 5 producing trendsetting dance tracks such as *Dancing Machine*, the family's string of hits for Motown lasted through 1975. As Michael matured, his voice changed, family tensions arose, and a contract stand-off ensued. The group finally broke with Motown, moving to Epic Records as the Jacksons. Jermaine remained at Motown as a solo performer and was replaced by his youngest brother, Randy Jackson (b. Oct. 29, 1961). As a recording act, the Jacksons enjoyed consistent success through 1984, and their sister Janet Jackson embarked on her own singing career in the early 1980s; however, Michael's solo albums took on an entirely different status.

Jackson's first solo effort for Epic, *Off the Wall* (1979), exceeded all expectations and was the best-selling album of the year. Produced by industry veteran Quincy Jones, *Off the Wall* yielded the massive international hit singles "Don't Stop 'til You Get Enough" and "Rock with You," both of which showcased Michael's energetic style and capitalized on the contemporary disco dance fad. Three years later he returned with another collaboration with Jones, *Thriller*, a tour de force that featured an array of guest stars and elevated him to a worldwide superstar.

*Michael Jackson's singles-studded solo album,* Off the Wall, *was released August 10, 1979, weeks before the singer's 21st birthday.* GAB Archive/Redferns/Getty Images

*Thriller* sold more than 40 million copies, captured a slew of awards, including a record-setting eight Grammys, and became the best-selling album in history. The first single on the album, "The Girl Is Mine," an easygoing duet with Paul McCartney, went to number one on the rhythm-and-blues charts and number two on the pop charts in the fall of 1982. The follow-up single, "Billie Jean," an electrifying dance track and the vehicle for Jackson's trademark "moonwalk" dance, topped the pop charts, as did "Beat It," which featured a raucous solo from famed guitarist Eddie Van Halen. Moreover, "Beat It" helped break down the artificial barriers between black and white artists on the radio and in the emerging format of music videos on television.

By 1984 Jackson was renowned worldwide as the "King of Pop." His much anticipated Victory reunion tour with his brothers was one of the most popular concert events of 1984. Further solo albums—*Bad* (1987) and *Dangerous* (1991)—solidified Jackson's dominance of pop music, and in 2001 he was inducted into the Rock and Roll Hall of Fame; the Jackson 5 were inducted in 1997.

Jackson's eccentric, secluded lifestyle grew increasingly controversial in the early 1990s. His reputation was seriously damaged in 1993 when he was accused of child molestation by a 13-year-old boy he had befriended; a civil suit was settled out of court. In 1994 Jackson secretly married Lisa Marie Presley, daughter of Elvis Presley, but their marriage lasted less than two years. Shortly thereafter Jackson married again, this marriage producing children, though it, too, ended in divorce. While he remained an international celebrity, his image in the United States was slow to recover, and it suffered even more in November 2003 when he was arrested and charged with child molestation. After a 14-week trial that became something of a media circus, Jackson was acquitted in 2005.

The singer was preparing a comeback tour in 2009 when he died suddenly of cardiac arrest. A widespread outpouring of grief culminated in a memorial celebration of his life on July 7, 2009 at the Staples Center in Los Angeles.

## PUBLIC ENEMY

The original members were Chuck D (original name Carlton Ridenhour; b. Aug. 1, 1960, New York, N.Y., U.S.), Flavor Flav (original name William Drayton; b. March 16, 1959, New York, N.Y., U.S.), Terminator X (original name Norman Lee Rogers; b. Aug. 25, 1966, New York, N.Y., U.S.), and Professor Griff (original name Richard Griffin).

Public Enemy was an American rap group whose dense, layered sound and radical political message made them among the most popular, controversial, and influential hip-hop artists of the late 1980s and early '90s.

Public Enemy was formed in 1982 at Adelphi University on Long Island, New York, by a group of African Americans who came primarily from the suburbs. Chuck D, Hank Shocklee, Bill Stephney, and Flavor Flav collaborated on a program on college radio. Reputedly, Def Jam producer Rick Rubin was so taken with Chuck D's booming voice that he begged him to record. Public Enemy resulted and brought radical black political ideology to pop music in an unprecedented fashion on albums with titles that read like party invitations for leftists and warning stickers for the right wing: *Yo! Bum Rush the Show* (1987), *It Takes a Nation of Millions to Hold Us Back* (1988), *Fear of a Black Planet* (1990), and *Apocalypse 91: The Enemy Strikes Black* (1991).

Acclaimed as Public Enemy's masterpiece, *Nation of Millions* revived the messages of the Black Panther Party and Malcolm X. On tracks such as "Night of the Living Baseheads," "Black Steel in the Hour of Chaos," and "Don't Believe the Hype," the strident, eloquent lyrics of Chuck

D combined with bombastic, dissonant, and poignantly detailed backing tracks created by Public Enemy's production team, the Bomb Squad (Shocklee, his brother Keith, Chuck D, and Eric "Vietnam" Adler), to produce songs challenging the status quo in both hip-hop and racial politics. The Bomb Squad sampled (composed with other recordings) a wide variety of genres and sounds, including classic funk tracks by James Brown, jazz, the thrash-metal of Anthrax, sirens, and agitprop speeches. Flavor Flav provided a comic foil for Chuck D.

Comments by Professor Griff to the *Washington Times* in 1989 brought charges of anti-Semitism, which ultimately resulted in his leaving the group. Public Enemy's open admiration for the Nation of Islam leader Louis Farrakhan also brought it into conflict with Jewish organizations. While Public Enemy's activism inspired other artists to take up topical themes, the group's influence waned in the early 1990s as younger, more "ghetto-centric" performers such as N.W.A. and Snoop Doggy Dogg came to the fore. The group seemed to have folded after *Muse Sick N Hour Mess Age* (1994), but in 1998 they produced a new album of songs for Spike Lee's film *He Got Game* and went on tour.

## U2

The members are Bono (byname of Paul Hewson; b. May 10, 1960, Dublin, Ire.), the Edge (byname of David Evans; b. Aug. 8, 1961, Barking, Essex [now in Greater London], Eng.), Adam Clayton (b. March 13, 1960, Oxford, Oxfordshire, Eng.), and Larry Mullen, Jr. (b. Oct. 31, 1961, Dublin, Ire.).

I rish postpunk band U2 had established itself by the end of the 1980s not only as one of the world's most popular bands but also as one of the most innovative.

Though forged in the crucible of punk rock that swept Europe in the late 1970s, U2 instantly created a distinctive identity with its grandiose sound; a merger of the Edge's minimal, reverb-drenched guitar; and Bono's quasi-operatic vocals. The band members were attending a Dublin secondary school when they began rehearsing, undeterred by their lack of technical expertise. The band's early records were characterized by an intense spirituality, and they commented on social and political issues, such as the civil strife in Northern Ireland, with compassion and tenderness. The group became renowned for its inspirational live performances and was a word-of-mouth sensation long before it made much of an impact on the pop charts. But, with the multimillion-selling success of *The Joshua Tree* album (1987) and the number one hits "With or Without You" and "I Still Haven't Found What I'm Looking For," U2 became pop stars. On *Rattle and Hum* (1988), a double album and documentary movie, the band explored American roots music—blues, country, gospel, and folk— with typical earnestness but were pilloried by some critics who found the project pompous.

U2 reinvented itself for the new decade, reemerging in 1991 with the album *Achtung Baby* and a sound heavily influenced by European experimental, electronic, and disco music. With this came a stage show that trafficked in irony and self-deprecating humour, qualities virtually absent from the band's music in the previous decade; the 1992 Zoo TV tour was one of the most technically ambitious and artistically accomplished large-scale rock spectacles ever staged. But, despite the flashier exterior, the band's lyrics remained obsessed with matters of the soul. The dehumanizing aspects of media and technology were a recurring theme on subsequent records, even as the band immersed itself in techno textures.

In 1997 the band rush-released the *Pop* album to fulfill obligations for a stadium tour and was greeted with its worst reviews since *Rattle and Hum*. Another reinvention was in store, but this time, rather than boldly pushing forward, the band sought to reassure fans by making music that referenced its 1980s roots. The aptly titled *All That You Can't Leave Behind* (2000) and *How to Dismantle an Atomic Bomb* (2004) were focused on riffs and songs rather than atmosphere and mystery, and they succeeded in reestablishing the quartet as a commercial force, but at what price? The band took five years before releasing its 12th studio album, *No Line on the Horizon* (2009). Longtime collaborators Brian Eno and Daniel Lanois played a bigger role in the production and songwriting, and the layered textures of the album's most experimental work crept back prominently in the mix.

## NIRVANA

The members were Kurt Cobain (b. Feb. 20, 1967, Aberdeen, Wash., U.S.—d. April 5, 1994, Seattle, Wash.), Krist Novoselic (b. May 16, 1965, Compton, Calif., U.S.), and Dave Grohl (b. Jan. 14, 1969, Warren, Ohio, U.S.).

Nirvana was an American alternative rock group whose breakthrough album, *Nevermind* (1991), announced a new musical style (grunge) and gave voice to the post-baby boom young adults known as Generation X.

From Aberdeen, near Seattle, Nirvana was part of the postpunk underground scene that centred on K Records of Olympia, Washington, before they recorded their first single, "Love Buzz," and album, *Bleach*, for Sub Pop, an independent record company in Seattle. They refined this mix of 1960s-style pop and 1970s heavy metal– hard rock on their first album for a major label, Geffen; *Nevermind*, featuring the anthemic hit "Smells Like Teen Spirit," was the first full expression of punk concerns to achieve mass market success in the United States.

Nirvana used extreme changes of tempo and volume to express anger and alienation: a quiet, tuneful verse switched into a ferocious, distorted chorus. In the fashion of many 1970s punk groups, guitarist-singer-songwriter Cobain set powerful rock against sarcastic, allusive lyrics that explored hopelessness, surrender, and male abjection ("As a defense I'm neutered and spayed," he sang in On a Plain). Imbued with the punk ethic that to succeed was to fail, Nirvana abhorred the media onslaught that accompanied their rapid ascent. Success brought celebrity, and Cobain, typecast as a self-destructive rock star, courted controversy both with his advocacy of feminism and gay rights and with his embroilment in a sequence of drug- and

*Nirvana singer Kurt Cobain performing with the band at a taping of the MTV show* Unplugged *in 1993.* Getty Images/Frank Micelotta

gun-related escapades—a number of which involved his wife, Courtney Love, leader of the band Hole.

Like *Nevermind*, the band's third album, *In Utero* (1993)—which contained clear articulations of Cobain's psyche in songs such as "All Apologies" and "Rape Me"—reached number one on the U.S. album charts. By this point, however, Cobain's heroin use was out of control. After a reputed suicide attempt in Rome in March 1994, he entered a Los Angeles treatment centre. In a mysterious sequence of events, he returned to Seattle, where he shot and killed himself in his lakeside home. Subsequent concert releases, notably *Unplugged in New York* (1994) and *From the Muddy Banks of the Wishkah* (1996), only added to Nirvana's legend. In 2002 the greatest-hits album *Nirvana* appeared and included the previously unreleased single "You Know You're Right." That year a collection of Cobain's journals was also published.

## RADIOHEAD

Formed in the mid-1980s at Abingdon School in Oxfordshire, Radiohead comprised singer-guitarist Thom Yorke (b. Oct. 7, 1968, Wellingborough, Northamptonshire, Eng.), bassist Colin Greenwood (b. June 26, 1969, Oxford, Oxfordshire, Eng.), guitarist Ed O'Brien (b. April 15, 1968, Oxford, Oxfordshire, Eng.), drummer Phil Selway (b. May 23, 1967, Hemingford Grey, Huntingdon, Cambridgeshire, Eng.), and guitarist-keyboardist Jonny Greenwood (b. Nov. 5, 1971, Oxford, Oxfordshire, Eng.).

The British rock group Radiohead arguably has been the most accomplished art-rock band of the early 21st century. This revered quintet made some of the most majestic—if most angst-saturated—music of the post-modern era.

Strongly influenced by American bands such as R.E.M. and the Pixies, Radiohead paid early dues on the local

*Singer Thom Yorke of Radiohead performs "15 Step" during the Grammy Awards in February of 2009.* Getty Images/Kevin Winter

pub circuit. With their university education completed, the group landed a deal with Parlophone in late 1991. Although its debut album, *Pablo Honey* (1993), barely hinted at the grandeur to come, the startling single "Creep"—a grungy snarl of self-loathing—made major waves in the United States.

*The Bends* (1995) took even the band's most ardent fans by surprise. A soaring, intense mix of the approaches of Nirvana and dramatic vocalist Jeff Buckley, the album's powerful sense of alienation completely transcended the parochial issues of mid-1990s Britpop. Driving rockers such as "Bones" were skillfully offset by sad ballads such as "High and Dry." The widely acclaimed *OK Computer* (1997) was nothing short of a premillennial version of Pink Floyd's classic album *Dark Side of the Moon* (1973): huge-sounding and chillingly beautiful, with Yorke's weightless voice enveloped on masterpieces such as "Lucky" by webs of dark, dense textures. In its live performances, Radiohead became one of pop music's most compelling acts.

The pressure to follow up one of the most acclaimed recordings of the 20th century told particularly on Yorke's fragile psyche. The band made false starts in Paris and Copenhagen before settling down back in England. When *Kid A* came out in October 2000, it signaled that Radiohead—and Yorke above all—wanted to leave the wide-screen drama of *OK Computer* behind. The resulting selection of heavily electronic, more or less guitar-free pieces (notably "Kid A" and "Idioteque") confounded many but repaid the patience of fans who stuck with it. Though the album was a commercial success, it met with mixed critical reaction, as would the similar *Amnesiac* (2001), produced during the same sessions as *Kid A*. But if Radiohead had seemingly disavowed its musical past on these two albums—moving away from melody and rock instrumentation to create intricately textured soundscapes—it found a way to meld this approach with its guitar-band roots on the much-anticipated album *Hail to the Thief* (2003), which reached number three on the U.S. album charts. In 2006 Yorke, who had reluctantly become for some the voice of his generation, collaborated with the group's modernist producer, Nigel Godrich, on a solo album, *The Eraser*.

The band, having concluded its six-album contract with the EMI Group in 2003, broke away from major label distribution and initially released its seventh album, *In Rainbows* (2007), via Internet download. An estimated 1.2 million fans downloaded the album within its first week of availability, paying any price they wished to do so. The novel distribution method generated headlines, but it was the album's content—a collection of 10 tracks that served as a confident, almost optimistic, sonic counterpoint to *The Bends*—that led critics to declare it the most approachable Radiohead album in a decade.

*In Rainbows* was released to retailers as a standard CD in 2008, and it immediately hit number one in both the United States and Great Britain. The group won its third Grammy for the album, and the *In Rainbows* box set, which featured CD and vinyl copies of the original tracks, a CD of eight bonus songs, and a booklet of original artwork, received the Grammy for limited edition packaging.

## JAY-Z

(b. Dec. 4, 1970, Brooklyn, N.Y., U.S.)

American rapper and entrepreneur Jay-Z (born Shawn Corey Carter) was one of the most influential figures in hip-hop in the 1990s and 2000s.

Shawn Carter grew up in Brooklyn's often dangerous Marcy Projects, where he was raised mainly by his mother. His firsthand experience with illicit drug dealing would inform his lyrics when he began rapping under the stage name Jazzy, soon shortened to Jay-Z (a name that may also have been derived from the proximity of the J and Z subway lines to the Marcy Projects). Jay-Z and two friends founded their own company, Roc-a-Fella Records, to release his debut album, *Reasonable Doubt* (1996), which climbed the *Billboard* charts, reaching number 23 on the pop chart and number 3 on the rhythm-and-blues chart.

A string of successful albums followed at a rate of at least one per year through 2003. *Vol. 2: Hard Knock Life* (1998) not only was the first of Jay-Z's releases to top the *Billboard* 200 album sales chart but also won a Grammy Award for best rap album. In 2001 he pleaded guilty to assault relating to a 1999 nightclub stabbing and received three years' probation. In 2003, with the release of *The Black Album*, Jay-Z announced his retirement as a performer. In 2004 he assumed the presidency of Def Jam Recordings, making him one of the most highly placed African American executives in the recording industry at the time.

Postretirement, Jay-Z stayed remarkably active, collaborating with the rock group Linkin Park in 2004 and appearing as a guest vocalist on the recordings of numerous other artists, including Kanye West and Beyoncé; Jay-Z and Beyoncé were married in 2008. He developed a large portfolio of business ventures and investments, including Roc-a-Fella Films, a clothing line, and a stake in the New Jersey Nets of the National Basketball Association. He formally returned to recording in 2006 with *Kingdom Come*. In December 2007 he stepped down as Def Jam president shortly after releasing the album *American Gangster*. Jay-Z proved that he remained one of rap's most bankable acts when he embarked on a highly successful tour with Mary J. Blige in 2008. The following year he won a Grammy Award for best rap performance for *Swagga Like Us*, a collaboration with T.I., Kanye West, and Lil Wayne.

# GLOSSARY

**agitprop** Political propaganda in the form of art, music, literature, film, etc.

**amalgam** A fusion of different elements.

**anathema** A person or thing that is detested, especially by the church.

**androgynous** Having both male and female characteristics.

**assiduity** Great and persistent attention and diligence.

**avant-garde** Experimental or progressive.

**blacklisting** Creating a list of people to be shunned, especially in reference to suspected Communist supporters in 1950s American culture.

**bravura** A style of music that is highly difficult and intended to show off the skill of the performer

**cantata** A poem set to music as a lyric drama, but not enacted.

**cantor** The person who leads singing during the liturgy.

**cantus firmus** An existing melody that forms the foundation of a polyphonic composition.

**chansons** Songs with French lyrics, from the Middle Ages to the present, in a variety of musical styles.

**chromatic** Notes that are half-steps or semitones apart; on a piano, the difference in sound between a white key and the closest black key.

**contralto** The lower range of the female voice.

**contrapuntal** Characterized by two or more independent melodies sounded together.

**diatonic** A scale of the type represented by the white keys on a piano.

**dissonance** Lack of a consonant (agreeable) sound between two or more tones.

**diurnal** Active during the day, as opposed to during the night (nocturnal).

**divertimenti** A light musical composition, usually written in several movements for a small group of instruments.

**dulcet** Characterized by soothing, melodious tones.

**ebullient** Overflowing with enthusiasm.

**ecclesiastical** Relating to the church.

**eponymous** Named after a particular person; self-titled.

**fugue** A musical structure in which multiple melodic lines repeat a single theme in various ways, often in a staggered or overlapping arrangement.

**glaucoma** An eye disease caused by increased pressure that damages the optic nerve.

**imam** The Muslim leader who leads prayers in a mosque.

**impecunious** Lacking money.

**impresario** A manager or producer in the entertainment industry.

**lieder** German songs, primarily from the Romantic period.

**lyceum** A school for students between elementary school and college (usually grades 9–12).

**masque** A dramatic verse composition usually performed by masked actors that represent mythological or allegorical figures.

**mazurka** A type of Polish dance and music, performed in triple time at a moderate tempo.

**mercurial** Liable to sudden and unpredictable change.

**minuet** A type of stately French music and dance, performed in triple time at a moderate tempo.

**mnemonic** A formula or rhyme intended to assist the memory.

**motet** A polyphonic vocal composition of the Middle Ages and Renaissance that is based on a sacred text and usually sung without accompaniment.

**neumes** Symbols used to note music in the Middle Ages.

**New Style** Time denoted according to the Gregorian calendar.

**oeuvre** An artist's complete body of work.

**Old Style** Time denoted according to the Julian calendar.

**opprobrium** Disgrace resulting from shameful conduct.

**oratorio** A musical composition for voices and orchestra that tells a sacred story without costumes, scenery, or dramatic action.

**papal** Pertaining to the pope or the Roman Catholic Church.

**pedagogic** Relating to the art and science of being a teacher.

**pizzicato** A playing technique by which the strings of an instrument are plucked, rather than bowed.

**polonaise** A type of stately Polish dance and music, performed in triple time at a moderate tempo.

**proletarian** A member of the working class.

**provost** A high-ranking university administrator.

**recapitulation** The final section of a musical composition that repeats the earlier themes.

**rondeau** A medieval French song form with two phrases, each repeated several times.

**scherzo** A lighthearted, rapid piece of music, often forming the third movement of a symphony; scherzo is Italian for joke.

**serenata (or serenade)** A dramatic musical composition, usually written in someone's honor.

**serenade** A type of 18th- and 19th-century instrumental music, usually written in several movements and performed in the evening.

**singspiel** A type of German comic opera that mixes light songs with spoken passages.

**solmization** Use of certain syllables to represent the tones of the scale.

**sonata** A musical composition for solo piano or another instrument with piano accompaniment, usually written in three or four movements.

**sycophant** A person looking for recognition by flattering the influential and powerful.

**tonality** The emphasis of a single pitch (tonic) as the centre of a composition.

**treatise** An extensive written composition detailing the principles of a subject.

**vibrato** A rapid, repetitive fluctuation of pitch on a sustained vocal or instrumental tone.

**virtuoso** An exceptionally skilled musician or artist.

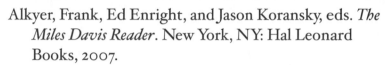

# FOR FURTHER READING

Alkyer, Frank, Ed Enright, and Jason Koransky, eds. *The Miles Davis Reader*. New York, NY: Hal Leonard Books, 2007.

Brower, Steven. *Satchmo: The Wonderful World and Art of Louis Armstrong*. New York, NY: Abrams, 2009.

Charles, Ray, and David Ritz. *Brother Ray: Ray Charles' Own Story*. Cambridge, MA: Da Capo Press, 2004.

Dylan, Bob. *Chronicles: Volume 1*. New York, NY: Simon & Schuster, 2004.

Gribbin, John. *Not Fade Away: The Life and Music of Buddy Holly*. London, England: Icon Books, 2009.

Köhler, Joachim. *Richard Wagner: The Last of the Titans*. London, England: Yale University Press, 2004.

Morris, Edmund. *Beethoven: The Universal Composer*. New York, NY: HarperCollins, 2005.

Nassour, Ellis. *Honky Tonk Angel: The Intimate Story of Patsy Cline*. Chicago, IL: Chicago Review Press, 2008.

Piaf, Edith. *The Wheel of Fortune: The Autobiography of Edith Piaf*. Chester Springs, PA: Dufour Editions, 2004.

Pignone, Charles. *The Sinatra Treasures*. New York, NY: Bullfinch Press, 2004.

Ritz, David, ed. *Elvis by the Presleys*. New York, NY: Crown Publishers, 2005.

Spaethling, Robert. *Mozart's Letters, Mozart's Life*. New York, NY: Norton, 2005.

Stark, Steven D. *Meet the Beatles: A Cultural History of the Band That Shook Youth, Gender, and the World.* New York, NY: Harper, 2006.

True, Everett. *Nirvana: The Biography.* Cambridge, MA: Da Capo Press, 2007.

Williams, Peter F. *J.S. Bach: A Life in Music.* Cambridge, England: Cambridge University Press, 2007.

Wyatt, Robert, and John Andrew Johnson, eds. *The George Gershwin Reader.* New York, NY: Oxford University Press, 2004.

Zwonitzer, Mark. *Will You Miss Me When I'm Gone?: The Carter Family and Their Legacy in American Music.* New York, NY: Simon & Schuster, 2002.

# INDEX

*Violin Concerto in D Major*
(Brahms), 94
*Violin Concerto in E Minor-Major*
(Mendelssohn), 69
*Violin Concerto No. 1*
(Shostakovich), 191
"Viva Las Vegas," 256
Vivaldi, Antonio, 20–23
*Voyevoda, The*, 102

# W

"Wabash Cannonball," 147
Wagner, Richard, 68, 80–85, 91,
95–96, 103, 108, 112–113, 119
"Waiting for a Train," 159
"Walking After Midnight," 249
*War*, 12
*Was Gott tut das ist wohlgetan*, 79
*Water Music*, 24, 27–28
Waters, Muddy, 10, 198, 204–
205, 300
"Weather Bird," 180
Weill, Kurt, 174–176
*We Shall Overcome: The Seeger
Sessions*, 322
"West End Blues," 180
*West Side Story*, 221
"What'd I Say," 248
*Wheels of Fire*, 310

"When Doves Cry," 329
"Where Have All the Flowers
Gone?," 223
"White Room," 309
Who, the, 301–304
"Whole Lotta Love," 299–300
"Wildwood Flower," 147
Williams, Hank, 231–234
*Winter Daydreams*, 102
"Without a Song," 209
Wonder, Stevie, 323–325
*Wonderful Town*, 221
"Won't Get Fooled Again," 303
*Wooden Prince, The*, 136
*Working on a Dream*, 322

# Y

"Yesterday," 275
*Yo! Bum Rush the Show*, 335
"You Are the Sunshine of My
Life," 324
*Young Americans*, 315
"Your Cheatin' Heart," 233
"You're the Top," 158
"You've Really Got a Hold on
Me," 270

# Z

*Zauberflöte, Die*, 52